BOOKS
THAT CHANGED
THE WORLD

The **50** most influential books in human history

A N D R E W   T A Y L O R

William Shakespeare

FIRST FOLIO

THE PRINCE
NICCOLO MACHIAVELLI

THE COMMUNIST MANIFESTO
KARL MARX

UNCLE TOM'S CABIN
Harriet Beecher Stowe

THE HISTORIES
HERODOTUS

THE INTERPRETATION OF DREAMS
SIGMUND FREUD

DON QUIXOTE
CERVANTES

THE WEALTH OF NATIONS
ADAM SMITH

Quercus

Contents

Introduction

How can we ever change the world? Military leaders, such as Genghis Khan or Napoleon have certainly managed to change large parts of it, though generally not for as long as they expected; scientists devising cures and vaccines for disease can spread a more benign influence across whole continents; the thoughts of religious leaders or philosophers, like Jesus Christ, Mohammed, Plato or Confucius, can sweep through generations like fire. But books?

Reading books is generally a solitary, unassuming pastime: bookishness is the very antithesis of the man-of-action qualities that seem to shake the world by the scruff of its neck. The pen may boast of being mightier than the sword, but it is generally the sword that wins in the short term. It is that phrase, though, which gives the game away: in the short term, writers can be bullied, imprisoned or executed, their work censored, and their books burned, but over the long sweep of history, it is books and the ideas expressed within them that have transformed the world.

From the first cave paintings 30,000 years ago, the passing on of thoughts and ideas from one person to another, from one generation to another, has been the key to civilization. For centuries, this could only be done by painstakingly copying one manuscript to another, or by memorizing long screeds of poetry – the works of Homer, for instance, survived for maybe 200 years before being written down. Then there was the transformative technology of print, first in the East, much later in the West. The *Diamond Sutra*, an ancient Buddhist text printed in China in AD 868, is thought to be the oldest printed book surviving, pre-dating Gutenberg's Bible in Europe by nearly six centuries. With print, philosophers, theologians, historians, scientists and poets could pass on their ideas – about life, about the world, about eternity and the present moment, about the way that people have thought and behaved in the past, and about how they always think and behave – to hundreds, even thousands of people at a time.

As a result, people who may never have heard of the Flemish cartographer Mercator of Rupelmonde still carry in their heads today a picture of the world that he devised 400 years ago; Odysseus, Don Quixote and Ebenezer Scrooge are familiar characters to children to whom the names of Homer, Cervantes and Dickens may mean nothing. The patient on the operating table may not know about William Harvey, but he has good reason to be grateful for *The Motion of the Heart and Blood*; because of the compilers of Shakespeare's First Folio, people who have never seen his plays may still describe themselves as 'tongue-tied' or tell others they are 'living in a fool's paradise'. In great ways and small, books spread their influence, even among those who never turn their pages.

But *which* books? There are few better ways of starting an argument than producing a list, whether it purports to rank the best opera singers, the most influential politicians or the greatest footballers, and I have been left in no doubt over the last few months about the passion with which people will defend favourite books and authors whom they feel to have been unjustly excluded. About some on the list, like the Bible and the Qur'an, Shakespeare's First Folio and Darwin's *On the Origin of Species*, there can be little argument – but where are Euclid's *Elements* or Thomas More's *Utopia*? Eliot, either George or T.S., depending on your point of view? How could you choose Dickens's *A Christmas Carol* rather than *Bleak House* or *David Copperfield*? Or *The Pickwick Papers*? What about Thomas Paine's *Rights of Man* or *A Vindication of the Rights of Women* by Mary Wollstonecraft?

The answer is that any list can only be subjective. These are the books that, in their different ways, have changed *my* world – but they are also books that I believe have demonstrably changed the world in one way or another for millions of other people. Often, they have enhanced the richness of human experience; sometimes, their civilizing effect, or otherwise, depends on the views one holds, a category that includes the great religious books. And very occasionally, books such as *The Protocols of the Elders of Zion* or Mao's *Quotations* (better known as the Little Red Book) are remembered like bad dreams, the tools of megalomaniacs and murderers.

Of course there are others – you could compile a list of a thousand books that have changed the world, and someone would still hold up the thousand-and-first, demanding indignantly how it could have been left out – but these fifty have helped to make the world what it is today.

Will they, or any books, help to make the world what it becomes tomorrow? Will books even exist by the end of the 21st century? Back in the 9th century, no doubt some elderly Chinese intellectual complained grumpily that this newfangled printing nonsense would spell the end of calligraphy and the hand-written manuscript – and today, there are increasing predictions of the end of the book as we know it. *Wikipedia*, the online encyclopaedia written and edited by its readers, without a traditional author or publisher, lives in cyberspace, with no place on the bookshelf; several manufacturers have tried to produce portable electronic screens that will enable people to carry hundreds of e-texts in their pocket, without having to bother about tiresome details like turning the page. No doubt, some day, someone will get it right.

But whatever the changes that come, they will only be in the way the writing is presented. The words that we want to survive, will survive, whether they are printed in books, electronically reproduced on screen or hand-written on parchment scrolls. All these 50 books have changed the present or the past. The deserving among them will continue to change the future, resonating, in whatever medium, a hundred years from now, and a hundred years from then.

The *Iliad*

*c.*8th century BC

Homer

The *Iliad* is the oldest work of poetry in the Western world. Conventionally credited to Homer sometime in the 8th or 9th century BC, it underpinned the astonishing flowering of Greek culture from the 5th century BC onwards, a culture that – via the Romans and the Renaissance – lies at the heart of Western civilization.

This epic poem adopts the 'hexameter', a form of stately poetic metre that later became known as 'heroic verse', though it was a form rarely adopted by English poets. Its subject is both a great military campaign and a single man. In its 24 books, it tells the story of the ten-year Greek siege of Troy, which followed the abduction of Helen, wife of King Menelaus of Sparta, by Paris, the son of the Trojan King Priam; but it also concentrates on one brief episode in the final year of the siege.

More specifically, it describes a quarrel in the Greek camp between Menelaus's brother, King Agamemnon, and the Greek champion Achilles, over Agamemnon's seizure of a captive slave girl. As a result, the Greeks are defeated in an assault on the city as Achilles and his forces keep out of the fight. Eventually, he relents and sends his friend Patroclus to rescue the struggling Greeks. When Patroclus is killed by Hector, another Trojan prince, Achilles joins the battle in a fury, kills Hector and defiles his body by dragging it behind his horse outside the city walls. Eventually, with the Greeks victorious, Priam pays a ransom, and the body is returned. The epic ends with the funeral of Hector.

The poem is traditionally thought of as the greater of a pair by Homer, the other being the *Odyssey*, an account of the journey back to Greece of the Greek commander Odysseus, who also figures in the *Iliad*. The story the *Iliad*, which tells of military virtues and the dealings between gods and men, was treated by the later Ancient Greeks as a kind of defining history, and knowledge of the poem was considered an essential part of a young man's education. It is possible that it was dictated by its author to a scribe; however, it may well be that the poem's 15,000 lines were not written down for decades after their original composition, having been composed to be recited from memory – probably in several sessions. By the 6th century BC, written versions did exist and were used at the Panathenaea, the great five-yearly festivals of poetry and athletics held in Athens.

The *Iliad*'s influence continued – helped by the editorial efforts of later Greek scholars who collated existing versions – through the Roman Empire,

Fathers and sons

In this passage, near the end of the *Iliad*, Achilles finally agrees to return Hector's body to his grieving father, Priam, who has come in disguise to the Greek camp. When Achilles praises Priam's 'heart of steel', there is an ironic echo of Hector's dying words to him. At last, the pitiless champion has attained the ability to feel sympathy.

> *'Alas, what weight of anguish hast thou known,*
> *Unhappy prince! Thus guardless and alone*
> *To pass through foes, and thus undaunted face*
> *The man whose fury has destroyed thy race!*
> *Heaven sure has armed thee with a heart of steel,*
> *A strength proportioned to the woes you feel.*
> *Rise, then: let reason mitigate your care:*
> *To mourn avails not: man is born to bear.*
> *Such is, alas! The gods' severe decree:*
> *They, only they are blest, and only free*
> *... Lo! To thy prayer restored, thy breathless son;*
> *Extended on the funeral couch he lies;*
> *And soon as morning paints the eastern skies,*
> *The sight is granted to thy longing eyes.'*

The *Iliad*, Book 14, translated by Alexander Pope, 1720

3000 years of the *Iliad*

c.800–700 BC Homer, whom the later Greeks identify as the *Iliad*'s author-compiler, may have lived at this time, perhaps in western Turkey.

6th century BC The *Iliad* and the *Odyssey* are recited at the Greek Panathenaea festivals.

3rd and 2nd centuries BC In Alexandria, Greek scholars collate and edit the known manuscripts of the *Iliad*: the basis for medieval manuscripts.

1488 The *Iliad* is printed for the first time, in Florence, by an expatriate Greek scholar.

1603–14 The first English translation, by George Chapman, is published.

1720 Alexander Pope's translation is published.

1846 William Munford publishes the first US translation, followed by William Cullen Bryant's better-known edition in 1870.

1945 E.V. Rieu launches the Penguin Classics series with his translation of the *Odyssey*, following it with the *Iliad* in 1950.

2002 The *Iliad* appears in translation online; a parallel Greek and English 'e-text' appears three years later.

and Virgil's *Aeneid*, written around 25 BC, was an attempt to create a Roman myth to match Homer's. The earliest surviving full manuscript of the *Iliad* was written during the 10th century AD and is believed to have been brought west from Constantinople (Istanbul) some 500 years later. A printed version appeared in 1488, and Homer was gradually rediscovered by the humanist scholars who were learning Greek.

Its literary legacy is huge. In its dramatic conflicts, the *Iliad* prefigures the great historical and tragic works of Western theatre, another art form with its roots firmly in the Greek world. In the intertwined conflicts of individual soldiers, armies and gods, and in the subtle interplay between the pride, bitterness, anger and savage remorse of Achilles, it has the beginnings of the fascination with plot and character which, centuries later, would feed the development of the novel. And the intensity of the poem's language looks forward to the whole range of European poetry, not just the long narrative epic.

Among its great and enduring themes are the relationship between men and the gods, the fragility of human life and the nature of warfare. Most of all, however, it is a poem about fury – the fury of military combat, the passionate anger of a proud man who believes he has been wronged, and the wrath that is engendered when each of two implacable sides believes in its own rightness.

Little is known about Homer himself. Early Greek legends suggested that he was blind, and that he may have been a wandering *aoidos*, or singer, who would have recited his work, accompanying himself on the lyre, to the guests at great feasts. We know that the Ancient Greeks themselves confidently ascribed the *Iliad* and the *Odyssey* to him – although they also credited him with many other works that modern experts agree could not possibly have been written by the same man. By the 5th century BC, various authors were writing his biography, although none of the 'facts' they included can be verified.

So what can we deduce about the *Iliad*'s author? It is likely, although not certain, that he would have been illiterate and would have composed his poems orally, for recitation. Linguistic evidence from within the poems, and descriptions of particular artefacts, suggest that they date from later than 1000 BC and

THE *ILIAD* IN ENGLISH

William Shakespeare, although said by his friend and rival Ben Jonson to have had 'small Latin and less Greek', was certainly familiar with the *Iliad*, at least by way of fellow playwright George Chapman's translation into English (1603–14). John Dryden tackled Homer later in the 17th century, as did the philosopher Thomas Hobbes (in part), and the poets Alexander Pope (1715–20) and William Cowper (in 1791) also produced translations. It was the 19th century, though, that raised the *Iliad* to the heights it now occupies, with studies and translations, several of the latter echoing the Homeric formalities of language. Among the most popular, and accessible, translations that the 20th century has offered are that by E.V. Rieu in England (for the paperback Penguin Classics) and in the United States that by Richmond Lattimore in 1965–7. In 1990, the Princeton University Hellenophile Robert Fagles produced a much-lauded version, which also entered the Penguin Classics portfolio, and in the 21st century the *Iliad* has become an online phenomenon.

before 700 BC. Both the *Iliad* and the *Odyssey* are written in a dialect that was spoken in Ionia, on the western coast of modern Turkey. This is at least consistent with the traditional account that Homer was born on the island of Chios in the eastern Aegean, although other islands also claim to be his birthplace.

There remain, however, arguments about whether the *Iliad* and the *Odyssey* were written by the same man, although the Greek philosopher Aristotle suggested in the 4th century BC that the *Iliad* seemed to have been written in the poet's maturity, and the *Odyssey* in his middle age. Further than that, though, we do not even know whether either poem had a single author, or was rather an accretion of versions by unnamed and unknown poets adding to each other's work over the centuries.

About Agamemnon, Achilles and the Greek siege of Troy, too, there is little certainty. Do the poems – almost certainly based on tales and legends that were already centuries old – carry echoes of the exploits of real people in a real military campaign? Archaeological excavations, particularly at the ancient city of Hisarlik on the Turkish coast, have revealed a succession of settlements on the site, which might correspond with ancient Troy, or 'Ilion' as the Greeks knew it. In its last incarnation, this city seems to have been destroyed by fire around 1250 BC, which roughly corresponds with Ancient Greek historians' dating of the Trojan War.

In the end, though, Homer's life – even his existence – is mysterious, and the events of Troy are lost in prehistory. What remains is the poetry and all that it inspired, directly and indirectly – from Aeschylus's tragic masterpiece the *Oresteia* in 458 BC to the Hollywood blockbuster *Troy* in 2004.

The *Histories*

5th century BC

Herodotus

The *Histories* of Herodotus, written in the 5th century BC, are the earliest prose work of Ancient Greece to survive intact. They tell the story of the expanding Persian Empire and the Graeco-Persian struggles of the 6th and 5th centuries. But beyond that, they are the source of much of our knowledge about the ancient world and the foundational work of history in Western literature.

It was Herodotus, the 'Father of History', who established the idea of investigating the past. He coined the term for the genre, the Greek word *historiai* translating as 'investigations', or 'inquiries'. With Herodotus, writers began to find first-hand accounts, look for evidence and describe what happened, and why, without reference to godly intervention or miracles.

The first five of the *Histories'* nine books cover the background to the Persian invasions of Greece, beginning in the mid-6th century BC. Book 1 describes Persian Emperor Cyrus's conquest of Lydia, in western Anatolia (Turkey), while Books 2 and 3 extend to Egypt and the expansion of the Persian Empire under Cambyses and then Darius I. Book 4 follows Darius into North Africa, while Book 5 contains the (unsuccessful) revolt of the Ionian Greek cities on the Anatolian coast in the 490s. The final four books then deal with the Graeco-Persian Wars (490–479 BC), until, as Herodotus says at the end of Book 9, 'the Persians departed with altered minds'.

Historical record and local legend

Herodotus's first words in the *Histories* are a declaration that the work will concentrate on what actually happened.

'These are the researches of Herodotus of Helicarnassus, which he publishes in the hope of thereby preserving from decay the remembrance of what men have done, and of preventing the great and wonderful actions of the Greeks and the Barbarians from losing their due meed of glory; and withal to put on record what were their grounds of feud ...'

But elsewhere, in digressions from his main story of the Greeks and Persians, he describes the religious rites, flora and fauna, and topography of 'exotic' peoples, in often colourful – if sometimes fanciful – evocations:

'The rites which the wandering Libyans use in sacrificing are the following. They begin with the ear of the victim, which they cut off and throw over their house: this done, they kill the animal by twisting the neck ... The eastern side of Libya, where the wanderers dwell, is low and sandy, as far as the river Triton; but westward of that, the land of the husbandmen is very hilly, and abounds with forests and wild beasts. For this is the tract in which the huge serpents are found, and the lions, the elephants, the bears, the aspicks, and the horned asses. Here too are the dog-faced creatures, and the creatures without heads, whom the Libyans declare to have their eyes in their breasts; and also the wild men, and wild women, and many other far less fabulous beasts.'

The Histories, Book 1, Introduction, and Book 4, pp. 188 and 191, translated by George Rawlinson, 1860

The traditional date for Herodotus's birth is 484 BC, at Helicarnassus, an Ionian Greek city on the site of Bodrum, southwestern Turkey – and much of the *Histories* is written in Ionian dialect. But little is known about Herodotus's life. He seems to have lived at various times on the north Aegean island of Samos, in Athens, and in the southern Italian city of Thurii (modern Taranto). Both Thurii and Pella, in Macedonia, claimed to have been the place of his death, sometime between 430 and 420 BC. (The last events mentioned in the *Histories* occur in 430 BC.)

Herodotus was thus about five years old when the wars he describes in Books 6–9 concluded. They began with an invasion of the Athenian hinterland by Darius I in 490 BC, in retaliation for Athenian support of the Ionian revolt. Herodotus describes in Book 6 how, even though the Persians ruled most of the known world at that time – their empire stretching from Asia Minor through the Middle East to Egypt – their expeditionary force was defeated by the Athenians on land at the Battle of Marathon (490 BC).

When Darius's successor, Xerxes, returned with an army ten years later to sack their city and conquer much of the Greek mainland, his initial success was overturned by the Athenian naval victory at the Battle of Salamis (480 BC), the turning-point of the war. The bulk of the Persian army withdrew, cut off from its supplies by the loss of the navy, and the remainder was finally defeated at the Battle of Plataea in 479 BC. Athens now began a period of imperial domination of, and competition with, other Greek city-states. The fact that Herodotus was writing during this period, with the Athenian forces now under increasing pressure from Sparta, has encouraged some commentators to suggest that the underlying purpose of the *Histories* was to warn his contemporaries about the transience of military power.

Within his work's broad structure, Herodotus introduces many digressions in which he explains how various peoples came into contact with their Persian conquerors, and he passes on travellers' tales – some more believable than others – about far-off tribes, their customs, their lands, and the animals that live there.

The *Histories* are thus both more and less than history as we understand it today. They are more, because Herodotus's interest ranges far more widely than his declared subject, the invasions of Greece. He was no book-bound researcher, but a traveller, whose journeys around the Eastern Mediterranean, Egypt and the Persian Empire would have taken him many years; and his subjects included not just history, but also geography, biology and ethnography, loosely bound together as a description of the lands and peoples conquered by the Persians.

But they are also less than what we think of as history, because Herodotus frequently appears to be carried away by his enthusiasm for a good story, and so the reader finds

The Persian invasions of Greece

521 BC Darius I becomes ruler of the vast Persian Empire in Asia and parts of North Africa.

499 BC Greek cities in Ionia, supported by Athens, rebel against their Persian-installed tyrants, until a Greek fleet is defeated in 494 BC.

490 BC An Athenian army under Miltiades defeats Darius's invading Persian army in the plain northeast of Marathon.

480 BC King Xerxes's Persian army overcomes the rearguard resistance of Leonidas and his 300 Spartans at Thermopylae, and proceeds to invade Attica and sack Athens.
   One month later, Themistocles leads the Athenian navy to a decisive victory over the Persian ships in the Bay of Salamis.

479 BC A Greek army under Pausanius, a Spartan, defeats the Persians on land, at Plataea, ending the Persian invasion.

TRUE LIES

Plutarch, the author of _Parallel Lives_ five centuries later and the founder of another historico-literary genre, biography, took a dim view of Herodotus's accuracy. But there are occasions when the claims Herodotus makes carry the ring of truth, even if unknown to him.

On one occasion Herodotus repeats – disbelievingly – a claim that Phoenician sailors had travelled westwards and around the southern tip of Africa. On his own travels in the Northern Hemisphere, the sun would always have been on his left when he was sailing west, and he describes how the Phoenicians claimed that on their journey they 'had the sun upon their right hand'. For Herodotus, this disproved their story. Ironically, this is the detail that proves the story is true: Herodotus did not know that the earth was round, and so could not realize that in the Southern Hemisphere the apparent position of the sun changes.

'fabulous' headless creatures with mouths in their chests (as illustrated on page 10) and great ants bigger than foxes scrabbling gold up from the earth. Additionally, Herodotus puts imagined speeches into the mouths of the often heroic protagonists as if they were characters in a drama.

In this respect, his closest literary ancestor is Homer. But in the _Histories_, unlike the _Iliad_, there are no sudden direct interventions by the gods to change the outcome of battles or rescue hard-pressed heroes. Although Herodotus, like Homer, appears to believe in the divine punishment of human greed, cruelty and arrogance, he concentrates on the effect of human actions on events – the first time such a realistic, rationalist approach had been seen in Greek literature.

Furthermore, Herodotus does at least attempt to evaluate the information he is given. Sometimes he admits that what he is reporting sounds unlikely; and at others, he offers his own restrained seal of approval: 'This seemed to me likely enough.'

There are also eye-witness accounts of his own from his travels, either to demonstrate the truth of what he is saying or simply for dramatic effect. In Egypt, for example, he describes a visit he made to the scene of the Battle of Pelusium, at which the Persians had seized the Egyptian town of Memphis more than a century earlier. There, he says, he saw the skulls of the dead soldiers, Persians in one part of the field, Egyptians in another, scattered where they fell – providing a sombre introduction to his account of the Egyptian defeat. Herodotus's infectious passion for information and insatiable appetite for tales, opinions, and theories make him the forerunner of today's travel writers as much as historians.

Despite the strong Greek national feeling that runs through the _Histories_, Herodotus attempts to be even-handed in his treatment of Greeks and Persians, to such an extent that in the 1st century AD the biographer-historian Plutarch accused him of being _philobarbaros_, a 'lover of the barbarians'. This has not, though, saved him from complaints by modern historians about a lack of objectivity in writing about other cultures.

The themes underlying Herodotus's writing – the dangers of absolute power, the importance of religion in society (although he is always reticent about his own beliefs) and the human cost of war – are also among the important themes of Western literature in the centuries that followed him. Herodotus, for all the inaccuracies and tall stories (which led him to be derided later as the 'Father of Lies' too), set the literary and philosophical agenda for centuries to come.

The *Analects*

5th century BC

Confucius

For much of the last 2500 years, the ideas of Confucius, expressed through his *Analects*, have been the dominant influence on Chinese thought. Confucius's stress on the desirability of virtue and self-discipline among rulers, on the need for good examples rather than legal sanctions, and on the individual rights of even the most wretched pauper, made the *Analects* a truly radical text for its time – and a lasting inspiration for later centuries.

Confucius lived between 551 and 479 BC. His real name was Kong Qiu. The title given him, 'Kong Fuzi', which translates as Master Kong, was a mark of honour and respect. It was Westernized as 'Confucius' in the 17th century by Jesuit scholars, who were preparing the first translations of his thoughts into Latin.

According to traditional Chinese accounts, his political career was brief and unsatisfactory. He had already developed his theory of humane or righteous government by around 500 BC, when he was appointed as a minister by Ding, the new ruler of the principality of Lu in eastern China. But within four years, disillusioned by Ding's frivolous attitude towards his governmental responsibilities, he had resigned his office and left to travel China as a wandering philosopher. His career in practical politics was over.

The traditional accounts have him spending 14 years on the road, gathering disciples as he went; some writers suggest that as many as 3000 people followed him from place to place. That figure seems unlikely, and many of the stories that are told about Confucius on his travels – his repeated expulsion from various royal courts, and the dangers and hardships that he faced – seem based on much older legends. No one knows.

The route to ethical living

Confucius concentrated not just on the duties of the individual in public life, but also on the way a man should behave in his personal relationships. These brief accounts of conversations with two of his followers, Zi Zhang and Fan Chi, illustrate the simplicity and directness of his philosophy.

'Zi Zhang asked: "What must a shi [scholar or minor official] be like to be considered distinguished?"

The Master said: "What do you mean by being distinguished?"

Zi Zhang replied: "Being always famous in a state, or always famous in a noble house."

The Master said: "That is fame, not distinction. A distinguished man is one who is upright in substance and loves righteousness, who examines people's words and observes their facial expressions, and who is anxious to remain humble to others. Such a man is always distinguished in a state and always distinguished in a noble house. A famous man, however, is one who, in appearance, upholds humanity but in action, departs from it and who, nonetheless, arrogates it without scruples."

... When Fan Chi asked about humanity, the Master said: "Loving men."

When asked about wisdom, the Master said: "Knowing men."

Fan Chi did not quite understand. The Master said: "Promote the upright, place them above the crooked, and you shall make the crooked upright."'

The Analects, 12.20–12.23, translated by Chichung Huang

Most accounts agree, however, that he returned to Lu in 484 BC, at the age of 67, and spent the rest of his life in scholarship and contemplation, arranging editions of ancient Chinese texts such as the *Book of Songs*, a collection of some of the oldest works of Chinese literature, dating back to around 600 BC, and the *Book of Documents* and the *Spring and Autumn Annals*, collections of speeches and government records dealing with the principality of Lu and elsewhere. He is believed to have died in 479 BC at the age of 72.

The *Analects* (*Lunyu* in Chinese) takes the form of accounts of conversations between Confucius and his disciples, arranged in 20 chapters and covering such subjects as learning, good government, humanity and the importance of ritual. There is no continuous thread to the thought, and there are still arguments about the arrangement of the different chapters.

The version that survives today is believed to have been gathered together sometime in the 2nd century BC – that is, some 300 years after the death of Confucius himself. It is drawn from the accounts of his disciples, handed down either orally or in separate documents, although arguments continue over how much of the text may have been added long after his death.

One of the main themes of the book is the importance of a rational moral philosophy, or *ren*, which has been variously translated as benevolence, humanity, compassion, virtue or loving others. It is not universal and unconditional brotherly love. Rather, Confucius says, *ren* should be graded according to the closeness of the family relationship, so that a man should love his parents more than his other relatives, his relatives more than his friends, and so on. It does not imply unconditional support, and demands occasional criticism and correction; but Confucius does stress the overriding importance of family relationships. If harmony could be brought to every family, he says, there would be peace throughout the empire. In dealing with the wider world, Confucius's prescription – very similar to the Christian commandment 'Love thy neighbour as thyself' – is that no-one should do anything to other people that he would not wish for himself. In the field of government, that means pursuing justice, honesty, and equality before the law.

The vision of the *Analects* is of an interdependent and mutually supportive society, in which both the rights and the responsibilities of all its members are fully acknowledged: 'you cannot deprive the humblest peasant of his opinion', Confucius says.

He repeatedly stresses that what he is putting forward is traditional Chinese thought – that he is, as he says at one point in the *Analects*, a passer-on of ideas, not a creator – and he concentrates on the importance of precedents, of *li* or strictly-observed ancient rituals, and the desirability of

CONFUCIUS GOES GLOBAL

In recent decades, Confucianism has enjoyed a resurgence of both popular and official Chinese support. Whereas in the 1960s, almost everyone in China possessed a copy of the *Quotations from Chairman Mao* – the so-called 'Little Red Book' – the more recent bestseller throughout China is a modern commentary on the *Analects*, published with a new translation.

Official approval is demonstrated by the rapidly increasing number of Confucian Institutes being opened by the Chinese government in cities throughout the world. These organizations, most of which are attached to universities, exist to promote Chinese language and culture, and to promote the teaching of the language in foreign countries. (They are thus similar in purpose to the German government's Goethe Institutes.) The first was opened in Seoul, South Korea, in 2004, and there are now more than 130 Institutes in 50 countries all over the world. Thus, a 2500-year-old philosopher plays his own part in the emergence of the world's next superpower.

learning from a teacher who is well versed in the ways of the past and the practices of the ancients. This backward-looking, slightly nostalgic aspect of the *Analects* may partly reflect the fact that they were composed at a time when China's traditional warrior society was falling apart and feuding states were launching raids and border wars against each other. It seemed that political institutions were breaking down, making the idea of political and personal harmony particularly compelling.

Confucius's reputation grew steadily after his death. The philosopher Mencius, writing about a hundred years later, said that 'ever since man came into this world, there has been no-one greater than Confucius', and 300 years later, Sima Qian, the early chronicler of Confucius, described him as the wisest of all philosophers. His ideas were influential largely because they were spread in Chinese schools. Confucius had run a school of his own – one of the first to educate the children of the poor as well as those of the nobility – and his philosophy was accepted as the bedrock of the whole Chinese education system. In the 2nd century BC, during the Han dynasty (206 BC–AD 220), Emperor Wu Di treated Confucius's thought almost as if it were a lay religion: he organized his state along Confucian lines, and he specifically declared that Confucianism was to be the only system taught in schools.

The study of Confucian philosophy also became central to the examinations that governed entry to the imperial civil service, and for almost 2000 years it remained the fundamental course of study for any Chinese scholar, passed down from generation to generation. It was only with the republican revolution of 1911 that it was declared to be decadent and reactionary; and later, Confucius was frequently attacked and vilified during the extremes of the 1960s' Maoist Cultural Revolution.

Even then, Confucius's writings never went away. Over history, different rulers, such as the Mongols in the 13th century, had instituted different political systems; and Buddhism and Taoism had emerged as systems of thought and belief competing with the secularist Confucianism. But Confucianism survived among the people as the most lasting political influence in the nation's history. While in recent times Confucius's concern for continuity has sometimes been blamed for China's slow modernization, political and technological, his emphasis on family relationships remains an important influence on thought in China to this day. He has, too, many modern admirers outside China. In January 1988, a conference of Nobel Prize-winners in Paris considered the great issues facing the world in the 21st century. One of their conclusions was: 'If mankind is to survive, it must go back 25 centuries in time to tap the wisdom of Confucius.'

2500 years of Confucianism

551 BC Kong Qiu, later titled Confucius (meaning Master Kong), is born in the Chinese state of Lu, now in the eastern coastal province of Shandong.

500 BC Having risen in government service, Confucius becomes a minister under Lu's ruler, Ding.

497 BC After falling out with Ding, Confucius leaves Lu and spends 14 years travelling, attracting followers and developing his philosophical thought.

484 BC Confucius returns to Lu, and spends last years teaching, writing and editing Chinese classics.

479 BC Confucius dies.

***c.*150 BC** Confucian sayings and aphorisms are collected as *Lunyu* (the *Analects*).

1687 Jesuit missionaries translate *Lunyu* into Latin.

1893 James Legge's English translation names it the *Analects*.

2004 The Chinese government opens the first of its international Confucius Institutes.

The *Republic*, written around 360 BC, set out Plato's ideas about justice and goodness, and how they could best be reflected in an ideal society. While his prescriptions for a city-state run by all-powerful philosopher-kings have yielded little practical application, his ideas about gaining enlightenment and practising goodness offered ethical guidelines for living. In particular, Plato's wider contrast between an imperfect, changeable physical world of mortal bodies and a permanent, immaterial realm of perfect forms and immortal souls exerted a significant influence on the development of both Christianity and Islam – and on Western philosophy generally.

Plato was born into one of the leading families of Athens in either 428 or 427 BC, during the Peloponnesian War against Sparta and her allies. His thoughts about justice may well have been sharpened by two events: his personal experience of oppressive government under the brief rule of the 'Thirty Tyrants' installed by the victorious Spartans in 404 BC; and in 399 BC the execution (enforced suicide by hemlock) of his close friend and mentor Socrates, by the democratic politicians who followed the Tyrants.

After the death of Socrates, Plato left Athens and is believed to have spent several years travelling in Greece, Egypt and Italy. After returning to the city, he founded an academy to train aspiring politicians around 387 BC, where astronomy, ethics, biology, geometry and rhetoric could be taught. He spent the rest of his life in teaching and research; one of his pupils, and later one of his teaching colleagues, was the philosopher Aristotle. Another pupil was Dionysius II, ruler of Syracuse, in whom Plato made some efforts to inculcate his concepts of philosopher-kingship during the 360s.

Scholars are confident that all of Plato's works have survived. Apart from the *Republic* and epistles – some of doubtful authenticity – he also wrote a famous account of the trial of Socrates, the *Apology*, along with a number of other dialogues exploring the nature of knowledge, belief, perception and reality. In the later dialogue, *Laws*, he returned to the *Republic*'s central theme of government. The *Republic* itself is one of a series of dialogues in which Plato lays out his philosophical ideas as a conversation among several characters. These often feature 'Socrates', a sign that Plato regarded himself as an intellectual heir to his great predecessor. In the *Republic*, the Socrates character tries to explain to Glaucon, a young Athenian who has been quizzing him about justice, that the concept means finding what is 'good' and acting in accordance with it. Their conversation is interrupted by Thrasymachus, a wandering intellectual who argues that justice is nothing more than the exertion of strength, and that there is no such thing as 'goodness'.

The life of Plato

427/428 BC Born into an aristocratic Athenian family.

c.407 BC Meets the philosopher Socrates, and becomes a disciple.

399 BC Socrates is executed by the state.

399–87 BC Travels around the Mediterranean and Aegean lands, including spells in Egypt and Sicily.

387 BC Returns to Athens and establishes his school of philosophy, the Academy, spending the remainder of his life teaching, debating and writing his Socratic dialogues (including the *Apology*, the *Republic*, and the *Laws*).

347 BC Dies in Athens.

Everyone in his place

Plato's conception of justice has nothing to do with modern ideas of equality. On the contrary, he says that the Guardians of his republic will be happier and more privileged than the rest of the population. But his aim, he says in this extract, is the happiness of the state as a whole – and that will best be achieved by everyone knowing his place.

'Our guardians may very likely be the happiest of men; but ... our aim in founding the state was not the disproportionate happiness of any one class, but the greatest happiness of the whole; we thought that in a state which is ordered with a view to the good of the whole we should be most likely to find justice, and in the ill-ordered state injustice: and, having found them, we might then decide which of the two is the happier.

At present, I take it, we are fashioning the happy state, not piecemeal, or with a view of making a few happy citizens, but as a whole; and by-and-by we will proceed to view the opposite kind of state ... And so I say to you, do not compel us to assign to the guardians a sort of happiness which will make them anything but guardians; for we too can clothe our husbandmen in royal apparel, and set crowns of gold on their heads, and bid them till the ground as much as they like, and no more. Our potters also might be allowed to repose on couches, and feast by the fireside, passing round the wine cup, while their wheel is conveniently at hand, and working at pottery only as much as they like; in this way we might make every class happy – and then, as you imagine, the whole state would be happy.

But do not put this idea into our heads; for, if we listen to you, the husbandman will be no longer a husbandman, the potter will cease to be a potter, and no one will have the character of any distinct class in the state.'

The *Republic*, Book 4, translated by Benjamin Jowett, 1892

Socrates sidesteps Thrasymachus's challenge, likening the concept of the 'good' to the light given by the sun, and he goes on to describe an ideal city where there is no private property, where wives and children are held in common, and where everything is sacrificed to the common good. The population, made up of foreign slaves, auxiliaries (soldiers, police and government officials) and the mass of workers and merchants, is controlled by learned rulers – philosophers – who know what is good.

While the *Republic* elaborates a rationalist philosophy of an ideal society, its form – as a dramatic and philosophical dialogue, rather than a political treatise – means there are still arguments over whether its suggestions were intended as realistic proposals for governing an actual state. *Republic*, itself, is a later title for the dialogue, from the Roman orator-politician Cicero some 250 years after Plato: it does not accurately represent Plato's Greek word *politeia*, which means 'system of government' or 'rights of citizenship'.

Certainly, the city-state that the Socrates character describes has little to do with any kind of elective, participatory republicanism as it might be understood today: censorship is strict, invalids may be left to die, and those regarded as irredeemably corrupt are to be executed. Rather, a small group of people holds power, supposedly for the sake of the majority. The philosopher-rulers and their auxiliaries (collectively referred to as the Guardians) have a harsh, austere lifestyle, with strict mental and physical training regimes, and their position of authority is reinforced by the spreading of what the Socrates character calls a 'noble lie' – that the gods have made them physically different from the lower classes.

They have, though, been educated so that they can see through the mental and sensory obstacles that clutter human minds to perceive truth, justice, beauty and reality – to use Plato's famous allegory of the cave, they are the citizens who have escaped the darkness and been taken into the light. And it is their enlightenment that qualifies them to rule. In this stress on enlightenment, Plato was offering Greek society a quite different notion of education from that which they were used to. For Greeks of the 4th century BC, memorizing the great poetic works of Homer was the backbone of learning; for Plato, famously, poets (and artists generally) were to have no place in his ideal society, for they toyed with perceptions and could turn falsehood into 'truth'.

No state has ever been deliberately organized along the lines that Plato proposed. Some modern totalitarian regimes have, though, reached similar destinations without recourse to Platonic philosophy, suppressing debate in favour of an oppressive rule vested in oligarchies who, perhaps, convince themselves that have attained their own 'enlightenment'. But the 'Socratic method' of constructing a philosophical case through a series of questions, which Plato passed on through the dialogues, proved highly influential.

'Neoplatonism' – the dominant pre-Christian philosophical umbrella until the 6th century AD – was, as its name suggests, deeply indebted to Plato, and it prepared the ground for early Christianity by elaborating a concept of dualism, whereby philosophical rationalism and ethical concerns on the one hand combined with mystical ideas of the soul and God on the other. The early fathers of the Christian church, such as St Clement (of Alexandria) and Origen, and most notably St Augustine (of Hippo), all combined Platonic reasoning with Christian doctrine in their thinking. Plato's contrast between everyday experience and a world of abstract perfection fitted well with Christian theology, where imperfect humans beset by Original Sin struggled to attain entry to Paradise.

The *Republic* and several other dialogues were also translated into Arabic, and frequently figured in the discussions of Islamic intellectuals, while the 1st-century AD Jewish philosopher Philo Judaeus of Alexandria is often seen as a channel by which Platonic thought reached Jewish culture. Plato's thinking, of which the *Republic* is such an important part, stands at the headwaters of the main channels of philosophy and ethical thinking in both Europe and the Islamic world.

INTO THE LIGHT

In Plato's famous allegory of the cave, in Book 7 of the *Republic*, Plato (through the character of Socrates) imagines people living chained in a hole in the ground, from where the only signs they can see of life outside the cave are the shadows of people walking about.

For them, he says, reality will be nothing but the shadows themselves. If one of the prisoners is then able to go outside the cave, he will be dazzled, and not see the people whose shadows are cast on the wall. Only when his eyes grow used to the light will he be able to see things as they really are. But if he then has to return to the cave, his eyes will not be used to the darkness, and he will no longer be able to see the shadows. 'Men would say of him that up he went and down he came without his eyes; and that it was better not even to think of ascending.'

The journey out of the cave, Socrates explains, represents the ascent of the soul out of the visible world of our everyday experience, where everything is imperfect and subject to change. The chained captives – ordinary people – live there, surrounded by illusions. Those who manage to leave find themselves in an intellectual world, where knowledge is perfect, eternal, and unchanging. Having attained that vision, he says, philosophers will be unwilling to return to the shadowy world that they had left behind.

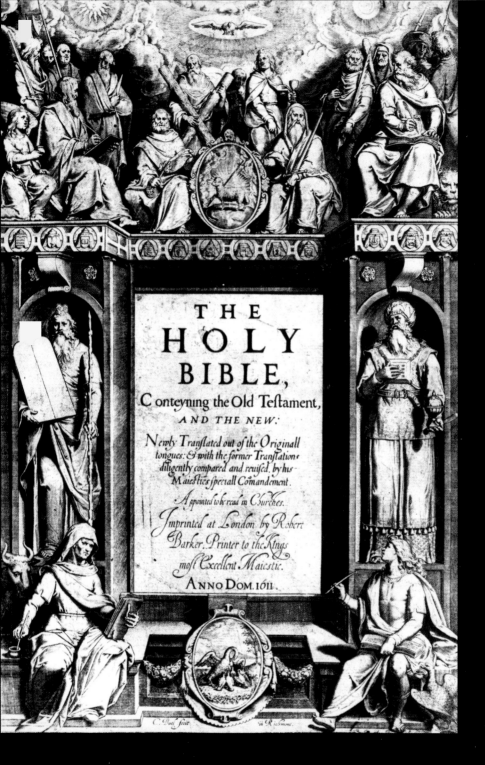

The Bible

2nd century BC – 2nd century AD

It is hard to exaggerate the influence of the Bible. The Old Testament lies at the core of Judaism and Jewish identity; and the New Testament constitutes the central text of Christianity, the principal belief system underpinning Western history, society and culture over the last 2000 years. There are many different versions of the Bible, but all consist of about 66 books, of which 39 in the Old Testament deal with the history, literature and religion of the ancient Jews, and 27 in the New Testament with the life of Jesus Christ and the activities of the early Christians.

The Old Testament books – which make up most of the Jewish Bible, or *Tanakh* (an acronym for its three sections) – were probably gathered from the 12th century BC onwards and compiled into a recognizable form around the 2nd century BC or a little later. (The Orthodox Christian churches have traditionally used an expanded Greek version of the Old Testament, the Septuagint.) The earliest texts would have been written on animal-skin scrolls, in Ancient Hebrew, though some parts were in Ancient Aramaic.

The Old Testament recounts the Hebrew creation myth of Adam and Eve, the turbulent histories of the kings and prophets of the Jewish world, and the story of how Moses led his people, God's chosen, out of captivity in Egypt to establish the land of Israel. In the Psalms, the Old Testament contains 150 religious songs, originally sung to an accompaniment on the harp and

The word and the spirit

The Bible has sustained beliefs about the creation of the world as well as providing a moral and ethical framework for living in it. For some Christians who reject modern physics and evolutionary theory, the first words of the Bible, in the Book of Genesis, carry literal truth:

'In the beginning God created the heaven and the earth.
And the earth was without form, and void; and darkness was upon the face of the deep. And the Spirit of God moved upon the face of the waters.
And God said, Let there be light: and there was light.
And God saw the light, that it was good: and God divided the light from the darkness.
And God called the light Day, and the darkness he called Night. And the evening and the morning were the first day.'

Genesis 1:1–5, Authorised Version, 1611

For a larger number of Christians, 'The Beatitudes' sum up the spiritual essence of a Christian way of life. They occur at the beginning of Christ's Sermon on the Mount, recounted in Matthew's Gospel, which also includes the Lord's Prayer and the instructions to 'Turn the other cheek' and 'Love thy neighbour as thyself'.

'Blessed are the poor in spirit: for their's is the kingdom of heaven.
Blessed are they that mourn: for they shall be comforted.
Blessed are the meek: for they shall inherit the earth.
Blessed are they which do hunger and thirst after righteousness: for they shall be filled.
Blessed are the merciful: for they shall obtain mercy.
Blessed are the pure in heart: for they shall see God.
Blessed are the peacemakers: for they shall be called the children of God.
Blessed are they which are persecuted for righteousness' sake: for their's is the kingdom of heaven.
Blessed are ye, when men shall revile you, and persecute you, and shall say all manner of evil against you falsely, for my sake.'

Matthew 5:3–11, Authorised Version, 1611

traditionally believed to have been composed by King David of Judah and Israel around 1000 BC. Parts of the books of Kings and Chronicles relate the magnificent reign of Solomon, son of David, in the 10th century BC, portraying a united Jewish kingdom at its zenith and the building of a temple to house the holiest of Jewish symbols: the Ark of the Covenant, containing the Ten Commandments.

The New Testament was compiled in Greek between about AD 50 and AD 150. The earliest known versions, tied together in bundles of papyrus sheets known as codices, date to the early 4th century – about the time when Athanasius of Alexandria established the present 27 books as the complete New Testament canon.

The four Gospels (from the Old English *god spel*, or 'good news'), written in the 1st century AD by Matthew, Mark, Luke and John – four of Christ's 12 Apostles – recount, with variations, the story of Jesus's birth, life, conflicts with the Jewish and Roman authorities, death, and resurrection in Palestine, along with the miracles Jesus is said to have performed and the parables with which he illustrated his preaching. For Jews, the Gospels are, at best, imaginative biographies of an errant preacher. For Christians, they are the bedrock of an evangelizing faith, with Christ the Son of God offering salvation to mankind through his death and resurrection.

The beginnings of the early Christian church are recounted in Acts of the Apostles, and in the Epistles traditionally ascribed to the Apostles Peter, John, James and Jude – and to Paul, who was converted to Christianity shortly after the Crucifixion. (Their actual authorship, like that of the Psalms, is hotly disputed.) Paul's epistles, addressed to individuals and to the inhabitants of cities such as Rome, Corinth and Ephesus, had a particularly significant influence on the development of the church in the first centuries after Christ.

There are remarkable inconsistencies in the Bible, most obviously between the vengeful, often angry, and occasionally even spiteful God of the Old Testament and the more mystical, loving Father of the New. Many of these arise because the Bible is, after all, a collection of books by different hands, written centuries apart.

Today, some Christians regard the Bible as the literal and revealed word of God, despite the inherent difficulties of that position. Many other Christians believe that large parts of the Bible are symbolically, rather than literally, true. And today's nominally Christian countries contain millions of people who profess no faith at all. Yet, even for the unreligious, no real

The invention of an English Bible

1380s The outspoken reformer John Wycliffe produces English manuscript translations.

1454 Johannes Gutenberg partially completes a Latin Bible using the technology of print, heralding the wider availability and lower cost of books.

1526 William Tyndale's New Testament in English is printed in Germany and smuggled into England, where it is denounced.

1535 Miles Coverdale's biblical translation is printed in Antwerp.

1539 The official Great Bible, drawing on Coverdale's and Tyndale's work, appears. Its frontispiece depicts Henry VIII handing down the word of God.

1560 The annotated and Calvinist-influenced Geneva Bible appears, translated abroad by dissident scholars; it is printed in England in 1575, to popular acclaim and official suspicion.

1568 Archbishop Matthew Parker and other clerics produce the Bishops' Bible (revised 1572) to replace the Great Bible in churches.

1611 The King James Bible (Authorised Version) is published, becoming the principal translation for over 200 years.

appreciation of the history of Western politics, society, art, architecture, music and literature can be had without at least a nodding acquaintance with their biblical influences.

Early biblical translations were made into Syriac, Coptic, and the Ge'ez language of Ethiopia, among others. Parts were also translated into Anglo-Saxon. But the version that achieved by far the widest circulation and authority was the Latin Vulgate Bible (from *lingua vulgata*, 'common language'), prepared in the early 5th century by St Jerome.

By the 14th century, the insistence of the Catholic Church that only its Latin version should be available was meeting growing resistance. The Oxford professor and theologian John Wycliffe and his followers produced dozens of unauthorized manuscript translations into English; 150 years later – and following the advent of print – William Tyndale was burned at the stake for producing

THE KING JAMES BIBLE

The King James Bible, also known as the Authorised Version, was created from 1604 by a committee of 47 leading scholars and linguists. Working with the explicit support and close personal involvement of England's Protestant king, James I, they completed their work in seven years, and the Bible was published in 1611.

The translators went back to the original Hebrew and Greek (so it contains the Apocrypha), but also relied heavily on earlier translations, notably that of William Tyndale (*c*.1494–1536). Despite some initial criticism, the new Bible rapidly established itself as the preferred version, and it remains so in many Protestant churches – and in the affections of those who love its stately and poetic language.

a printed English translation of his own, copies of which were smuggled into England. At issue was the authority of the church to determine how the Bible was interpreted and transmitted to the people: vernacular translations meant that the literate could read it, and the illiterate could listen to it, which potentially opened up the church's teachings and practices to all manner of debate. In England, as elsewhere, politics played its part, and when Henry VIII broke with the Church of Rome to become supreme governor of a Church of England, an English Bible – the Great Bible of 1539 – became not only acceptable but officially authorized.

Thus, the continuing desire for Bibles that people could read played its part in the bloodletting of the Reformation in the 16th century and the establishment of the Protestant churches. By the late 16th century, the Catholic Church had accepted that it could not prevent translations out of Latin, and issued its own English versions of the Old and New Testaments, translated respectively at Douai and Rheims in France. Other English translations followed – most famously, the King James Bible of 1611.

The spread of Bibles in the 17th century was instrumental in the establishment of nonconformist churches in Britain, Europe and America. Missionaries worked over succeeding centuries to win converts with new translations – the first Bible to be printed in America was in the Algonquin language – but it was not until the 19th century that a popular new version in English appeared. Noah Webster produced a translation in the United States in 1833, and in 1881 the English Revised Version appeared, based on the original Greek and Hebrew texts.

Since then, several new translations have tried to make the Bible more accessible to a modern audience – notably the Revised Standard Version of 1952, the New English Bible of 1961 (New Testament) and 1970 (Old Testament), and the English Standard Version of 2002. At the same time, the work of translation has continued, so that in 2007 it was estimated that at least parts of both the Old and New Testaments were available in a total of nearly 2500 languages.

Odes

The *Odes*, by the Roman poet Horace, are four books of short poems about love, friendship, the pleasures of wine and Nature, and the Roman virtues of dignity and serenity. Simple, restrained and dignified, but always passionate, they are the timeless poems of a man who thinks as well as feels; and they have inspired poets, artists and writers for the last 2000 years. If any one poet has shown us that it is possible to experience deep and lasting emotion but still live in the real world, it is Horace.

Quintus Horatius Flaccus, to give him his proper name, is relatively well documented, not least because the historian Suetonius wrote his life. So we know that he was born in 65 BC in Apulia, in the Latin-speaking heel of Italy, the son of a freed slave who had acquired a modest farm. He had a surprisingly good education, including a spell in Athens, and he was in Greece when the Roman Republic was convulsed by the assassination of Julius Caesar in 44 BC. In the subsequent civil war, at the age of about 21, he joined the army of Brutus and Cassius, two of the conspirators who had assassinated Caesar, and he fought at the Battle of Philippi in 42 BC.

Their defeat by the forces of Mark Antony and Octavian – the future Emperor Augustus – marked the end of the Republic and seemed to do the same for Horace's hopes of prosperity. The family farm had been seized, and Horace seemed to be not only penniless but also friendless. However, he obtained a pardon from the Augustan regime, and with the help of the wealthy literary patron Gaius Maecenas, he gained a junior government post – and wrote poetry.

All the works that Horace published have survived, and they include two books of satires and a volume of poems known as *Epodes*, a series of verses that wistfully suggest a new Golden Age might be found among the islands of the western ocean. He wrote an influential verse treatise on poetry, *Ars poetica* (*The Art of Poetry*), two books of verse letters and a hymn to the Roman gods, *Carmen saeculare* (*The Song of the Ages*), which was commissioned by Augustus himself for public games. Significantly, the early satires seemed to support Augustus's declared intention of restoring traditional morality and promoting self-made men to stand alongside the traditional Republican aristocracy. Horace was balancing his own independent spirit with the

Seize the present

In this extract from Horace's first book of *Odes*, he urges the reader not to worry about the future or indulge in fortune-telling as the Babylonian astrologers do. In other words, 'Gather ye rosebuds while ye may', as the 17th-century English poet Robert Herrick put it.

'Ask not ('tis forbidden knowledge), what our
   destined term of years,
Mine and yours; nor scan the tables of your
   Babylonish seers.
Better far to bear the future, my Leuconoe, like
   the past,
Whether Jove has many winters yet to give, or
   this our last;
This, that makes the Tyrrhene billows spend their
   strength against the shore.
Strain your wine and prove your wisdom; life is
   short; should hope be more?
In the moment of our talking, envious time has
   ebb'd away.
Seize the present; trust to-morrow e'en as little
   as you may.'

Odes 1, xi, translated by John Conington, 1870

The life of Horace

65 BC Born Quintus Horatius Flaccus, in the Roman colony of Venusia, Apulia. Educated in Rome and Athens.

44–42 BC Serves with the Republican army of Marcus Junius Brutus in Rome's civil wars, until their defeat at the Battle of Philippi, in Macedonia.

38 BC Having turned to writing to supplement a meagre income, obtains the patronage of Maecenas, an influential member of the new Augustan regime in Rome.

35 BC His first book of ten *Satires* appears.

***c.*33 BC** Is granted a country villa in the Sabine hills, where he spends much time. Probably begins work on the *Odes*.

30 BC Publishes 17 lyric poems, the *Epodes*, together with a further 8 satires.

23 BC Publishes Books 1–3 of the *Odes*, containing 88 poems.

20 BC Publishes first book of *Epistles*, with more appearing in 14 BC.

***c.*18 BC** Writes the literary essay *Ars poetica* (*The Art of Poetry*).

17 BC Writes the long ode *Carmen saeculare* to celebrate the public games.

13 BC Publishes Book 4 of the *Odes* (15 poems).

8 BC Dies the same year as his patron, Maecenas.

practical need to be loyal to his patron and support the new ruler. Indeed, so successful was Horace in his conversion to Augustan Rome that he was offered the influential and profitable post of private secretary to the emperor: he turned it down, but with such grace that he managed to remain in official favour. By the time of his death, in 8 BC, Horace's star was sufficiently high for his work to have become standard reading in the Roman syllabus.

Horace's lyric poetry was written at what was both the dawn of the Roman Empire and a period of peace and cultural awareness, and he tried to set out a framework for Roman culture, which was already spreading across Europe. It was a time of astonishing literary achievement – Horace's contemporaries included the poets Virgil (70–19 BC) and Ovid (43 BC–AD 17), the older orator-politician Cicero (106–43 BC), the historian Livy (59 BC–AD 17) and the rhetorician Seneca the Elder (*c.*55 BC–*c.*AD 37).

The *Odes* appeared in four separate books, the first three (containing 88 poems) published when Horace was in his early forties. The fourth, with 15 poems, appeared ten years later. Their themes were common enough, for Horace – as with many of his compatriots – was torn between a fascination with wealth, power and glory on the one hand, and an uneasy sense that the better life was one of bucolic calm and simplicity on the other. The *Odes* shiver with that tension, which was felt not just by the Romans of the 1st century BC, but by so many readers in the centuries to follow. Although Virgil's masterpiece the *Aeneid* became the defining poetic epic of the Empire, it describes the way the Romans would like to have seen themselves, aspiring for grandeur and glory. Horace's *Odes*, by contrast, deal with friendship, love and the simple life – as well as the harsher realities of politics.

Unusually for a Roman poet of the period, Horace himself takes a central role in his poems. They dramatize his personal experiences and depict his everyday world, although particular incidents are often drawn from earlier classical models. He mixes calm serenity with blazing passion: he can warn the reader to be guided by 'the golden mean', while in a different poem declaring that he prefers his wine triple-strength, urging: 'I hate your penny-pinching handfuls – scatter roses generously!'

Horace referred to his odes as *carminae*, 'songs', although it is not certain whether they were set to music or simply recited to the accompaniment of a lyre. Their simplicity is deceptive, and their structure, adopting various metrical styles, was highly innovative for Rome. Horace was the first Roman poet to write a significant body of lyric verse, and he claimed to be the first to draw on the classical metres of 7th-century Greek poets Sappho and Alcaeus, and (in some of the more stately odes) the traditional master of the public ode in the 5th century, Pindar.

The *Odes* provided both an image of society in Horace's own day and a model of patriotism and civilized values for the centuries that followed. However close to reality the character he presented in his poetry may have been, the restraint, affection, and easy-going irony that it exemplified were a lasting moral influence. Those qualities, along with Horace's technical mastery, his occasional deprecating references to himself – he is no soldier, he suggests, and tells how he threw away his shield to escape at Philippi – and above all his all-embracing humanity have given his poetry enduring appeal.

For one thing, some of Horace's lines have gained a life of their own, so we have, for example, *Carpe diem!* ('Seize the day') and *Nil desperandum* ('No cause for despair'). The concept of *aurea mediocritas*, 'the golden mean', which Horace borrowed from the Greeks, remains familiar; and it is to Horace that the 19th century owed the popular aphorism *dulce et decorum est pro patria mori* ('it is sweet and fitting to die for your country'), which was given a bitterly ironic twist as 'the old Lie' in Wilfrid Owen's famous war poem 'Dulce et decorum est' (see page 154).

But the literary influence of the *Odes* is much more than that of a collection of Latin tags. Five hundred years after his death they were being quoted by St Jerome, one of the first Latin translators of the Bible. In the early 14th century, Dante, in the *Divine Comedy*, placed Horace alongside Homer and Virgil as one of the three great poets of the ancient world. His influence is clear in the poems and plays of Ben Jonson and Shakespeare, while his imitators over the centuries have included the Renaissance writers Ariosto and Montaigne, John Milton and Andrew Marvell from England in the 17th century, and Alexander Pope and John Dryden in the 18th. 'Horace still charms with graceful negligence, / And without method talks us into sense,' wrote Pope in his *Essay on Criticism*. The 18th-century polymath Voltaire was a French admirer, and Lord Byron – even though he referred to 'Horace, whom I hated so', thinking back on painful Latin lessons as a boy – offered his own versions of the *Odes* and other poems. The echoes are there in the poems of a quite different 19th-century poet, Gerard Manley Hopkins, as well as in W.H. Auden in the 20th, who applauded Horace's ability to look at 'this world with a happy eye / but from a sober perspective'. As that quotation suggests, it was not only Horace's technical skill and classical learning that attracted these and scores of other poets from all over Western Europe, but also the character of the poet that emerges in the *Odes*.

Horace knew that while life was ephemeral, words might be forever. In the third book of *Odes* he staked his claim to a long legacy with the words *Exegi monumentum aere perennius / regalique situ pyramidum altius*, which Ezra Pound translated a millennium later as 'This monument will outlast metal and I made it / More durable than the king's seat, higher than pyramids.' And so it proved to be.

Geographia

c.AD 100–170

Ptolemy

The eight books of Ptolemy's *Geographia* provide our best account of the state of geographical knowledge in the 2nd century AD. But more than just repeating what was already known, Ptolemy strove to achieve the accurate measuring and recording of coastlines, cities, rivers and mountains. He set standards for practical geography, for the assessment of evidence, and for the management of information that later geographers strove to meet over the next 1500 years.

For centuries afterwards, the calculations, discoveries and groundbreaking scientific works produced by Ptolemy – Claudius Ptolemaeus of Alexandria – were forgotten knowledge in Western Europe. There are no original manuscripts, and the *Geographia* survived only in Arabic translations from much later. Out of Arabic, the work was subsequently translated into Greek, and then, in the early 15th century, from Greek into Latin.

Although Ptolemy left no maps of his own, his description of the three continents of Europe, Asia and Africa, and his calculations of the location of some 8000 different towns, rivers, mountains, and headlands were the intellectual foundation on which a great development of new cartography was constructed in the Renaissance. Respect for him was almost universal among Renaissance scholars, and afterwards. Before Gerard Mercator produced his own *Atlas* of the world in the late 16th century (see page 54), he spent more than seven years compiling a book of maps based entirely on the work of the man who became known as the 'Father of Geography'. Even as the map-makers who charted the great discoveries of the 16th century were proving the inadequacy of Ptolemy's vision of the world, they still looked up to him as the ancient fount of geographic wisdom.

Measuring the world

At the beginning of the *Geographia*, Ptolemy sets out his intention to represent the known world as accurately as he can, and also to record the observations of ancient travellers. Accurate measurement, he says, rather than the philosophical pondering of his predecessors, is the true key to geography.

'It is the prerogative of Geography to show the known habitable earth as a unit in itself, how it is situated and what is its nature; and it deals with those features likely to be mentioned in a general description of the earth, such as the larger towns and the great cities, the mountain ranges and the principal rivers. Besides these it treats only of features worthy of special note on account of their beauty … Now, as we propose to describe our habitable earth, and in order that the description may correspond as far as possible with the earth itself, we consider it fitting at the outset to put forth that which is the first essential, namely, a reference to the history of travel, and to the great store of knowledge obtained from the reports of those who have diligently explored certain regions; whatever concerns either the measurement of the earth geometrically or the observation of the phenomena of fixed localities; whatever relates to the measurement of the earth that can be tested by pure distance calculations to determine how far apart places are situated; and whatever relations to fixed positions can be tested by meteorological instruments for recording shadows.'

Geographia, Book 1, i–ii, translated by E.L. Stevenson, 1932

Ptolemy was either Greek or Egyptian by descent, and he lived in the cosmopolitan Roman-Greek city of Alexandria, on Egypt's Mediterranean coast, during the 2nd century. The precise dates of his birth and death are unknown, as are all the other facts about his life. But he was evidently a man of wide interests, for the books he left behind dealt with geography, astronomy, mathematics, astrology, physics and music – virtually the whole range of contemporary learning.

The *Geographia*, in particular, reveals a talented artisan and experimental thinker, as well as a dedicated scholar. Ptolemy was well aware that the geographical knowledge of his day extended at best over only about a quarter of the globe. The known world stretched from the 'Fortunate Isles' in the western Atlantic (probably the Cape Verde Islands) to central China in the east, and from the Shetlands in the north to the eastern coast of Africa in the south. But much was based on conjecture or unreliable reports. Where reliable measurements could be obtained, he said, the map-maker should rely on them: elsewhere, he would have to use his judgement as to what figures to use, 'deciding what is credible and what is incredible'.

Much of the material in the *Geographia* was directly derived from earlier scholars: Ptolemy saw his role as collecting and preserving scientific thought as well as developing his own theories. But, unlike his predecessors from the classical age, he believed that geography was essentially a mathematical enterprise, depending on accurate measurement and calculation. The location of a place, he knew, could be fixed by taking precise observations of the stars, and he constructed a grid to cover the world – an early form of latitude and longitude. Since his figures have been altered, improved, and miscopied by generations of scribes, it is impossible to know how accurate he was; but one short extract, dealing with the path of the Danube in Germany, demonstrates that it was a work of staggering ambition – the first time anyone had used mathematical coordinates in such a way:

> *The headwaters of the Danube 30° 0´ 46° 20´*
> *Alongside where the river first turns into Germania*
> *   32° 0´ 47° 15´*
> *Where the river turning bears towards the south,*
> *   being called Ainos 34° 0´ 47° 20´*

Geography before Ptolemy

c.2000 BC First known map is inscribed on rocks at Bedolina, in the Italian Alps.

6th century BC By tradition, Anaximander produces a map of the known world.

5th century BC Hecateus, an Ionian Greek traveller, creates a map and guide of the Mediterranean world, surrounded by the vast mythical Oceanus, or 'stream of river': fragments survive. Herodotus describes, sometimes fancifully, peoples, lands, animals and customs on the basis of information gained at first and second hand in his *Histories*.

4th century BC Ctesias, a Greek at the Persian court, writes a book about India and a work of theoretical geography. Alexander the Great's conquests encourage geographical curiosity and make available new information. Aristotle offers proof of Pythagoras's view that the world is spherical. Pytheas of Massilia sails around the northern coast of Britain.

3rd century BC Eratosthenes, in charge of Alexandria's library, writes his three-book *Geographica* about the known world, now lost, but reportedly including a map; his *On the Measurement of the Earth* attempts calculations of longitude and latitude, with a meridian running through Alexandria.

1st century BC Roman expansion spreads knowledge of Northern and Western Europe in the Mediterranean world. The historian and traveller Strabo updates Eratosthenes's work with his 17-book *Geography*, the first all-embracing attempt at a physical, descriptive geography of the world, in which the single super-continent (from Spain to India, Britain to Ethiopia) is surrounded by water.

1st century AD Chang Heng, the Chinese astronomer royal, creates a grid system for constructing world maps.

Where the river turning bears towards the north and another river against the Gambretan Forest, 36° 0′ 46° 40′

Next where the river turning against the Lunan Forest by a mountain stream from the north, 39° 20′ 47° 20′

For all Ptolemy's ambitions, the *Geographia* is strewn with mistakes – most of them due to the unreliability of the information on which he had to rely. He underestimated the circumference of the world by some 25 per cent, and exaggerated the length of the Mediterranean and the distance across Asia – mistakes which, by drastically reducing the west-to-east distance across the Atlantic to the 'Indies', may have encouraged Christopher Columbus to set out on his great voyage of 1492.

It is not known whether there were any maps in the original book but the *Geographia* was planned, too, as a practical handbook of geography, in which Ptolemy gave precise instructions as to how they should be constructed. He knew that the world was round, not flat, and laid down guidelines for constructing a globe to show it in three dimensions – although he warned future geographers that they would find a globe either too small to fit enough information on, or too big to be of any use. Better by far, he said, to represent the round world on a flat sheet of paper – and the mathematically-designed projections that he designed for doing so remained the basis of most serious cartography until Mercator designed his own projection some 1450 years later.

Ptolemy's view of the physical world dominated Western geography for almost 1500 years, and the *Geographia* still provides historians with most of what they know about how his contemporaries understood their world. Despite the shortcomings of his magnum opus, Ptolemy proposed a scientific method that represented a huge leap forward in gathering, assessing and combining knowledge. The real importance of the *Geographia*, however, was that it raised the possibility of a world outside. Geographers before Ptolemy had presented a view of a finite world, with the encircling waters of one great ocean, 'Oceanus', lapping at its shores. Ptolemy introduced the concept of *terra incognita*, the 'unknown lands' beyond the sea that explorers would one day reach.

THE *ALMAGEST*

Ptolemy's other books included the *Optica*, a study of reflection, refraction, and colour; *Tetrabiblos* ('Four Books'), dealing with astrology; *Harmonics*, on musical theory; and, most notably, the *Almagest*, in which Ptolemy developed his view of the universe. The earth was at its the centre as a stationary sphere around which the stars, the planets, the sun and the moon revolved in a succession of larger celestial spheres.

This view of creation was derived, like much of the information in the *Geographia*, from the work of earlier Greek scholars, particularly Aristotle. Other Greeks such as Aristarchus of Samos (*c*.310–230 BC) had actually suggested that it might be the earth, rather than the heavens, that moved. But in the *Almagest*, Ptolemy demonstrated to almost universal satisfaction that what became known as the Ptolemaic system, with the earth comfortably at the centre of creation, conformed to mathematical laws.

He was wrong – but this was the view that dominated scientific and religious thought throughout the Middle Ages in Europe and the Islamic world, until, in the 16th century, Nicolaus Copernicus (in *De revolutionibus*) and then Galileo Galilei began a new intellectual revolution.

Kama Sutra

2nd or 3rd century AD

Mallanaga Vatsyayana

No-one knows exactly when the *Kama Sutra* was written. The world's best-known classic of erotic literature is believed, though, to date from before the early 4th century AD. Since the orientalist and explorer Sir Richard Burton famously translated it in the 19th century, it has flourished in the Western imagination as an exotic manual of sexual experimentation. But it is actually far more than this, possessing an underlying philosophical message about the place of sensual pleasure in a serious and religious life.

Type 'Kama Sutra' into an internet search engine, and you will get more than 16 million results, listing intimate gifts and services, love beads, escort agencies, and calendars that you would not send to your mother. But that says more about the internet and the West than it does about the *Kama Sutra*.

Its seven short volumes were written in Sanskrit, the classical language of the Hindu religion, probably during the 2nd or 3rd centuries. They are mostly in prose, with brief sections of verse scattered through them. Little is known about their supposed author, the philosopher Mallanaga Vatsyayana. The whole tenor of the book suggests that he could have spent part of his life as a religious student, possibly in the holy city of Varanasi (Benares) on the Ganges; he is also believed to have written influential commentaries on the 2nd-century BC *Nyaya Sutras* of the Hindu philosopher Aksapada Gotama.

Vatsyayana declares in the opening chapters of the *Kama Sutra* that he is drawing on a lengthy tradition of erotic writing. He names writers such as Auddalaki, Babhravya, Dattaka and Charayana – although we have no surviving works by any of them – and he claims that his own work represents a final distillation of their wisdom.

The first volume provides a general introduction to the whole work and stresses a need to achieve piety, worldly success and sensual pleasure – the Hindu trinity of *dharma*, *artha*, and *kama*. The second volume describes how a man might perfect his sexual skills, the third how a virgin might be seduced, and the fourth how a man should treat his wife (or wives). The fifth

Serenity and sensuality

Although Vatsyayana seems to assume that his readers will mostly be prosperous men, who have the free time to pursue their sexual pleasures, and he generally concentrates on sex from a man's point of view, he also explicitly says that women, too, should take advantage of the instruction he is offering. And true sensual happiness, he insists, is only possible as part of a balanced and contemplative life.

'A man should study the Kama Sutra *and its subsidiary sciences as long as this does not interfere with the time devoted to religion and power and their subsidiary sciences. A woman should do this before she reaches the prime of her youth, and should continue when she has been given away, if her husband wishes it … '*

'… A man who knows the real meaning of this text
Guards the state of his own religion, power, and
*   pleasure*
As it operates in the world, and he becomes
A man who has truly conquered his senses.
The man who is well taught and expert in this text
Pays attention to religion and power;
He does not indulge himself too much in passion,
And so he succeeds when he plays the part of a lover.'

Kama Sutra, 1.3 and 7.2, translated by Wendy Doniger
and Sudhir Kakar, 2002

Erotic classics of East and West

Late 7th century BC On the island of Lesbos, Sappho writes poems of intense feeling about her circle of women friends.

6th century BC The Greek poet Anacreon writes precise and witty poems on the subjects of erotic (and homoerotic) love and wine, invoking the gods of both: Eros and Dionysius.

411 BC In *Lysistrata*, a play by the Athenian comic dramatist Aristo-phanes, the wives of the men of Athens and Sparta deny their husbands sex in order to persuade them to end their Peloponnesian War.

***c.*65–55 BC** The autobiographical Roman poet Catullus describes the pain and ecstasy of a love affair, in verse.

***c.*1 BC** The Roman poet Ovid's popular *Ars amatoria* (*The Art of Love*) offers light-hearted instructions to men and women on techniques of seduction.

11th century AD Fakhruddin As'ad Gorgani's epic poem *Vis and Ramin* describes the tribulations and passionate consummation of the relationship of a Persian prince and princess.

***c.*1524** The poet Pietro Aretino writes sonnets to accompany a book of etchings of sexual positions, *Sei dici modi* (*Sixteen Postures*).

17th century The anonymous *Jin Ping Mei* (translated as *The Golden Lotus*) tells the story of the wives and concubines of a merchant in Ming dynasty China.

1676 The Buddhist scholar Kitamura Kigin collects Japanese homoerotic poems, published 37 years later as *Iwatsutsuji* (*Wild Azaleas*).

volume considers ways of gaining the trust of other men's wives – although Vatsyayana, possibly ironically, stresses that he is not writing to encourage potential seducers but to warn husbands when they should take special care of their wives. In the sixth volume, he describes courtesans – those who 'find sexual pleasure and a natural way of making a living in their sexual relations with men' – and in the seventh he deals with medical, pharmaceutical, herbal and magical ways to improve performance, virility and desirability.

The *Kama Sutra* seeks to place all these sexual subjects within the context of a rounded and fulfilled life. Childhood, Vatsyayana says, is the principal time for education and for acquiring the knowledge that will lead to political and material advancement in later life; the prime of youth is the time for pleasure; and old age is the most important time for the development of the religious attitudes that may enable the individual to escape the Hindu cycle of rebirth.

However, he also stresses that throughout life, the cultivation of the religious sense and piety – *dharma* – is the most important of the three goals; *artha* is the second; and *kama* is only to be pursued once virtue and material prosperity are assured. It is perhaps this hierarchy that enables Vatsyayana to claim that the *Kama Sutra* was written 'in chastity and the highest meditation'.

Vatsyayana presents the book initially as an attempt to distil and impart knowledge, rather than an imaginative work of art. He describes in detail how the earlier authors summarized an initial version of 100,000 chapters, which was given to mankind at the creation of the world as a guide to living a balanced and holy life. This original source of wisdom, he says, was reduced first to 1000 verses and then to 150, until his own work cuts it down to 36 chapters, in 64 sections, arranged into 1250 passages in seven books. (Although recent Western editions have been illustrated with sexually explicit paintings and pictures of erotic carvings from various periods of Hindu history, the original texts – and Burton's translation in the 19th century – were without pictures.)

The *Kama Sutra* claims to offer objective evidence for its propositions and, as do many such Hindu texts, presents apparently complete and exhaustive lists. Vatsyayana specifies 64 arts that an educated person should master, including, for instance, playing musical

EROTICISM IN STONE

Several centuries after the *Kama Sutra* was written, the Chandela Rajput dynasty of India constructed temples at their religious centre, Khajuraho, in modern Madhya Pradesh. They are decorated with world-famous erotic carvings. More than 80 temples are believed to have been built around the end of the 10th century. Most were Hindu, though a few were dedicated to Jain gods. Twenty-two temples remain, now listed as UNESCO-protected monuments.

There is no agreement about the purpose of the erotic carvings, which appear only on the outer walls of the temples and are mingled with other scenes showing farmers, potters and villagers going about their everyday life. Sexually explicit or suggestive images, carvings and dances were an integral part of some Hindu rituals, partly as a celebration of human sexuality, partly to test the devotion of the worshippers, and occasionally also as a way of focusing erotic emotion on the deity itself.

What they do suggest, however, is the very element that gives the *Kama Sutra* its identity: the acceptance of the erotic within a culture and belief system, as a natural part of life.

instruments, preparing wines and drinks, writing verses, the use of disguise, and athletics. There are, he claims, 16 specific ways in which lovers may bite each other, 17 different kisses, and 12 types of embrace.

Some of the numbers Vatsyayana chooses have a magical or philosophical resonance – 64, for instance, which is 2 to the power of 6, was considered to be a sacred figure, and, apart from the number of desirable arts, it is also given as the number of different positions for sexual intercourse.

There is, though, a more poetic and imaginative layer to the *Kama Sutra*. Vatsyayana insists several times that there is more to the subject of sensual pleasure than dry facts: 'This is no matter for numerical lists or textbook tables of contents,' he says at one point; and at another, 'When the wheel of sexual ecstasy is in full motion, there is no textbook at all, and no order.' The moment of experience must always move beyond words.

Each individual volume ends with a verse passage, in which Vatsyayana considers the preceding section and draws general conclusions about it. These verse sections, together with other brief verses scattered throughout, make up about one tenth of its total length. They tend to offer views of a more personal nature, whether they are presented as quotations from earlier writers or written by Vatsyayana himself. Together with the occasional dialogues, in which Vatsyayana – always referring to himself in the third person – argues with other scholars, or in which imaginary characters create situations that he then goes on to resolve, these verse passages help the *Kama Sutra* to transcend the typological and the objective and enter the world of imaginative literature.

In India, the *Kama Sutra* remains an important strand of ancient philosophy. Its history in the West, where Christianity and sensuality/sexuality have always been uneasy bedfellows, is rather different. Burton's translation, in 1883, caused a furore in Victorian Britain, even though with Burton (and for some years afterwards) its eroticism was disguised by a veneer of high-minded scholasticism. Since the relaxation of sexual inhibitions in the 1960s, and following a resurgence of interest in Indian culture and thought in that decade, one of the *Kama Sutra*'s legacies is the huge number of sex manuals that have been published. The most famous of these, *The Joy of Sex* by Dr Alex Comfort (1920–2000), sold over 8 million copies between 1972 and 2000, when it was updated and reissued. In its own way, Comfort's book broke down inhibitions and raised awareness, 'changing the world' for some who read it. But it is a long way from its forebear, the philosophic-erotic classic, *Kama Sutra*.

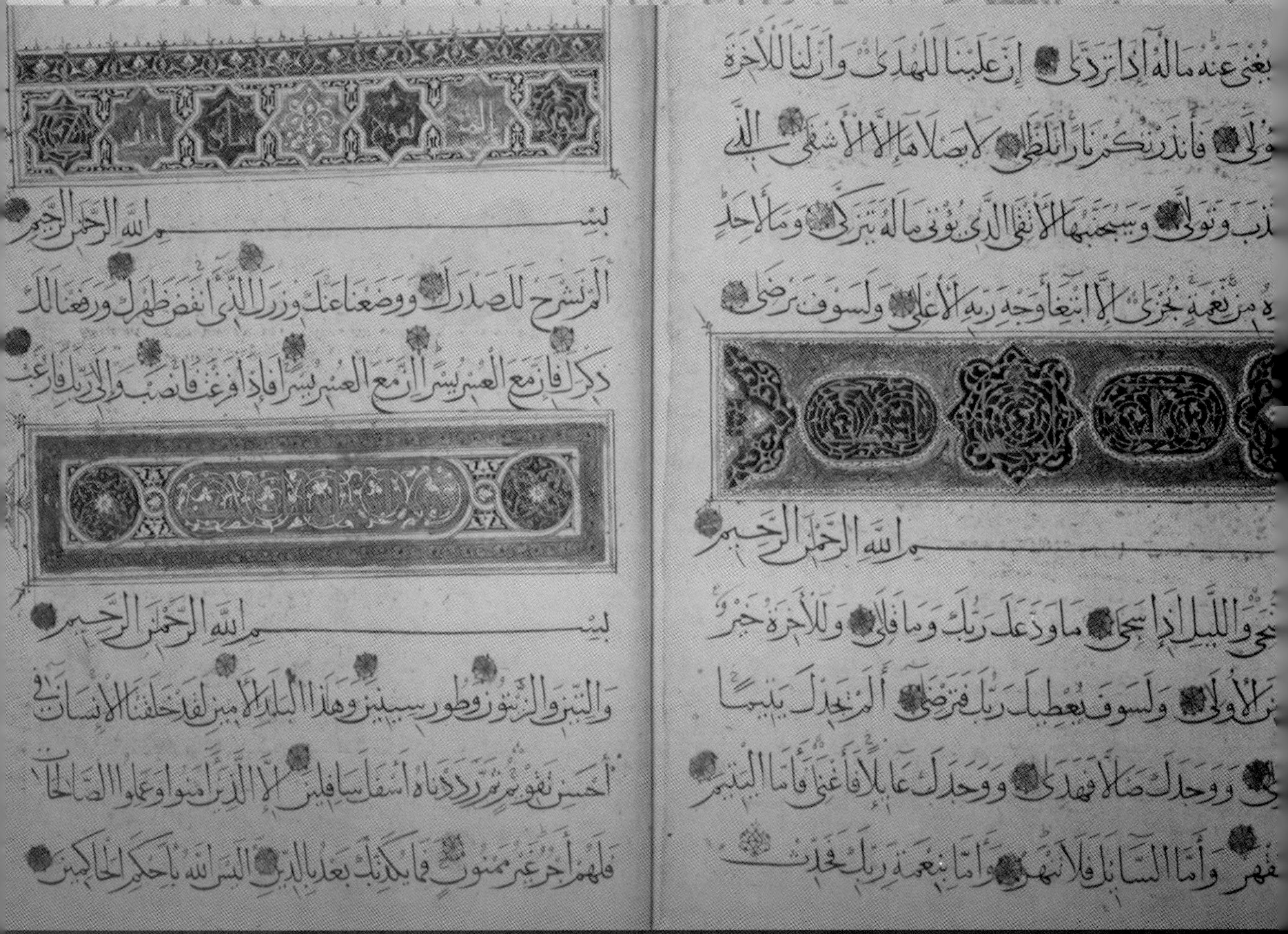

The Qur'an

7th century

For Muslims, the Qur'an – the holy book of the Islamic faith – is unique, unchallengeable, and ultimately untranslatable. Christians refer to the New Testament figuratively as the 'Word of God', but accept that it was written down by followers of Christ during the 1st century AD. Muslims, by contrast, believe the Qur'an is the literal word of God, as revealed to the Prophet Mohammed through the Archangel Gabriel between AD 610 and 632.

Mohammed was born in Mecca in 570, grew up in the Arabian desert, and was later cared for by his uncle Abu Talib after his parents died. He acquired a reputation for devoutness and spirituality, as well as for his skills at settling disputes among men. From 610, when he first reported receiving the holy revelations to his wife Khadijah, he began to preach and don the mantle of the Prophet, acquiring an ever larger following, but earning the hostility of the unconverted and polytheistic Meccans. In 622, three years after the death of his wife and uncle, he took his supporters away to Medina. The next few years saw armed conflict between Mohammed's converts and the Meccans, but in 629 the first pilgrimage (*haj*) to Mecca took place. The breaking of the truce saw Mohammed leading thousands of followers to capture Mecca in 630. Two years later the Prophet was dead. But the ramifications of the previous 20 years of his life were were immense.

It was the Qur'an and the example of the Prophet that brought together the Arabian tribes and which, in the 7th and 8th centuries, inspired the great Muslim empires such as the Umayyad and the Abbasid, which dominated the Middle East, southwestern Asia and much of North Africa for 600 years. Although the followers of Mohammed split their allegiances among differing groups of his family's descendants, resulting in the two denominations of Sunnis and Shi'ites, those divergences of view are about traditions of leadership and descent, and not about the nature or text of the Qur'an.

The name 'Qur'an' (or Koran) is derived from the Arabic for 'recitation', and it is significant that, according to

'In the name of Allah'

The Qur'an opens with the verse known as the 'Bismillah' ('In the name of Allah'), from its first three Arabic words. This phrase, testifying to the goodness and mercy of God, precedes almost all the *surahs*, and it occurs in the call to prayer and in the five daily Muslim prayers. It is also often offered as a brief prayer before any important activity. The *surah* continues to pray for God's help in obeying his laws.

'In the name of Allah, the Beneficent, the Merciful.
Praise be to Allah, Lord of the Worlds,
The Beneficent, the Merciful.
Master of the Day of Judgment,
Thee (alone) we worship; Thee (alone) we ask for help.
Show us the straight path,
The path of those whom Thou hast favoured;
  Not the (path) of those who earn Thine anger nor
  of those who go astray ...'

The Qur'an's final *surah*, An-nas ('The Men'), is the shortest. It offers a prayer for God's protection from evil, both from the *jinn*, or angels of the Devil, and from mankind.

'... Say: I seek refuge in the Lord of mankind,
The King of mankind,
The God of mankind,
From the evil of the sneaking whisperer,
Who whispereth in the hearts of mankind,
Of the jinn and of mankind.'

The Qur'an, 1:1–7 and 114: 1–6, translated by
Marmaduke Pickthall, 1930

TRANSLATING THE QUR'AN

The Arabic Qur'an is ubiquitous throughout the polyglot Islamic world. Most Muslims who speak no other Arabic are at least acquainted with the words of the Qur'an, and there has always been a strong feeling among many Islamic scholars that the original Arabic should be respected as the actual words of God. Translators have thus always faced theological difficulties, but also linguistic ones. Many Arabic words have more than one meaning, and can be interpreted differently according to context, which makes the dense and often mystical text almost impossible to reproduce in another language.

Nevertheless, translations of parts of the Qur'an are believed to have been sent during Mohammed's lifetime to Christian leaders, including the Byzantine Emperor Heraclius and Emperor Negus of Abyssinia; and shortly after Mohammed's death, the first translation into Farsi was made by one of his followers, 'Salman the Persian'.

A 12th-century Latin version, prepared by the English theologian Robert of Ketton, was the basis for translations into other European languages for some 400 years. But it was written, like most of the European versions that followed it, specifically to denigrate the Muslim faith. In England, the 16th-century Arabist William Bedwell published commentaries on the Qur'an, but a full English edition had to wait until the 17th century.

Muslim ideas of its origin, it was heard by Mohammed, and not read as a text. It fits most comfortably, in other words, into an oral, rather than a written, tradition. Although there are different views about exactly how it was passed on after Mohammed's death in 632, there is no doubt that it existed for several years simply as a holy recitation, remembered and repeated by his followers. The language shares some of the rhythms and other characteristics of ancient oral poetry, like Homer's *Iliad* or *Odyssey*, which make it possible, with determination, to commit the book to memory despite its great length – some 80,000 words. Today, a Muslim who achieves this feat is highly honoured, and referred to as a *hafiz*.

Some Muslims believe that Ali ibn Abi Talib, Mohammed's son-in-law, compiled the first written version of the Qur'an shortly after the Prophet's death, from his memories of Mohammed's recitations, and showed it to the people of Medina; others contend that the first text was created by scholars on the orders of the first caliph, Abu Bakr. There is no dispute, though, about what constitutes the canonical text of the Qur'an, which Muslims believe was established about 20 years later, when the third caliph, Uthman, ordered that a final authoritative version should be written down.

However, there are different views even among Muslims about how the book may have reached its final written form, and many Western scholars, challenging the Muslim belief in its divine origin, suggest that this may not have happened until much later.

Like the Bible – which, along with the Jewish Torah, is also considered by Muslims to be a divine revelation – the Qur'an is divided into chapters (114 *surahs*) and then verses (*ayat*), although its overall structure, with no clear storyline, is very different. The first of the *surahs*, al-Fatihah ('The Opening'), is recited daily as part of a Muslim's prayers. The rest are arranged according to length, with the longest, al-Baqarah ('The Cow'), coming immediately after al-Fatihah. Among other *surahs* are ar-Ra'd ('Thunder'), bani Isra'il ('The Israelis'), Maryam ('Mary') and al-Anbiya ('The Prophets'). There are further divisions into thirty sections, or *juz* – which means that devout Muslims can read the entire book over the thirty days of the holy month of Ramadan – and into seven *manazil*, which means it can be read over a single week.

The Qur'an refers to many events and stories that are also described in the Bible and the Torah, although with important differences. Adam and Eve are tempted, eat the forbidden fruit, and are expelled from the garden in both books, for instance. However, while the Bible blames Eve for leading Adam to eat, the Qur'an shares the blame equally between them; and where the Bible story ends with the punishment of Adam and Eve, the Qur'an stresses their forgiveness. Original Sin is a Christian, not an Islamic, concept.

In the third *surah*, al-i-Imran ('The Family of Imran'), the Qur'an tells how the angels told Mary that she was to be the mother of Jesus ('Isa'). But while in St Luke's Gospel the Archangel Gabriel goes on to say: 'He shall be great, and shall be called the Son of the Highest,' the Qur'an honours Jesus simply as one of the prophets following on from Moses.

At the centre of the Qur'an's philosophy is godliness, *tawhid*, the acceptance of God's divine truth as revealed to Mohammed, with everything that implies for the way one leads one's life: Islam means 'surrender to God', and there is therefore a sharp distinction between those who believe and become part of the community and those who live in *kufr*, disbelief. The Qur'an structures everyday life for millions of people to an extent that the Bible has rarely done. In particular, Islamic law, or *Shari'ah*, is based on the Qur'an as well as the *hadith* (or traditions about the life and sayings of the Prophet Mohammed). Indeed, scholars and religious leaders claim to be able to find guidance within these two 7th-century sources to enable them to give rulings on virtually every aspect of modern life.

Nevertheless, as with the Bible and every other inspirational religious text, its influence over individuals varies widely, and in the 21st century debate about how to live life as a 'true' Muslim is fertile. While a minority might claim to find justification in the Qur'an for blowing up strangers in a café, others are led to establish schools and hospitals. The answers the book gives ultimately depend on the questions asked of it.

From Arabic revelation to English interpretation

610 The Archangel Gabriel's first revelations are made to Mohammed, by Muslim tradition.

619 Mohammed's 'year of sorrows' witnesses the death of his uncle and wife, but also his most intense periods of revelatory experience.

632 Mohammed dies in Medina, after which the Qur'anic chapters and verses are preserved orally.

***c*.650** Caliph Uthman orders the preparation of the first written, canonical Qur'an.

1143 Robert of Ketton is commissioned by the Abbot of Cluny to denigrate the 'pseudo prophet' Mohammed in the first Latin translation of the Qur'an.

1649 Scottish cleric Alexander Ross's translation of the Qur'an, from a French version, is the first full English edition but is unreliably loose.

1734 George Sale publishes an important translation, the best known until the early 20th century.

1914 Eight English translations now exist, half by Muslim scholars.

1930 The orientalist scholar and Muslim convert 'Mohammed' Marmaduke Pickthall publishes an acclaimed English translation.

1934 A translation by Abdullah Yusuf Ali, a Cambridge-educated Indian civil servant, proves popular among the Muslim community.

1985 An American English version appears, published by Dr Thomas B. Irving, a Muslim convert.

21st century The University of Southern California hosts parallel translations, by Pickthall, Yusuf Ali and M.H. Shakir, on the Web.

Canon of Medicine

Avicenna's encyclopedic *Canon of Medicine* formed a crucial 11th-century bridge in the history of medicine. It brought together the knowledge and theories of Ancient Greek luminaries – largely forgotten in medieval Europe – with the traditions of Persia and India and the best of contemporary medical understanding. The *Canon* preserved the history of medicine up to that time, but also laid the foundations of modern, experience-based, medical science.

The *Canon*, more than a million words long, was completed in 1025, and translated into Latin in the 12th century, and into Hebrew a hundred years later. Its compiler was the prodigiously talented and polymathic Avicenna, whose name is the Latin form of 'Aven Sina', the Hebrew version of 'Ibn Sina' (in full, Abu Ali al-Husayn Ibn Abd Allah Ibn Sina). He was born around 980 near the ancient city of Bukhara, in modern Uzbekistan, and educated by a private tutor. Intellectually precocious, by the age of 18 he was discovering new treatments for disease, and by his early twenties he was personal physician to Sultan Nuh Ibn Mansur al-Samai, of the Persian Samanid dynasty in Bukhara.

Curing the sultan of a dangerous illness led to the young Avicenna being granted access to his rich and extensive library, where he researched and wrote books on science, mathematics, law, and ethics. However, the fall of the Samanids and the death of his father left him a wandering scholar, moving from city to city, and settling briefly in Rai, near modern Tehran, and Qazvin, in northwestern Iran. For a while, in the city of Hamadan in west-central Iran, he was appointed court physician to Prince Shams al-Dawlah of the Buyid dynasty, one of the family that had seized control of the Abbasid Empire in Baghdad. Following his father into government service, he was twice appointed vizier or chief minister.

During this period, Avicenna is believed to have begun work on the three-volume *Canon* (in Arabic, *Al-Qanun fi al-Tibb*). In it, the learning of Hippocrates and Aristotle from the 5th and 4th

Traditional theories, experimental practices

The *Canon of Medicine* was the first book of medicine to base its theories on evidence and objective experimentation, but Avicenna also accepted many traditional ideas about the human body. These extracts demonstrate both the conservatism of his philosophy and the radicalism of his medical treatments.

'Natural philosophy speaks of four elements, and no more. The physician must accept this. Two are light, and two are heavy. The lighter elements are Fire and Air; the heavier are Earth and Water.

Light: equivalents: weak, male (because conferring or inceptive), positive, active. Heaven.
Heavy: equivalents: strong, female (because recipient), negative, passive. Earth ...'

'... There are three groups of agents which alleviate pain: (i) Some contrary to the cause of pain, which removes the cause, e.g. Anethum, linseed, made into a poultice and applied over the painful place; (ii) any agent which counteracts the acrimony of the humours, or soothes, induces sleep, or dulls or soothes the sensitive faculties and lessens their activity, e.g. inebriants, milk, oil, aqua dulcis, etc.; (iii) an agent which infrigidates as dulls the sensation in the painful part, e.g. all narcotics and somniferous drugs. The first of the three is the most certain.'

Canon of Medicine, Book I, pp. 34 and 251, translated by O. Cameron Gruner

centuries BC co-exists with that of another famous Greek doctor, Galen, from the Roman Empire of the 2nd century AD. Added to them are the writings of Persian and Indian physicians, as well as Avicenna's own observations and the writings of his contemporaries.

Different sections of the book deal with anatomy, physiology, general pathology and detailed studies of individual diseases, along with descriptions of simple and compound drugs that might be used to cure them. It is a triumph of organization and categorization – for example, Avicenna lists 15 different types of pain: boring, compressive, corrosive, dull, fatiguing, heavy, incisive, irritant, itching, pricking, relaxing, stabbing, tearing, tense and throbbing. But the breadth of his references and the detail of his understanding were matched by a resolutely practical interest in surgery and the application of medical knowledge. For example, among the procedures spelled out were clearing out the airways with a length of reed wrapped in soft material to assist breathing, inserting a tube – 'gold or silver', he insisted – into the pharynx, or, as a last resort, performing a tracheotomy to allow air to reach the lungs.

Avicenna recommended techniques for anaesthetizing patients and relieving pain, including the use of mandrake root or opium – not more than two grains, or a dose the size of a large lentil, he says – taken orally to bring about sleep before the amputation of a limb or the excision of a cancerous tumour (another surgical procedure that he proposed). Opium, he suggested, could also be used locally for pain relief.

Many of the herbs that he recommended for their curative properties had not been used in medicine before. Avicenna suggests that wounds should be washed in wine, implying that he understood the antiseptic effects of alcohol, and he set out rules for the testing of medicines, including the need for purity, blind testing and close observation of timings and results. The *Canon* was also one of the first surviving medical texts to suggest that the pulse was caused by the beating of the heart, and Avicenna proposed checking a patient's pulse rate by feeling his wrist. He was said to be able to diagnose certain diseases solely by using this method.

Although the learning of ancient times was largely forgotten or ignored in the Europe of Avicenna's day, in the Arab world the study of Ancient Greek, Persian, and Indian medicine was

FATHERS OF MEDICINE

Avicenna was not the first man to be called the 'Father of Medicine'. Earlier claimants to the title include the Greeks Hippocrates of Cos (c.460–c.370 BC) and Galen (AD 129–200). Hippocrates is credited with abandoning superstitious and religious beliefs about the divine origin of illness in favour of the treatment of symptoms and an awareness of the importance of personal habits, diet and environmental factors in preserving good health. And the professional oath that many doctors swear today is derived from the traditional Hippocratic Oath, thereby honouring Hippocrates' legacy.

Galen wrote a number of commentaries on Hippocrates. Born in Pergamum, Asia Minor (modern Turkey), he travelled to Rome and became personal physician to Emperor Marcus Aurelius. In his life he achieved a reputation for painstaking dissections and for carrying out complex surgical operations, including one for cataracts.

Avicenna built on the knowledge of these two 'fathers', but brought to it a much wider experience and a greater breadth of reference from Western, Arab and Eastern sources than they could command. He deservedly became known to later generations as the leading authority on everything to do with medicine, and perhaps the title 'Father of *Modern* Medicine' belongs to him.

already well established. Scholars at the famous philosophical and medical school at Gundishapur, in southern Iran, studied Greek texts translated into Arabic, Syriac and other Middle Eastern languages by monks from Byzantium and Alexandria centuries earlier. The *Canon of Medicine* was the first book to bring together all these different sources of medical knowledge, and it became the most widely used and comprehensive work on medicine during the Middle Ages, both in Europe and in the Arab world. It was clear, concise, and authoritative, and it gave ready guidelines to which doctors could refer in treating disease.

In some respects, and despite his innovations, Avicenna's acceptance of the wisdom of the past perpetuated medical red herrings. He did not question such fundamental theories as the belief in the four bodily 'humours' of blood, yellow bile, black bile, and phlegm, representing air, fire, earth and water respectively, whose imbalances in the body he believed to be responsible for most sickness. Indeed, partly through his authority, this belief became the bedrock of later medieval medicine. But his actual observations were acute and his remedies as reliable as any to be found in his day – and his recommendation of experience, observation and practical experimentation as the basis of progress justifies the reputation of the *Canon* as one of the original texts of medical science.

With the invention of the printing press in Europe in the 15th century, the book spread across the continent, and its Latin version was reissued 16 times between 1470 and 1500, going through another 20 editions in the hundred years thereafter. Added to, commented on, and revised by generations of scholars, it remained one of the most influential textbooks in the medical schools of Europe well into the 17th century.

As for Avicenna himself, his later years saw prolific work but also imprisonment and exile. As he was writing the *Canon* he was also working on another literary triumph, the mammoth scientific and philosophical *Kitab al-shifa*, or *Book of Healing*. The death of Shams al-Dawlah in 1022, however, meant that Avicenna was briefly imprisoned and then forced into exile. He took refuge in Isfahan, in central Iran, where he spent the remaining 15 years of his life. Here, honoured at the court of Ala al-Dawlah, he completed his two great books. He also composed an account of his own philosophical development, the *Kitab al-isharat wa al-tanbihat* (*Book of Instructions and Words*), a summary of the *Kitab al-shifa*, and over 200 short treatises on various philosophical and scientific subjects, as well as books now lost. He died in 1037, accompanying the ruler on a military campaign against the town of Hamadan, where he had once lived. With a posthumous reputation as one of the greatest philosophers of medieval Islam, his tomb is still venerated there today.

The Life of Avicenna

***c.*980** Avicenna (Ibn Sina) born near Bukhara, in modern Uzbekistan, a cultural centre of the Persian Samanid dynasty. As a child, he demonstrates early talent.

***c.*1001** Becomes physician to Sultan Nuh Ibn Mansur al-Samai, in Bukhara, and produces his first of many books.

1004 The fall of the Samanid dynasty to the Turks pushes Avicenna into exile and itinerant life in Khorasan (eastern Persia and western Afghanistan), working variously as a physician, teacher and administrator, until finding favour as physician and vizier under Prince Shams al-Dawlah in Hamadan, Persia.

1022 Moves to Isfahan, and into the service of its ruler, Ala al-Dawlah. Works on his two major books, the *Canon of Medicine* (completed 1025) and the encyclopedic-philosophic *Book of Healing*.

1037 Dies at Hamadan.

The Canterbury Tales

1380s–90s

Geoffrey Chaucer

Geoffrey Chaucer's collection of tales told by a group of pilgrims as they travel to Canterbury can lay claim to be England's first masterpiece of creative literature in the vernacular English of its time, rather than in the French or Latin used at court and in church. But Chaucer did not only 'give the people a voice'; he also produced a work whose breadth and variety of tone and character ranks with Shakespeare and Dickens.

Geoffrey Chaucer (*c.*1343–*c.*1400) combined a life as a royal official with his writing. His other works include *The Book of the Duchess,* an elegy for the Duchess of Lancaster; *The House of Fame* and *The Parlement of Foules* (Fowls), two 'dream-vision' poems; and *Troilus and Criseyde,* a poem about Troilus and Cressida in the Trojan Wars, which some critics consider to be one of the finest love poems in the language. But it is *The Canterbury Tales* with which his name is indelibly associated.

In the *Tales,* the pilgrimage to St Thomas Becket's shrine in Canterbury – a popular act of medieval religious devotion – is a simple device linking a succession of disparate stories. Each of the pilgrims is briefly introduced in the General Prologue, and then presented in more detail in separate prologues to their own tales. All this is interspersed with squabbles, bickering and boisterous exchanges with Harry Bailly, landlord of the Tabard Inn, in Southwark, London, where the group gathers at the start of the poem. Not all the pilgrims introduced (such as the Ploughman) eventually reappear to tell their tales, so there is evidence the poem was never fully finished. The General Prologue sets the scene, in its Middle English vernacular:

> Whan that Aprille, with his shoures sote [showers sweet]
> The droghte [drought] of March hath perced [pierced] to the roote
> And bathed every veyne in swich [sweet] licour,
> Of which vertu [by virtue of which] engendred is the flour [flower] …
>
> Thanne longen folk to goon on pilgrimages …
>
> In Southwerk at the Tabard as I lay,
> Redy to wenden on my pilgrymage
> To Caunterbury, with ful devout corage,
> At nyght [night] were come into that hostelrye
> Wel nyne [nine] and twenty in a compaignye
> Of sondry folk, by aventure yfalle [by chance we met]
> In felaweshipe, and pilgrimes were they alle,
> That toward Caunterbury wolden ryde.

A pilgrimage was one of very few occasions in the Middle Ages when a cross-section of society might be gathered together in an informal way, which is crucial for the social commentary of Chaucer's poem. There are no aristocrats – the Knight is the highest-ranking member of the party, and fittingly tells the first story – and no member of the lowest social classes; but the pilgrims still cover a wide spectrum. Many of them, such as the Prioress, the Monk and the Friar, have close connections to the church, but the group also includes a doctor, a lawyer, a merchant and various tradesmen. There is the five-times-married and well-travelled Wife of Bath, who is particularly conscious of her social position, and the vulgar Miller, with a hairy wart on his nose, a red beard and mouth as big as a

CHAUCER'S 24 PILGRIMS' TALES

The Knight's Tale a courtly romance about two knights who fight a duel over a lady.

The Miller's Tale a bawdy farce about jealousy and infidelity.

The Reeve's Tale a tale of black humour about two students who avenge themselves on a dishonest miller by sleeping with his wife and daughter.

The Cook's Tale the unfinished account of the exploits of a lusty young apprentice who goes to live with a friend and his prostitute wife.

The Man of Law's Tale an exotic tale about a Christian princess betrothed to an Arab sultan and later shipwrecked on the English coast.

The Wife of Bath's Tale the romantic story of a knight's quest to find what women really desire.

The Friar's Tale a satire describing the misdeeds of summoners or church officials.

The Summoner's Tale a riposte to the Friar's Tale, describing how a cheating friar gets his comeuppance.

The Clerk's Tale the story of the ruler of the Italian town of Saluzzo, and how he tests the fidelity of his new wife.

The Merchant's Tale the story of the cuckolding of a wealthy, blind old man by his young wife.

The Squire's Tale an unfinished epic romance, which starts with the appearance of a mysterious knight carrying gifts for the king.

The Franklin's Tale a romantic story of the love of a young knight and his lady, and of her refusal to betray him.

The Physician's Tale the classical story of a noble Roman who kills his own daughter rather than allow her to be seized by a corrupt and licentious judge.

The Pardoner's Tale a fable in which three drunks agree to kill Death, but fall out and kill each other.

The Shipman's Tale the bawdy story of a merchant robbed and cuckolded by a visiting monk.

The Prioress's Tale an anti-Semitic Christian story about the murder of a young child by Jews.

The Tale of Sir Topas an unfinished story told by Chaucer himself as one of the pilgrims, about the quest of a child knight to find a fairy queen.

The Tale of Melibeus a long prose story, also told by Chaucer, on the ethics and philosophy of vengeance.

The Monk's Tale a collection of 17 short stories on the theme of tragedy.

The Nun's Priest's Tale the fable of a cockerel's escape from a fox.

The Second Nun's Tale the story of the martyrdom and miracles of St Cecilia.

The Canon's Yeoman's Tale an attack on the fraudulent practices of alchemists.

The Manciple's Tale a fable about Apollo, his unfaithful wife and a crow who reveals her secret.

The Parson's Tale a long prose sermon on penitence and the virtuous life.

furnace. There is the prosperous Franklin or landowner, of whom Chaucer says, 'It snowed in his house of meat and drink', and a humble Ploughman, fresh from laying dung in the fields.

Chaucer presents himself as a wide-eyed, trusting and naïve narrator – but his acute observations reveal the foibles and hypocrisies of all the pilgrims, except for the Knight, the Parson and the Ploughman. These three are depicted as moral and upright representatives of military, religious and civil life. In contrast, the Prioress wears a brooch with the motto *Amor vincit omnia* ('Love conquers all'), suggesting a life not wholly devoted to religion; while the Monk has no time for sacred texts that forbid holy men from hunting; and, although the Man of Law appears 'discreet and full of reverence', he still 'seemed busier than he was'. All but two tales are in verse, but they vary greatly in their style and mood, from the courtly language of the Knight's Tale to the crude humour of the Miller's and the Merchant's. The overall effect is one of light, subtle and reflective satire. There is little doubt that Chaucer intended the poem as a whole to cast an ironic light on the manners and morals of his time.

One of the triumphs of the poem is that, at a time when French was the language of the Court, the law and high society in general, *The Canterbury Tales* was written largely in English, the language of the people. Chaucer's style is often mannered and almost courtly in tone, with an abundance of French borrowings and Latin words – but in the speech of some of his pilgrims he brings the rough vernacular of ordinary people into English literature.

The pronunciation of *The Canterbury Tales* reflects a radical change in spoken English during Chaucer's time, as the language emerged from more than two centuries of French domination. Words like *droghte* (drought) or *nyght* (night), as in the extract above, were pronounced with the 'gh' sounding almost like the 'ch' in the Scottish 'loch'; *perced* (pierced), with a vowel that would sound Scottish today, and the final 'ed' spoken as a separate syllable, so that the word would have been pronounced 'pairs-ed'; *licour* (liquor, or sap) would have a long final syllable, as in the modern 'tour'; the long vowel in *swete* (sweet) would be more like 'ay' than 'ee'; and the final 'e' would be pronounced, so the word would sound like 'swayt-uh'.

The continuing influence of the French language meant that a word such as *engendred* would have had a nasal 'on' sound, and the '-age' suffix in *pilgrimage* and *corage* (courage) would have a long 'ah' vowel and a soft Gallic 'g' like a 'zh'.

Chaucer added to his mix of elements aspects of the high culture of contemporary Europe. He had travelled widely, and he borrowed stories from Boccaccio, Dante and contemporary French literature. The total combination probably accounts for the most important literary influence of *The Canterbury Tales*, in the way that the pilgrims and their tales juxtaposed high and low culture, the language and manners of the court with those of the village, in a way that became characteristic of the English tradition.

The life of Geoffrey Chaucer

*c.*1343 Born in London.

1357 Appointed page for Elizabeth, Countess of Ulster, and her husband Prince Lionel.

1359 Serves in Edward III's army, which invades France, starting the Hundred Years War; is captured and ransomed.

*c.*1366 Marries Philippa Roet, sister of the future wife of John of Gaunt, who will become a lifelong patron.

1367 Becomes a member of the royal household.

*c.*1370 Writes *The Book of the Duchess*, honouring the Duchess of Lancaster, John of Gaunt's first wife, who died in 1369.

1370s Writes the dream-poem *The House of Fame*.

1374–86 Is appointed Controller of Customs for the Port of London.

1380s Writes the dream-poem *The Parlement of Foules*

1380s–90s Writes *The Canterbury Tales*.

*c.*1385 Writes *Troilus and Criseyde*.

1386 Becomes Knight of the Shire for Kent.

*c.*1400 Dies and is buried in Westminster Abbey.

The Prince

1532

Niccolò Machiavelli

The Prince, a revolutionary analysis of power-politics, was written in 1513 with a specific aim: to win back the favour of the powerful Medici family in Renaissance Italy for its author, Niccolò Machiavelli. It has, though, been read for centuries as a cynical and ruthless blueprint for gaining and keeping power by any means necessary, and 'Machiavellian' entered the language to denote deceit and treachery.

Il principe (*The Prince*) was written after Machiavelli (1469–1527), a moderately successful public servant and diplomat, had been sent into exile following a change of leadership in his native city-state of Florence. Its fulsome dedication to the young Lorenzo II de' Medici (1492–1519) – grandson of Lorenzo the Magnificent – makes clear that Machiavelli's prime aim was to win the support of a powerful patron and escape the 'great and relentless malice of fortune'. Machiavelli's advice in *The Prince* was that the leader of a resurgent Italy – by implication, Lorenzo himself – could succeed by following the precepts set out in the book and paying unswerving attention to his duties as head of state. *The Prince* was written in 1513, the year in which Lorenzo began his Florentine rule, but in the event it was not published until 1532, five years after its author's death.

Through historical observation and practical advice, Machiavelli was putting forward a coherent view of the way that Italian states ought to be governed. 'I have thought it proper to represent things as they are in a real truth, rather than as they are imagined,' he wrote. Thus, Machiavelli's ideal prince claims power solely on the basis of his own ability to seize it and considers any policy justifiable if it reinforces his own position. It was a blatant rejection of the traditional view (to which at least lip-service was paid) that authority was God-given and/or inherited through royal bloodlines. The man who should control the state, Machiavelli said, was the man with the strength and single-mindedness to do so. The discussion of that reality makes *The Prince* the first serious work of empirical political science in Western literature.

When not engaged in war, a prince should be preparing for war: his own safety and the stability of the state demand that he should always concentrate on military affairs, and he should organize daily life within his realm so as to maintain the security of his rule. These requirements come

Ends justify means

Machiavelli reiterates throughout *The Prince* that the ruler personifies the state and thereby he ensures his own power by ensuring the safety of the state. He needs the goodwill of the people – but cruelty and deceit may be justified by the overarching importance of maintaining order. The ordinary ethical rules simply do not apply.

'The fact is that a man who wants to act virtuously in every way necessarily comes to grief among so many who are not virtuous ... You must understand, therefore, that there are two ways of fighting: by law or by force. The first way is natural to men, and the second to beasts ... So, as a prince is forced to know how to act like a beast, he must learn from the fox and the lion; because the lion is defenceless against traps, and a fox is defenceless against wolves. Therefore, one must be a fox in order to recognise traps, and a lion to frighten off wolves. Those who simply act like lions are stupid. So it follows that a prudent ruler cannot, and must not, honour his word when it places him at a disadvantage.'

The Prince, Chapters XV and XVIII, translated by George Bull, 1961

The life of Niccolò Machiavelli

1469 Born in Florence, which was ruled until 1492 by Lorenzo de' Medici, 'the Magnificent'.

1498–1512 Emerges from obscurity to head the Second Chancery in Florence's new republic, dealing with foreign affairs.

1513 Imprisoned, then exiled, after Medici rule re-established. Writes *Il principe* (*The Prince*), dedicated to Lorenzo II de' Medici, ruler of Florence to 1519. The new pope, Leo X, is also a Medici.

1513–17 Writes *Discorsi sopra la prima deca di Tito Livio* (*Discourses on the First Ten Books of Titus Livy*).

1517 Completes *Asino d'oro* (*The Golden Ass*), reworking in verse a comedy by the Roman playwright Terence.

1518 Writes *Mandragola* (*The Mandrake*), an original comedy.

1520 Writes *Dell'arte della guerra* (*The Art of War*), a dialogue. Appointed Florence's official historian by its new Medici ruler, Cardinal Giulio, who becomes Pope Clement VII in 1523.

1525 Writes his *Istorie fiorentine* (*Florentine Histories*), and receives papal reward.

1527 Dies at Casciano, outside Florence.

1532 *The Prince* is finally published.

before any other considerations: *The Prince* is therefore an outspoken, unvarnished textbook of *Realpolitik*. 'A prince must have no other object or thought, nor acquire skill in anything, except war, its organization, and its discipline,' Machiavelli says.

It is better to be cruel than merciful, he advises, and more important to be feared than loved. If keeping promises would be against the interests of the ruler, then promises should be broken without hesitation. Princes should avoid making themselves hated and despised, but only because a prince's greatest safety lies in retaining the goodwill of his people.

There had been many other books that recommended how kings, princes and other leaders should behave, but none before that so overtly eschewed morality or ethical considerations. Machiavelli referred to a host of (often unpleasant) classical and modern rulers – Agathocles of Syracuse, for example, who butchered the entire senate on his route to power; or, in Machiavelli's own time, Cesare Borgia, who installed a cruel and efficient ruler to impose his will on the Romagna and then had him murdered and mutilated once his reign of terror had served its purpose. It is on stories such as these that *The Prince's* reputation for amoral cynicism is built. The bloody implication was that power was there for the taking.

Machiavelli was, after all, steeped from his earliest days in the complex political infighting of Renaissance Italy. He was born of a middle-class Florentine family, which had traditionally held middle-ranking government posts. By the time he was 30, he was involved in the deposing of Girolamo Savonarola, the Dominican priest who effectively ruled Florence as a harsh religious republic for four years until he was overthrown and burned at the stake in 1498.

After Savonarola's fall, Machiavelli was appointed as a government servant, and spent 14 years working both in domestic politics and on sensitive foreign diplomatic missions, rising to the post of assistant to the head of the Florentine Republic, Piero Soderini. Soderini's fall, following a Spanish invasion of Italy – at the behest of the pope – in 1512, brought the Medicis back to power, and Machiavelli, along with many other republican sympathizers, was imprisoned, tortured, and sent into exile in his family home in the nearby village of Percussina. There he wrote *The Prince* and another political commentary, his *Discourses on Livy*. He also wrote plays, poetry, and classical translations.

The *Discourses* concentrate on the idea of republican government. They are quite different from *The Prince*'s concern with the autocratic rule of a single individual, based, as Machiavelli freely admits, on the character of the young Roman warlord Cesare Borgia, whom he had come to know during his diplomatic career. With Italy torn apart by infighting among the city-states, as the French and Spanish armies rampaged across the country, *The Prince* concludes with an impassioned plea for the Medici family – its members now wearing the papal tiara as well as running Florence – to drive the foreigners from Italy, and establish a powerful and unified Italian state.

Machiavelli was only moderately successful in winning favour. It was not until after Lorenzo's death that, in 1520, he was appointed official historian of Florence and went on to receive a series of minor government appointments. His unsentimental and severely pragmatic view of the nature of government was never likely to recommend itself to those in authority, and in 1559 *The Prince* was placed on the papal *Index* of banned books. Machiavelli became a figure of hatred across Protestant Europe as well, a stereotype of evil for William Shakespeare, Ben Jonson, and the other dramatists of the Elizabethan and Jacobean ages: Shakespeare's Richard III, boasting of his deviousness, declares (anachronistically): 'I can … set the murderous Machiavel to school.'

That distrust survived the centuries: in the 19th century, the historian Lord Macaulay declared that it was doubtful 'whether any name in literary history be so generally odious', and in the 20th century the philosopher Bertrand Russell wrote of *The Prince* as 'a handbook for gangsters'. The fact that Machiavelli was admired by the power-hungry, such as Napoleon Bonaparte and Benito Mussolini, only added to the general opprobrium.

Modern critics vary in their interpretations of the book. Some see it as simply an objective chronicle of the way that despotic Renaissance princes thought and behaved during a turbulent period of history; others view it as a carefully veiled satire on contemporary attitudes; and still others regard it as a work of intense and passionate patriotism, pre-dating the eventual unification of Italy by more than three centuries. What they do agree on, however, is the lucidity of Machiavelli's writing and the understated mastery of his prose. Even more importantly, the message of *The Prince* – that men have the power to create their own fortune through seizing their opportunities and imposing their will – chimed perfectly with the wider spirit of the Renaissance, and still resonates today.

BANNED BOOKS

The Prince was one of the first books to be placed on the Catholic Church's formal list of banned books, established by Pope Paul IV in 1559, as the church tried to control the flood of printed matter across Europe.

The declared aim of the *Index auctorum et librorum prohibitorum* ('Index of Prohibited Authors and Books') was to prevent books that encouraged immorality or put forward views contrary to the church's teachings from being circulated among Catholics, although several of the books listed – including *The Prince* – were also banned in some Protestant countries. The *Index* went on to encompass works by the Dutch humanist Desiderius Erasmus (1456–1536), the astronomer Nicolaus Copernicus (1473–1543), the essayist and philosopher Francis Bacon (1561–1626) and the astronomer and physicist Galileo Galilei (1564–1642).

The *Index* endured for over 400 years, with its final updating taking place in 1948, by which time it also included works by the poet John Milton (1608–74), the novelists Gustave Flaubert (1821–80) and James Joyce (1882–1941), and the philosopher Jean-Paul Sartre (1905–80). Its publication ceased under Pope Paul VI in 1966.

Atlas, or,
Cosmographic
Meditations

1585–95

Gerard Mercator

The first volume of the great *Atlas, or, Cosmographic Meditations on the Creation of the World and the Image of Creation* by Gerard Mercator appeared in 1585, and the work represented the cartographic culmination of the great European age of exploration. With discoveries in the Americas and East Asia, Europeans' understanding of the size of the known world had more than doubled during the previous hundred years. Mercator's book – the first to be called an 'atlas' – eventually incorporated all the new lands in a series of maps drawn to a single scale. It changed the whole conception of geography and set the standard for map-makers for generations to come.

The Flemish geographer, cartographer and globe maker Gerard Mercator was, in fact, Gerard de Cremer of Rupelmonde, Flanders, born in 1512. It was not until he was 73 that the first volume of his *Atlas* appeared, containing 51 specially created maps of France, the Low Countries and Germany. It was followed 4 years later by a second volume, comprising a further 22 maps of Italy and the Balkans. Mercator died before his task was finished: the third volume of his maps, covering Britain, the Arctic, Iceland, Scandinavia, the Baltic and Russia, appeared in 1595, a year after his death, and his son and grandsons eventually completed the project with maps of Africa, Asia and America.

The design and research that went into the *Atlas* were the result of years of study in Mercator's little workshop in the German city of Duisburg, as he desperately squirrelled away reports and maps from correspondents who were scattered across a continent riven by religious and political conflict, with Catholic forces clashing with Protestants. By the time Mercator started work on the *Atlas*, his eyes were failing and he had to employ craftsmen to produce the plates from which the

Mapping politics

Apart from the new maps of the world, Mercator's *Atlas* contained a lengthy Introduction – originally in Latin, of course – to explain the concept of the new book and set down guidelines for future geographers. The idea of maps suggesting political boundaries and other features as well as raw data about the natural world seems commonplace today, but it was not so at the time.

'Geography will add greatly to the knowledge of forms of government if it describes not only the position of various sites, but also their character and political condition. A painter fails to satisfy the demands of his craft if he draws a man according to the proportions of his limbs but ignores his complexion and the signs of his face and does not study his character and emotions; so too, a geographer will create what I might call a lifeless geographic corpse if he simply marks locations according to their distances, without indicating their mutual political relationships ...'

Preface to Volume 1 of the *Atlas, or, Cosmographic Meditations*, 1585

THE MERCATOR PROJECTION

Gerard Mercator's name still appears on most maps of the world. More than four centuries after his death, the technique he devised to reproduce the round world on a flat page – the Mercator Projection – remains the most common way of setting out a map. In the last hundred years, though, there have been increasing criticisms of the way the Mercator Projection distorts distances: countries are the correct shape, but their size becomes more disproportionate the nearer they lie to the north and the south of the map. China, for instance, appears to be much smaller than Greenland on a Mercator map; but at around four million square miles it actually covers more than four times as much of the earth's surface as Greenland does.

Repeated attempts have been made to devise projections that are less misleading, but they all have their disadvantages. The most famous, the Peters Projection in the 1970s, makes landmasses the right size but grotesquely distorts their shape. Other attempts have produced maps based on circles, triangles – and even doughnut-rings!

None, though, has proved to be as popular as the Mercator Projection. For all its faults, the Mercator map still represents the picture of the world that most people carry in their heads.

maps were printed – although as a younger man, he had been known as the most skilful and delicate engraver in Europe.

In 1569, sixteen years before the first volume of the *Atlas* appeared, Mercator had produced a famous map of the world, with the curved surface of the globe transferred to the flat sheet of paper according to a new mathematical projection, which he had devised. But that map was huge – more than 83 inches (208 cm) from east to west, and more than 52 inches (130 cm) from north to south. It was hard to store, difficult to consult, and easy to damage – and even at such an unwieldy size, it was simply too small to contain all the information that Mercator had at his disposal.

His aim, even then, was to produce a collection of maps in a series of books that would provide a complete record of the geographical knowledge of the world. The areas depicted on the maps would overlap to some extent, so that a careful reader would be able to follow them from one page to another across continents. They would be drawn to a single, consistent scale, so that one map could easily be compared with another. They would show the political relationships of one place with another. Finally, the maps would be drawn according to Mercator's projection, so that the shape of the countries and continents would be accurately represented. In short, the *Atlas* would present the most up-to-date and authoritative depiction of the world that Mercator's extensive scholarship could achieve.

Mercator's original plan, though, had been even more ambitious – the *Atlas* had been intended to be part of a greater *Cosmography,* which would bring together Christianity, history and geography in one huge synthesis of learning. But if that was too great a task even for him, the *Atlas* nevertheless aimed to revolutionize the study of geography: instead of simply describing the relative positions of rivers, seas, cities and mountains, as previous scholars had done, Mercator's aim, he said, was to show how political relationships might be reflected in the landscape. The *Atlas* contained a detailed essay setting out this aspect of his work. 'The two branches of study, those of geography and political government, can throw light upon each other,' he noted.

It was not, of course, the first book of maps to have been produced. Mercator himself had compiled a collection of maps based on the writings of the classical geographer Ptolemy, and his good friend Abraham Ortelius had produced a book of his own maps, the *Theatrum orbis terrarum,* in 1570. But Mercator was the first cartographer to design maps *specifically* to be bound together in

The evolution of an atlas

1512 Gerard de Cremer born in Rupelmonde, Flanders, in the Spanish Low Countries.

1530 De Cremer takes name 'Mercator' at the University of Leuven.

1546 His manual of italic script is published.

1552 Moves to Duisburg in the German Duchy of Cleves and opens a cartographic workshop.

1569 Mercator's *Chronologia* (a chronicle of world history) appears, part of his planned *Cosmography*.

1569 Mercator's world map is published, with his new projection.

1584 A new edition of Ptolemy's *Geographia* is published.

1585 The first volume of Mercator's *Atlas* appears, covering France, the Low Countries and Germany.

1589 The second volume adds Italy and the Balkans.

1594 Mercator dies in Duisburg.

1595 The third volume of the *Atlas* incorporates maps by Mercator and his son and grandsons, and the volumes together eventually cover the known world.

a book, with a single style and scale. Where earlier map-makers had been forced to admit defeat by leaving large spaces blank or decorating them with discursive legends and pictures of monsters and sea serpents to cover their ignorance, Mercator painstakingly filled his pages with detailed geographical references. His maps sought to represent what was – not what might have been.

Mercator wrote in Latin, and his thoughts were dense, philosophical and intense. The essays that he prepared as prefaces to his maps – 'To the studious and benevolent reader' in the first volume, for instance – are almost unread today. His maps, too, while still startling historical examples of the cartographer's art, have inevitably been superseded by the discoveries and techniques of the last four hundred years. But the *Atlas* was unrivalled in its day. Thirty years after Mercator's death, it was still selling across Europe, and it set the standard for geographical study for the next three hundred years. Its importance, though, cannot be measured simply in terms of the numbers of copies that were bought and used: the *Atlas* was part of the most significant shifts in human awareness that had ever taken place.

Just 20 years before Mercator's birth, Christopher Columbus was still convinced that his voyage across the Atlantic had taken him literally to the gates of Eden. Jerusalem was traditionally placed at the centre of world maps, because that was where the Bible decreed that it stood. In such ways, the traditional understanding of geography was inextricably bound up with religion, and cartographers turned to ancient authorities like Ptolemy, from 1400 years earlier, with unquestioning reverence.

Mercator was one of the first map-makers to draw on the new knowledge that the explorers brought back and reflect it in a new view of the world. Where his predecessors had assumed that only ancient learning was valuable or reliable, he demonstrated that new discoveries were possible. That understanding of the primacy of experience and experimentation would be the trigger for all manner of scientific discoveries in the centuries that followed.

EL INGENIOSO

HIDALGO DONQVI-
xote de la Mancha.

Compuesto por Miguel de Ceru. tes
Saauedra.

DIRIGIDO AL DVQVE DE
Bejar, Marques de Gibráleon, Conde de Benalcaçar, y
Bañares, Vizconde dela Puebla de Alcozer, Señor
de las villas de Capilla, Curiel,
y Burguillos.

Impresso con licencia, en Valencia, en casa de
Pedro Patricio Mey, 1605.

A costa de Iusepe Ferrer mercader de libros,
delante la Diputacion.

Don Quixote
1605–15
Miguel de Cervantes

Don Quixote, by Miguel de Cervantes, has been described as the first modern novel. Written in two parts, nine years apart, it appeared early in the 17th century, at the peak of Spanish literature's Golden Age. It was enormously influential in its time and down the ages, bringing characterization and perspective to the forefront of modern prose literature. Its central character is one of literature's most enduring and appealing protagonists, whose idealistic, if deluded, impulses have given the word 'quixotic' to the English language.

Miguel de Cervantes (1547–1616) published *Don Quixote* in Madrid at the age of 59, after 25 years of struggling to make enough money to live on, whether from government work or from writing. Earlier, he had had an adventurous life, serving as a soldier and seeing action on several occasions, including at the naval Battle of Lepanto against the Ottoman Empire, in which he lost the use of his left hand and was wounded in the chest. Returning to Spain, he was captured by Barbary pirates in the Mediterranean and sold into slavery. Despite four escape attempts, it was five years before he was eventually ransomed and returned home.

Back in Spain, he applied unsuccessfully for several government posts, both at home and in Spain's American possessions, before eventually being appointed to a position arranging supplies for the armada that was being gathered to invade England. By now he had started writing poetry and in 1585 he had published a pastoral romance, *La Galatea*, which achieved some success; but it did not justify a sequel. He also started writing drama and produced a number of plays, of which only two survive from the period.

His money worries continued, despite another official appointment as a government tax collector, and he had at least two stays in prison – during one of which, according to his own

Tilting at windmills

In this famous extract, Don Quixote has just started his travels with Sancho Panza when he sees a group of about 40 windmills, which he believes to be evil giants. His actions and perceptions typify his delusions:

'He spurred his horse, Rocinante, paying no attention to the shouts of his squire, Sancho, who warned him that, beyond any doubt, those things he was about to attack were windmills and not giants … Well protected by his shield, with his lance in its socket, he charged at Rocinante's full gallop and attacked the first mill he came to; and as he thrust his lance into the sail, the wind moved it with so much force that it broke the lance into pieces and picked up the horse and the knight, who then dropped to the ground and were very badly battered …

"God save me," said Sancho. "Didn't I tell your Grace to watch what you were doing, that these were nothing but windmills, and only somebody whose head was full of them wouldn't know that?"

"Be quiet, Sancho my friend," replied Don Quixote. "Matters of war, more than any others, are subject to continual change; moreover I think, and therefore it is true, that the same Freston the Wise who stole my room and my books has turned these giants into windmills in order to deprive me of the glory of defeating them: such is the enmity he feels for me."'

The Ingenious Hidalgo Don Quixote of La Mancha, Part I, Chapter 8, translated by Edith Grossman, 2003

account, he conceived the idea for *Don Quixote*. He began writing stories without much success, and when he managed to persuade a publisher to take the manuscript of his new book in 1604 he was glad to sell all his rights to it, for an unknown amount. Even though the novel was an immediate success, with new editions published over the next five years in Madrid, Lisbon, Brussels and Milan – at the time all part of Spain's European territories – Cervantes still failed to make a significant profit. The first English translation appeared in 1612.

During the following few years, Cervantes concentrated on securing the patronage of various wealthy Spanish aristocrats, and he published a book of short stories, *Novelas exemplares* (*Exemplary Stories*), the long allegorical poetic work *Viaje del Parnaso* (*Journey to Parnassus*) and a collection of plays.

The second part of *Don Quixote* appeared in 1615, a few months after an unauthorized sequel, brought out by an anonymous author taking advantage of the first book's popularity. Cervantes' second part was as great a success as the first, and new editions were quickly published across Spain and in Portugal, the Low Countries and England. The first edition of both parts of the novel appeared two years later, and the two parts have been treated as a single novel ever since.

The protagonist of *Don Quixote* is Alonso Quixano, a middle-aged *hidalgo* (nobleman) who lives in La Mancha, a Spanish province just south of Madrid, and who has become obsessed with books about chivalry. Renaming himself 'Don Quixote of La Mancha', he equips himself with an old suit of armour and a makeshift helmet, asks his fat and none-too-intelligent neighbour Sancho Panza to be his squire, and embarks on a life as a wandering knight, astride his stumbling old nag renamed Rocinante.

Much of the book relates their adventures on the road and the misunderstandings that arise as Don Quixote, by now clearly mad, mistakes an inn for an enchanted castle from the romantic stories he has read, a barber's tin basin for a magical helmet, and – most famously of all – a number of windmills for a group of dangerous and evil giants. He imagines that a farm-girl who lives close by – and who never actually appears in the novel – is his romantic lady-love Dulcinea, in whose honour he fights many battles. Sancho Panza, who tries repeatedly to keep his master out of trouble and is occasionally roundly berated for his pains, is promised the eventual governorship of an enchanted

The life of Miguel de Cervantes

1547 Born in Alcalá de Henares, Spain.

1567–8 Studies at the Estudio de la Villa, Madrid.

1569–70 In Rome, working in the service of a cardinal.

1571 Now in military service, is wounded at the Battle of Lepanto while serving with the Spanish fleet.

1572–5 Serves as a soldier around the Mediterranean and North Africa.

1575–80 Enslaved by Moorish pirates and held in Algiers until ransomed.

1581 Works as a tax inspector in Spain.

1585 Publishes the pastoral novel *La Galatea*, and writes a number of plays in these years, including *La Numancia* (*Numantia*) and *El trato de Argel* (*The Commerce of Algiers*).

1597 Imprisoned for bankruptcy (and again in 1602).

1605 Part I of *Don Quixote* is published in Madrid.

1612 English translation of Part I by Thomas Shelton.

1613 Publishes a short story collection, *Novelas exemplares* (*Exemplary Stories*).

1614 Publishes the poetic work *Viaje del Parnaso* (*Journey to Parnassus*).

1615 Part II of *Don Quixote* is published in Madrid.

1616 Dies in Madrid.

island (*insula*) in reward for his service as a faithful squire. The novel ends with Don Quixote's disillusionment, his recovery from his madness and his eventual death. On his death-bed, he declares of Sancho: 'If, when I was mad, I was party to giving him the governorship of the insula, now, when I am sane, if I could give him the governorship of a kingdom, I would, because the simplicity of his nature and the fidelity of his actions deserve it.'

Such a stark outline of the plot does little justice to the richness and originality of *Don Quixote*. It is partly a comic novel, partly – as in the final death-bed scene – a moving story in which the simplicity of the language and the benevolence and good-heartedness of the central character increase the pathos, partly a parody of the popular chivalric romances of the time, partly a social commentary about contemporary Spain, and partly a philosophical novel about the nature of truth, deception and falsehood.

> ## THE LEGACY OF DON QUIXOTE
>
> **Cervantes' great creation is one of the few characters in world literature whose name has passed into not one but several languages** – *quixotic* in English, *quijotesco* in Spanish, *donchisciottesco* in Italian, *donquichottesque* in French and *Donquichotterie* in German, to name only a few. The terms embody the 'extravagantly romantic' and 'absurdly generous and unselfish' qualities of Cervantes' hero – as *Chambers English Dictionary* defines 'quixotic'.
>
> Since it was published, there have been more than 20 different translations into English. The literary influence is deep and long. The 18th century exhibited a fondness for picaresque-type adventures: Henry Fielding described his novel *Joseph Andrews* in 1742 as being 'in imitation of the manner of Cervantes', while Laurence Sterne's structurally freewheeling *Tristram Shandy* (1759–67) also owes a debt. Critics have discerned Cervantes' influence, too, in 19th-century novelists as different as Charles Dickens and Gustave Flaubert.
>
> Beyond literature, composers such as Telemann, Massenet, Ravel and Richard Strauss have produced ballets, song cycles and orchestral music in homage to Don Quixote, and there have been more than a dozen films based on his adventures. And in art, Honoré Daumier and Pablo Picasso are just two of the painters drawn to Cervantes' creation.

The chivalric romances to which Cervantes looked back had a simple 'picaresque' progression, in which a series of separate episodes were linked only by the central character's travels. At first sight, this seems to be *Don Quixote's* arrangement too, but Cervantes allows the characters of Don Quixote and Sancho Panza to develop through the book and charts the changes in their relationship.

But he also plays with the reader's perspective, describing a number of different supposed sources for his tale. Firstly, there is the narrator figure, who complains bitterly at the start of the second part of *Don Quixote* about the previously published unauthorized continuation of the original story. However, he admits from the start that he has himself drawn on the accounts of several other writers who have dealt with the subject of Don Quixote before him; much of the story is allegedly culled from the writings of an unreliable Moorish historian named Sidi Hamid Benengali (invented by Cervantes); and there are frequent diversions as other characters tell long stories that last for several chapters. This 'story-within-a-story' technique keeps the perspective of the novel constantly changing.

Such factors – the complex and artful structure, the development of the characters and the close psychological observation – all help explain why, in the words of Mexican writer Carlos Fuentes, *Don Quixote* is 'the first modern novel, perhaps the most eternal novel ever written'.

Mr. WILLIAM SHAKESPEARES

COMEDIES, HISTORIES, & TRAGEDIES.

Published according to the True Originall Copies.

First Folio

1623

William Shakespeare

LONDON

Printed by Isaac Iaggard, and Ed. Blount. 1623.

William Shakespeare is generally held to be the greatest writer in the English language. Yet it was seven years after his death before many of his plays appeared in print, in the collection known as the First Folio. Properly titled *Mr. William Shakespeares Comedies, Histories, & Tragedies*, it contains 36 plays and is the sole source for 18 of them. Its influence is incalculable: Shakespeare, more than any other writer, has changed a language, defined a literary and theatrical tradition, and charted the highs and lows of the human condition.

During Shakespeare's life (1564–1616), there was comparatively little demand for published plays. The professional theatre was young and regarded by its practitioners and audience alike as the stuff of ephemeral events, not of lasting literature. Although Shakespeare took great care over the publication of his two long poems, *Venus and Adonis* and *The Rape of Lucrece* during the 1590s, he was typical in demonstrating little interest in preserving his plays: they were practical tools for performance. (By contrast, his friend and rival Ben Jonson appeared rather pretentious in supervising his published *Works* in 1616.) The plays that did appear were often pirated and inaccurate versions, sometimes cobbled together from the memories of people who had watched performances or, slightly better, acted in them.

Shakespeare spent more than 20 profitable years in London's theatre, as writer, actor and company shareholder. But after 1614 he gave it all up and retired to his family and life as a country gentleman in sleepy Stratford-upon-Avon, dying shortly afterwards. Some years later a memorial to him was placed in the local church – and a scheme was hatched to publish his plays. John Hemynge and Henry Condell – both actors from his theatre company, the King's Men – joined a syndicate with booksellers and stationers.

Hemynge and Condell wrote a Preface and acted as editors. They worked from Shakespeare's original drafts, from fair

Tributes and valedictions

In their Preface to the First Folio, Hemynge and Condell offer a rare and touching description of their friend:

'It had been a thing, we confess, worthy to have been wished, that the Author himself had lived to have set forth, and overseen his own writings ... Who, as he was a happy imitator of Nature, was a most gentle expresser of it. His mind and hand went together; and what he thought, he uttered with that easiness, that we have scarce received from him a blot in his papers ... Read him, therefore; and again, and again: And if then you do not like him, surely you are in some manifest danger, not to understand him.'

And in Act V, Scene i, of *The Tempest* – believed to be one of Shakespeare's last plays – occurs what some scholars take as the playwright's own farewell to his craft. The god-like figure of Prospero declares that, with the conflicts of the play resolved, he will no longer practise his magic:

*'... the strong-based promontory
Have I made shake, and by the spurs pluck'd up
The pine and cedar: graves at my command
Have waked their sleepers, oped, and let 'em forth
By my so potent art. But this rough magic
I here abjure, and, when I have required
Some heavenly music, which even now I do,
To work mine end upon their senses that
This airy charm is for, I'll break my staff,
Bury it certain fathoms in the earth,
And deeper than did ever plummet sound
I'll drown my book ...'*

COMEDIES, HISTORIES AND TRAGEDIES

The First Folio is arranged in this order but gives no information about when the plays were written. The dates of possible composition, below, are based on clues provided by contemporary documents, references within the plays and stylistic evidence.

Comedies

The Tempest (1610–11), *The Two Gentlemen of Verona* (early 1590s), *The Merry Wives of Windsor* (1590s), *Measure for Measure* (1603–4), *The Comedy of Errors* (early 1590s), *Much Ado About Nothing* (late 1590s), *Love's Labour's Lost* (mid-1590s), *A Midsummer Night's Dream* (mid-1590s), *The Merchant of Venice* (1595–8), *As You Like It* (1599–1600), *The Taming of the Shrew* (early 1590s), *All's Well That Ends Well* (early 1600s), *Twelfth Night* (c.1601), *The Winter's Tale* (unknown, first known performance 1611).

Histories

King John (before 1598), *Richard II* (before 1597), *Henry IV, Part I* (before 1597), *Henry IV, Part II* (between 1596 and 1599), *Henry V* (1599), *Henry VI, Part I* (1588–90), *Henry VI, Part II* (c.1591), *Henry VI, Part III* (early 1590s), *Richard III* (c.1591), *Henry VIII* (before 1603?).

Tragedies

Troilus and Cressida (before 1603), *Coriolanus* (c.1608?), *Titus Andronicus* (before 1594), *Romeo and Juliet* (early 1590s), *Timon of Athens* (c.1604), *Julius Caesar* (1599), *Macbeth* (1603–6), *Hamlet* (between 1599 and 1602), *King Lear* (before 1606), *Othello* (probably 1603), *Anthony and Cleopatra* (before 1608), *Cymbeline* (before 1611).

copies made by him and the company's official scrivener, from the prompt book used during performances, and from some of the earlier editions of individual plays. They also arranged the plays into 'Comedies', 'Histories', and 'Tragedies', a classification that broadly persists to this day. Their aim, they declared in their Preface, was 'only to keep the memory of so worthy a friend and fellow alive as was our Shakespeare'.

The resulting book contained almost all the plays now securely ascribed to Shakespeare (*Pericles* was added to a later edition), and generally in their most authoritative versions where previous ones had existed. As well as boasting the great tragedies of *Hamlet*, *Othello* and *King Lear*, it contains such plays as *The Tempest*, *Julius Caesar*, *Macbeth* and *Twelfth Night*, which had never been published previously, and which – without the First Folio – would almost certainly have been lost to us.

The book was adorned with a now-famous portrait of the playwright, by engraver Martin Droeshout, and a dedicatory poem by Jonson. The first printing ran to 750 copies of over 900 pages each, and around one third of those copies survive today, 79 of them alone in the US Folger Shakespeare Library. Most have leaves missing, and because proofreading continued while the pages were being printed, there are slight differences in the text. The initial price of the book was £1 (around £100/ $200 in today's equivalent), but of course each could now sell for millions. It is a quirk of literary history that the collection became known as the First Folio rather than by its name. 'Folio' refers to the page size: a large printer's sheet was folded once to make two leaves, or four individual pages, making the book around 15 inches tall. This was the format considered suitable for serious tomes such as Bibles, atlases, and histories, in contrast to the 'quarto' size (where the printer's sheet is folded twice) in which the earlier, unauthorized copies of individual plays had appeared. (Scholars refer to 'good' and 'bad' quartos of the plays, according to the presumed integrity of their texts.)

As for the Folio's contents, Shakespeare took the stories for his plays where he could find them – from Homer, from Geoffrey Chaucer, from the chronicler Ralph Holinshed (d. *c.*1580). But he enriched them to such an extent that they provided the backbone for the entire English dramatic tradition and penetrated the world's imagination, recycled for every age and every medium. Verdi's opera *Macbeth*, the musicals *West Side Story* (based on *Romeo and Juliet*) and *Kiss Me Kate* (based on *The Taming of the Shrew*), the sci-fi film *Forbidden Planet* (inspired by *The Tempest*), Akira Kurosawa's samurai masterpiece *Throne of Blood* (from *Macbeth*), or Tom Stoppard's play *Rosencrantz and Guildenstern are Dead* (indebted to *Hamlet*): these, and many more, are the children of the First Folio.

His influence on language itself is more thoroughgoing than any other writer's. People who have never read or watched a Shakespeare play may say they are 'more sinned against than sinning' (like King Lear); they may describe something or someone as 'dead as a doornail' (from *Henry VI*) or demand their 'pound of flesh' (like Shylock in the *The Merchant of Venice*). The list could go on 'for ever and a day', another of Shakespeare's phrases. He also brought new words into the language – 'domineering', 'fashionable', 'misquote', 'puke' and 'swagger' are just five of scores of words whose first usage, as listed in the *Oxford English Dictionary*, is Shakespearian.

Perhaps his biggest contribution, though, is that he demonstrated the power of language and its incarnation in performance. His language, 400 years ago, was different from ours, and reading or watching his plays today demands a degree of effort and concentration from most people – but the plays still show how effectively anger, pain, love, fear, doubt, jealousy, remorse, ambition, guilt or desire can be expressed in words. His emotional range was immense, and in his thematic range he grappled head-on with the great questions of life and death, right and wrong, loyalty and love, in ways that have permeated the way we look at the world and the way we feel about ourselves and others. We may not have read *Hamlet*, but we know about doubt – and we know a little more about it because what Shakespeare wrote resonated so forcefully beyond the play itself.

Shakespeare, ultimately, endures because he helps us to see who we are – and without the First Folio, the legacy of the plays through which he does that might have been lost.

The life of William Shakespeare

1564 Born in Stratford-upon-Avon, Warwickshire, the son of a glover, and later attends local 'petty' and grammar schools.

1582 Marries Anne Hathaway, daughter of a local farmer.

1592 A written reference to an 'upstart crow' by fellow writer Robert Greene shows that he is established in London's theatre world.

1593 Writes poem *Venus and Adonis*, while theatres are closed because of plague.

1594 Joins the Lord Chamberlain's Men as actor, writer and shareholder.

1599 The company begins performing at the new open-air Globe Theatre.

1603 The Lord Chamberlain's Men become the King's Men, on the accession of James I.

1608 The company takes over the lease of the enclosed, 'upmarket' Blackfriars Theatre.

1614 Writes *The Two Noble Kinsmen* with John Fletcher, probably his last play.

1616 Dictates his will and dies a few months later, having retired to Stratford.

1623 A memorial bust to him is erected in Stratford's Holy Trinity Church, Anne Hathaway dies, and *Mr. William Shakespeares Comedies, Histories, & Tragedies* – the First Folio – is published.

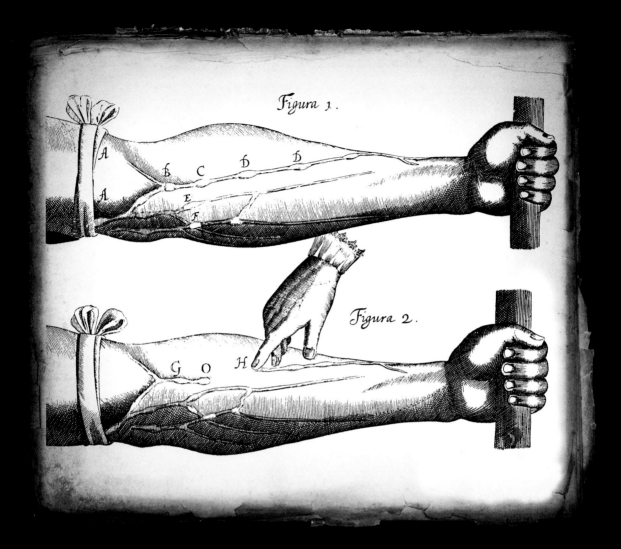

An Anatomical Study
of the Motion of the Heart
and Blood in Animals

1628

William Harvey

William Harvey's *An Anatomical Study of the Motion of the Heart and Blood in Animals* (1628), published originally in Latin, was a milestone in the development of modern medicine. In it, he announced his discovery that the circulation of the blood was brought about by the beat of the heart. It was a radical departure in the understanding of the function of the heart and lungs and of the purpose of the blood, and it opened the way for the modern practice of medicine.

For European doctors, Harvey's ideas marked a decisive break with the 2nd-century Graeco-Roman physician Galen. He had taught that in two separate systems dark red (venous) blood was produced in the liver and bright red (arterial) blood in the heart, and that blood ebbed and flowed through the arteries like a tide. That doctrine had been held to be true right up to Harvey's time.

William Harvey studied first at Cambridge, and then at the renowned University of Padua, where his interest in the question of how blood flowed through the body was aroused by his teacher, the Italian anatomist Hieronymus Fabricius (Girolamo Fabrici), who discovered – but did not realize the significance of – valves in the veins. Harvey was also very interested in the anatomical work of Andreas Vesalius (Andries van Wesel), who had studied at Padua and discovered in 1542 that there was no connection between the two sides of the heart.

The conclusions set out in Harvey's book followed his own observations of a succession of post-mortem examinations of humans and vivisections of animals. 'Careful observation is needed in every discipline, and sensation itself is often to be consulted,' he said. 'One's own experience is to be relied upon, not that of someone else.'

Harvey describes his studies of live animals, in which he showed that blood is pushed out when the heart contracts, and that both ventricles contract together. Harvey also describes experiments that showed that blood in the veins would move towards the heart, but not in the opposite

'An unceasing, circular sort of motion'

These two extracts summarize Harvey's conclusions about the 'closed' circulation of the blood, which were based on careful reasoning and observations from his dissections.

'I think it will be manifest that the blood goes round and is returned, is driven forward and flows back, from the heart to the extremities, and thence back again to the heart, and so executes a sort of circular movement ... Since calculations and visual demonstrations have confirmed all my suppositions, to whit, that the blood is passed through the lungs and the heart by the pulsation of the ventricles, is forcibly ejected to all parts of the body, therein steals into the veins and the porosities of the flesh, flows back everywhere through those very veins from the circumference to the centre, from small veins into larger ones, and thence comes at last into the vena cava and to the auricle of the heart ...'

'... I am obliged to conclude that in animals the blood is driven round a circuit with an unceasing, circular sort of movement, that this is an activity or function of the heart which it carries out by virtue of its pulsation, and that in sum it constitutes the sole reason for the heart's pulsatile movement.'

An Anatomical Study of the Motion of the Heart and Blood in Animals, Chapters 9 and 14, 1628

The life of William Harvey

1578 Born in Folkestone, Kent. As a boy, attends King's School, Canterbury.

1597 Graduates from Gonville and Caius College, Cambridge.

1602 Graduates in medicine from University of Padua.

1604 Marries Elizabeth Browne, daughter of Elizabeth I's physician.

1609 Becomes physician at St Bartholomew's Hospital, London.

1615 Appointed Lumleian Lecturer at the Royal College of Physicians, London.

1616 Makes his first public reference to circulation theory.

1618 Becomes 'physician extraordinary' to James I and then (from 1625) Charles I.

1628 Publishes *Exercitatio anatomica de motu cordis et sanguinis in animalibus* (*An Anatomical Study of the Motion of the Heart and Blood in Animals*) at the Frankfurt Book Fair.

1649 Publishes the essay *De circulatione sanguinis* ('The Circulation of the Blood').

1657 Dies in London.

direction. He describes how he had tied a bandage tightly around his subject's arm, cutting off blood from both the arteries and the veins. The arm below the bandage was left cool and pale, in contrast to above the bandage, where it was warm and swollen. Then, Harvey says, he slightly loosened the binding, allowing blood from the arteries – which are deeper in the arm than the veins – to flow again. The swelling between the heart and the now unblocked artery went down, while the vein on the side away from the heart swelled up. The obvious conclusion, Harvey was convinced, was that blood in arteries must flow *from* the heart whereas blood in veins flows *back* to the heart.

In similar experiments he found that he could easily push the blood in veins up the arm, but not in the opposite direction. However, when he tried the same experimentwith the veins on the neck, blood would flow down, but not upwards. He also tried pushing rods through veins in dissections, and realized that one-way valves in veins must prevent blood from flowing in both directions.

In addition to careful observations, Harvey's book also contains careful mathematical reasoning. He shows that the long-held theory of Galen, that blood was produced in the liver and then consumed by the other organs in the body, would have required impossible quantities of blood to be produced. In his dissections, Harvey had observed that the left ventricle of the heart held 1.5–3 ounces of blood. About a sixth of this was pumped out at every beat. With the heart beating over 2000 times an hour, some 500 ounces, or more than the total amount of blood in the whole body, would have to be produced every half-hour if Galen's supposition were true. Harvey concluded that 'blood is incessantly infused into the arteries in larger quantities than it can be supplied by the food … it is matter of necessity that the blood perform a circuit'.

Harvey's conclusions were accurate as far as they went – but he could not say how blood was transferred between the peripheral arteries into the veins. All he could conclude was that there were spaces or areas of 'free exchange'. This gap in his theory was filled in 1661, when an Italian scientist, Marcello Malpighi, used the newly developed microscope to observe capillaries in a frog's lungs, identifying these as the smallest blood vessels that close the circulatory loop between arteries and veins. Although the revelations of Harvey's book were new to European physicians, scholars in the Arab world had come close to an understanding of the circulation of the blood several centuries earlier. In the 11th century the Arab philosopher-physician Avicenna (Ibn Sina) had suggested that the beating heart might be responsible for pulses elsewhere in the body, and in the 13th century the Syrian scholar and physician Ibn Al-Nafis had described the circulation of blood from one side of the heart through the lungs then back to the heart. These views had, however, not been absorbed in Europe.

Harvey's first reference to his ideas about the circulation of the blood was in lectures on anatomy he gave at the Royal College of Physicians in 1616, and he continued to work on these ideas privately for more than ten years. Criticism of Galen's long-held ideas could not be undertaken lightly, and Harvey explained the delay in publishing by saying that the theory was 'of so novel and unheard-of character, that I not only fear injury to myself from the envy of a few, but I tremble lest I have mankind at large for my enemies, so much does wont and custom … influence all men'.

Occasional references to his theories before the book was published caused great anger among some doctors. After publication, this opposition continued. Harvey's contemporary, the memoirist John Aubrey, noted later in his *Brief Lives* that 'I have heard him say that after his book of the circulation of the blood came out, that he fell mightily in his practice, and that 'twas believed by the vulgar that he was crack-brained, and all the physicians were against his opinion, and envied him; many wrote against him.' Harvey's idea that there was a fixed amount of blood in the body suggested that there was no need for the widespread practice of blood letting: many physicians had difficulty accepting that this core practice should be abandoned.

Despite continuing antagonism, however, Harvey's theories were eventually accepted during his lifetime. In personal letters addressed to Jean Riolan, a critic of the circulation theory, and which he published in 1649, Harvey refuted his critics' arguments and drew on new observational evidence from dissection. Soon, scholars at universities throughout Europe were teaching Harvey's theory of the circulation of the blood.

THE UNIVERSITY OF PADUA

The University of Padua, where Harvey studied under one of the leading anatomists of the day, Hieronymus Fabricius (1537–1619), was reputed to be the finest medical school in Europe in the 16th and 17th centuries. It attracted students from all over the continent.

Among Harvey's medical predecessors at Padua were the Flemish scholar Andreas Vesalius (1514–64), who carried out detailed anatomical examinations of the human body and wrote an influential seven-volume textbook of anatomy, *De humani corporis fabrica* ('On the fabric of the human body'), and Gabriele Fallopio (1523–62), whose studies of the human reproductive organs led to a much greater understanding of what became known as the fallopian tubes in women.

John Keys (1510–73) left Cambridge's Gonville Hall in 1539 to study medicine there, sharing a room with Vesalius, and graduating in 1541. Having Latinized his name to 'Caius', he pursued a flourishing medical career in London, and in the 1550s his large-scale philanthropy resulted in his Cambridge *alma mater* being renamed Gonville and Caius College – which Harvey would attend 30 years later.

Another Padua scholar, Realdo Colombo (1516–59), studied the way blood moves between the heart and the lungs and also carried out detailed observations of the working of the heart. Harvey was able to build on these discoveries in his own research.

Dialogue
Concerning the Two
Chief World Systems

1632

Galileo Galilei

The publication of Galileo's *Dialogue* in 1632 under licence from the Vatican was possibly the most important episode in the gradual discrediting of Aristotle's view that the heavenly objects circled a fixed and non-rotating earth. The subsequent arrest and prosecution of its author was one of the last rearguard actions of the Roman Catholic Church against the new astronomy. But after Galileo, the universe – or at least man's view of it – would never be the same again.

The full title of Galileo's book is *Dialogue Concerning the Two Chief World Systems, Ptolemaic and Copernican* (in Italian, *Dialogo sopra i due massimi sistemi del mondo, tolemaico e copernicano*). In it, Galileo contrasted the idea of the earth-centred ('geocentric') universe, which had been put forward by Aristotle in the 4th century BC and developed by Ptolemy in the 2nd century AD – and was accepted by the church – with the later sun-centred ('heliocentric') system of Copernicus. The Polish astronomer Nicolaus Copernicus (1473–1543) had argued in his 1543 book *De revolutionibus orbium coelestium* (*On the Revolutions of the Celestial Spheres*) that the earth and the other planets moved around the sun. His book initially caused little controversy: he dedicated it to Pope Paul III, and a Preface, written by Copernicus's theologian friend Andreas Osiander, suggested that 'These hypotheses need not be true or even probable.'

   Galileo Galilei had, by the end of the 16th century, held prestigious academic positions at the leading universities of Pisa and Padua. A mathematician, he had made important discoveries in the study of moving bodies, which were later extended by Isaac Newton. He also used the newly invented telescope to study the stars and planets, and in 1610 discovered four moons orbiting the planet Jupiter – one of the first observations to convince him that, as Copernicus had contended, Aristotle was wrong. He published this discovery, along with observations of the mountains on the moon in 1610, in a brief treatise called *Sidereus nuncius* (*The Starry Messenger*), which brought him instant fame and a court position with Grand Duke Cosimo of Tuscany, to whom he had dedicated the work.

   In 1613 three letters by Galileo were published in *Istoria e dimostrazioni intorno alle macchie solari* ('Account and Evidence of the Sunspots'). The letters challenged the idea of the sun as a perfect body, and stated that the spots appear to move because the sun itself is revolving. In 1613 he further set out his views in a letter to his former student Benedetto Castelli, declaring openly

GALILEO AND THE TELESCOPE

It was with the newly invented telescope – first manufactured by the Dutch-German lens-maker Hans Lippershey in 1608 – that Galileo made the observations that eventually led to the publication of his *Dialogue*. He built one of the new instruments during 1609, after 'a rumour came to our ears that a spyglass had been made by a certain Dutchman', and he gradually made several improvements to it, using different combinations of lenses. Pointing it at the night sky, he was able to see that the surface of the moon, instead of being perfectly smooth as had always been supposed, was covered with mountains and craters like that of the earth. Observing Jupiter and the movement of its 'little moons', he noted that Jupiter could have satellites while itself orbiting the sun.

   While Copernicus's theory had been entirely mathematical, Galileo's observations suggested that the earth, being so similar to the moon and the planets, might itself be just another planet in the universe, rather than the Aristotelian centre of everything.

his belief that the sun was at the centre of the universe, and that the earth both rotated and moved around the sun. Castelli had discussed these ideas with Grand Duchess Cristina, Cosimo's interested mother, and the letter spread widely by hand, reaching cardinals in Rome; in 1615 Galileo revised it into an essay addressed to the grand duchess herself – this, too, circulated widely.

By now, advisers to Pope Paul V were arguing that the heliocentric view directly contradicted church teaching, and in 1616 a panel of theologians concluded that these views were heretical. Copernicus's book was placed on the church's infamous *Index auctorum et librorum prohibitorum* ('Index of Prohibited Books') a few weeks later, prohibiting Catholics from reading it until it had been 'corrected'.

The Starry Messenger was not banned, but Galileo was formally warned by representatives of the pope not to defend Copernicus's ideas any further. Galileo's next book, *Il saggiatore* (*The Assayer*), published in 1623 as a case for a mathematical and experimental basis for science, was approved by the church's censors and was widely praised. The new pope, Urban VIII, to whom Galileo dedicated the book, declared himself pleased with it, but other senior churchmen were offended by its outspoken attacks on a Jesuit astronomer.

Encouraged by Pope Urban's initial support, and by the success he had enjoyed so far in avoiding outright condemnation by the church while openly espousing the supposedly heretical new ideas, Galileo published the *Dialogue* in 1632. In order to satisfy the Vatican's censors, Galileo had to promise that he would treat the comparison of the Ptolemaic and Copernican systems in theoretical terms only. Partly for that reason, the book is arranged as a conversation about cosmology between three characters named Salviati (representing Galileo), Sagredo (a neutral, open-minded observer) and Simplicio (a convinced Aristotelian).

Science versus philosophy

Much of Salviati's proof that the earth rotates and also orbits the sun is based on detailed geometric diagrams and arguments. Towards the end of the third day's conversation, he challenges the others to accept his conclusions. Sagredo has no hesitation in agreeing; Simplicio does not, but has no counter-proofs to offer. Geometry and observation compete with abstraction and philosophy.

'Salviati: "See, then, how two simple non-contradictory motions assigned to the earth, performed in periods well suited to their sizes, and also conducted from west to east as in the case of all movable world bodies, supply adequate causes for all the visible phenomena. These phenomena can be reconciled with a fixed earth only by renouncing all the symmetry that is seen among the speeds and sizes of moving bodies, and attributing an inconceivable velocity to an enormous sphere beyond all the others, while lesser spheres move very slowly … I leave it to your judgment which has the more likelihood in it." …

Simplicio: "If I must tell you frankly how it looks to me, these appear to me to me some of those geometrical subtleties which Aristotle reprehended in Plato, when he accused him of departing from sound philosophy by too much study of geometry. I have known some very great Peripatetic philosophers, and heard them advise their pupils against the study of mathematics as something which makes the intellect sophistical and inept for true philosophizing." '

Dialogue Concerning the Two Chief World Systems, 'The Third Day', translated by Stillman Drake, 1953

The life of Galileo Galilei

1564 Born in Pisa.

1581 Begins studies at the University of Pisa.

1589–92 Professor of Mathematics, University of Pisa.

1592–1610 Professor of Mathematics, University of Padua.

1610 Publishes *Sidereus nuncius* (*The Starry Messenger*), a well-received treatise; appointed chief mathematician at Pisa, and mathematician and philosopher to Grand Duke Cosimo de' Medici.

1613 Publishes the letters *Istoria e dimostrazioni intorno alle macchie solari* ('Account and Evidence of the Sunspots').

1615 His letter to Grand Duchess Cristina circulates, affirming his heliocentric views.

1623 Publishes *Il saggiatore (The Assayer)*, concerning scientific method.

1632 Publishes his *Dialogo ...* (*Dialogue Concerning the Two Chief World Systems, Ptolemaic and Copernican*).

1633 Tried for heresy and placed under house arrest at his villa in Arcetri, near Florence.

1637 Goes blind, but continues to work.

1638 Publishes *Discorsi e dimostrazioni matematiche, intorno a due nuove scienze* (*Mathematical Discourses Concerning Two New Sciences*).

1642 Dies at Arcetri.

The conversation takes place over four days, the first being devoted to a discussion of Aristotle's belief that the heavens, the stars and the planets are all made from a different substance from the earth, and that they are all smooth and perfectly formed. On the second day, Salviati, the man of science, puts forward arguments to demonstrate that the earth could be rotating daily without there being any sensation of motion. On the third day, he demonstrates that Aristotle is mistaken in believing that everything beyond the earth is permanent and unchanging, and begins his proof that the earth both rotates on its own axis and also orbits the sun. On the fourth, he continues this exposition and relates it to the movement of the tides on earth.

In his Introduction to the book, Galileo protested that its arguments were simply hypothetical, as the church had demanded, and stressed his own religious orthodoxy: his three characters, he said, 'resolved to meet together on certain days during which, setting aside all other business, they might apply themselves more methodically to the contemplation of the wonders of God in the heavens and upon the earth.'

In principle, the book is even-handed, simply presenting the competing arguments for each system – but in fact, Simplicio is frequently caught out in his arguments and made to look foolish; further, and to his detriment, Galileo put some of Pope Urban's own arguments into the mouth of Simplicio. Within months, Galileo was summoned before the Holy Office of the Inquisition in Rome, which ruled at a trial that he was strongly suspected of heresy. He was forced to recant the 'false belief' that the earth moves and is not the centre of the universe and was then sentenced to life imprisonment – although his 'prison' for the remaining nine years of his life was a comfortable villa in Arcetri, in the hills near Florence.

Part of the judgement was that no further works by Galileo should be published. The *Dialogue* was placed on the next edition of the *Index*. Galileo's last book, *Discorsi e dimostrazioni matematiche, intorno a due nuove scienze* (*Mathematical Discourses Concerning Two New Sciences*), which dealt with the strength of materials and the physics of motion, was published in 1638 in the Protestant Dutch Republic, where the Inquisition's ruling could be safely ignored. Both Copernicus's *De revolutionibus* and Galileo's *Dialogue* were formally – and belatedly – removed from the *Index* in 1828. But the general prohibition against Copernicanism had been removed in 1758.

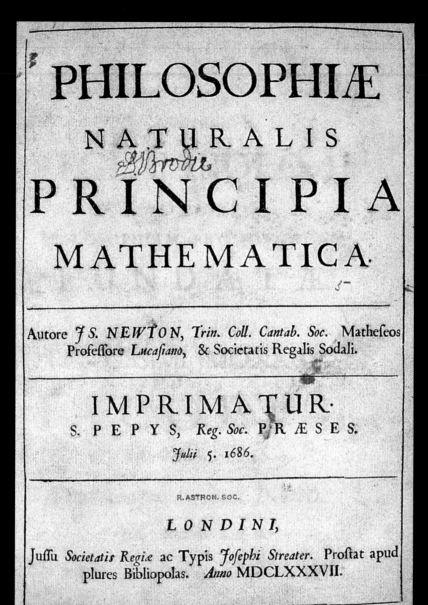

PHILOSOPHIÆ
NATURALIS
PRINCIPIA
MATHEMATICA.

Autore *JS. NEWTON*, *Trin. Coll. Cantab. Soc.* Matheseos
Professore *Lucasiano*, & Societatis Regalis Sodali.

IMPRIMATUR·
S. PEPYS, *Reg. Soc.* PRÆSES.
Julii 5. 1686.

LONDINI,

Jussu *Societatis Regiæ* ac Typis *Josephi Streater*. Prostat apud
plures Bibliopolas. *Anno* MDCLXXXVII.

Principia
mathematica

1687

Isaac Newton

Sir Isaac Newton's *Philosophiae naturalis principia mathematica* (*Mathematical Principles of Natural Philosophy*), generally known as the *Principia*, is a seminal book in the history of physics and mathematics. Published in 1687, at the pinnacle of the Scientific Revolution, it brought together discoveries about motion on earth and in the heavens. The laws of motion and gravity that Newton developed, and the method he developed to prove them, laid the foundations for much of modern physics and mathematics.

The century before the *Principia* was a period of startling advances in physics and astronomy. In 1543, the Polish astronomer and mathematician Nicolaus Copernicus had suggested that the sun, and not the earth, was at the centre of the solar system, and in 1609, the German astronomer Johannes Kepler had established that planets moved in elliptical orbits around the sun. In Italy, Galileo Galilei's observations of falling objects and experiments with inclined planes had demonstrated that acceleration under gravity was constant. Galileo also produced an equation that showed falling objects travel in 'parabolas', or curves.

In 1665 Isaac Newton returned to his home town in Lincolnshire from Cambridge University, which had closed because of the plague. He said later that the plague years of 1665 and 1666 were 'the prime of my age for invention'. Still less than 25 years old, he laid the basis of his work on light and colours and, prompted by seeing an apple fall from a tree, began to consider if the force that acted on the apple could also explain why the moon revolved around the earth. Newton realized there had to be a force pulling the moon towards the earth to make it continuously divert from the straight path that it would otherwise follow. He probably also deduced at this time that this force was weakened by the distance involved, measurable by applying the 'inverse square law'. Thus the force (gravity) decreased in inverse proportion to the square of the distance between the earth and the moon, which he was able to confirm.

It was in the plague years that Newton also invented what is now called 'calculus', a branch of mathematics that analyses rates of change at any instant using the idea of increments produced during an infinitely small time interval. Although Newton circulated his work among friends, he did not publish the calculus method until the *Principia* in 1687. This led to a dispute about priority of the invention between Newton and Gottfried Wilhelm Leibniz, who independently developed the calculus method and published his account in 1684.

Crucially, Newton had still not established that the force he described between the earth and moon would apply to all bodies in the universe. Correspondence with his rival Robert Hooke in 1679 about the nature of gravity and the motion of projectiles may have been the trigger for Newton to generalize the inverse square law for gravity.

In 1684 the astronomer Edmond Halley visited Newton to ask if he could show that the planets moving in elliptical orbits, which Kepler had described, were subject to an inverse square law – in other words, that the force required to keep the planets in orbit came from the sun. Newton said that he already had a proof of this, but could not find it. Within three months, however, Newton sent Halley a brief paper, *De motu corporum in gyrum* ('On the Motion of Revolving Bodies'), with the proof. Halley urged Newton to publish a full treatment, and this document, revised and expanded over the next 18 months, became the basis of the *Principia*. It was published with help from Halley, who paid all the costs, and also from the diarist Samuel Pepys, President of the Royal Society.

The laws of motion

Newton's famous three laws of motion come at the beginning of the *Principia*, in a section dealing with the principles of dynamics. The first law, as Newton acknowledged, is a restatement of what Galileo had described earlier, that a moving object keeps moving as long as friction does not slow it enough to stop it. The second law, which can be written as the equation 'Force = Mass x Acceleration', is often considered to be one of the most important in physics. The third law is often simply stated as 'action and reaction are equal and opposite'. The three laws together form the basis of what is often referred to as Newtonian or classical mechanics.

Law I

Every body perseveres in its state of rest, or of uniform motion in a right line, unless it is compelled to change that state by forces impressed thereon.

Projectiles persevere in their motions, so far as they are not retarded by the resistance of the air, or impelled downwards by the force of gravity. A top, whose parts by their cohesion are perpetually drawn aside from rectilinear motions, does not cease its rotation, otherwise than as it is retarded by the air. The greater bodies of the planets and comets, meeting with less resistance in more free spaces, preserve the motions both progressive and circular for a much longer time.

Law II

The alteration of motion is ever proportional to the motive force impressed; and is made in the direction of the straight line in which that force is impressed.

If any force generates a motion, a double force will generate double the motion, a triple force triple the motion, whether that force be impressed altogether and at once, or gradually and successively. And this motion (being always directed the same way with the generating force), if the body moved before, is added to or subtracted from the former motion, according as they directly conspire with or are directly contrary to each other; or obliquely joined, when they are oblique, so as to produce a new motion compounded from the determination of both.

Law III

To every action there is always opposed an equal reaction: or the mutual actions of two bodies upon each other are always equal, and directed to contrary parts.

Whatever draws or presses another is as much drawn or pressed by that other. If you press a stone with your finger, the finger is also pressed by the stone. If a horse draws a stone tied to a rope, the horse (if I may so say) will be equally drawn back towards the stone: for the stretched rope, endeavoring to relax or unbend itself, will draw the horse as much towards the stone as it does the stone towards the horse. It will obstruct the progress of the one as much as it advances that of the other. If a body impinge upon another and by its force change the motion of the other, that body also (because of the equality of the mutual pressure) will undergo an equal change in its own motion towards the contrary part. The changes made by these actions are equal, not in the velocities but in the motions of bodies; that is to say, if the bodies are not hindered by any other impediments. For, because the motions are equally changed, the changes of the velocities made towards contrary parts are reciprocally proportional to the bodies.

Principia mathematica, translated by Andrew Motte, 1729

In Book 1 of the *Principia*, Newton built on Galileo's discoveries to set out his three laws of motion, which mathematically define the concepts of 'acceleration', 'force', 'momentum' and 'mass' and how forces change the motion of bodies. Book 2 deals with the motion of bodies through resisting fluids, including the movement of a pendulum through air, and the way that fluids themselves move in waves with comparison to the movement of light and sound. Book 3 concentrates largely on the development of Newton's law of universal gravitation – that every particle of matter in the universe attracts every other particle even though they are not in contact. This gravitational force increases with the mass of the bodies – the bigger each mass, the bigger the force – and decreases in proportion to the square of the distance between them. Newton expressed the law in an equation:

$$F = \frac{G\,M\,m}{r^{\,2}}$$

(F = the gravitational force between the two bodies;
G = a constant called the gravitational constant;
M = the mass of the first body, m = the mass of
the second body, and r = the distance between them.)

In passing, Newton also explained the motion of the tides on earth by referring to the attraction exerted on the waters of the sea by the sun and the moon.

At the time of publication, Newton's critics acknowledged the importance and mathematical rigour of his analysis but objected that the universal law of gravitation had no logical basis. In a note to the second edition in 1713, Newton said he had not been able to find a cause for gravity, admitting that it seemed absurd that a force could act 'at a distance' between two bodies.

Newton's laws were refined in the 20th century by Einstein's theories of relativity – which relate to objects travelling close to the speed of light or to gravitational fields much stronger than those on earth – and by the development of quantum mechanics, which describes the behaviour of particles within atoms and molecules. Einstein's theory of gravity also described gravity as a consequence of the warping of space-time in the presence of a large mass. However, Newton's equations for the dynamics of moving bodies remain highly accurate tools for calculating the motion of everyday objects, where relativistic and quantum effects can be neglected.

The life of Isaac Newton

1642 Born in Woolsthorpe, Lincolnshire; as a boy, attends Grantham Grammar School.

1661–5 Attends Trinity College, Cambridge.

1668 Receives MA degree and a senior fellowship at Trinity, subsidizing his future researches.

1669 Becomes Lucasian Professor of Mathematics at Cambridge University.

1684 His work *De motu corporum in gyrum* ('On the Motion of Revolving Bodies') is presented to astronomer Edmond Halley.

1687 Publishes *Philosophiae naturalis principia mathematica* (*Mathematical Principles of Natural Philosophy*), better known as *Principia mathematica*, in three volumes.

1689–90 Member of Parliament for Cambridge University (again in 1701–2 and 1705).

1693 Suffers a possible nervous breakdown.

1696 Leaves Cambridge for appointment as Warden of the Royal Mint; made Master of the Mint, 1699.

1701 Resigns his fellowship and professorship.

1702 Elected President of the Royal Society.

1704 Publishes, in English, his *Opticks, or a treatise of the reflections, refractions, inflections and colours of light*.

1727 Dies in London.

SAMUEL JOHNSON, LL.D.

A

DICTIONARY

OF THE

ENGLISH LANGUAGE:

IN WHICH

THE WORDS ARE DEDUCED FROM THEIR ORIGINALS,

AND

ILLUSTRATED IN THEIR DIFFERENT SIGNIFICATIONS

BY

EXAMPLES from the best WRITERS.

TO WHICH ARE PREFIXED,

A HISTORY OF THE LANGUAGE,

AND

An ENGLISH GRAMMAR.

BY SAMUEL JOHNSON, LL.D.

THE SEVENTH EDITION.

LONDON:

Printed for J.F. and C. Rivington, L. Davis, T. Payne and Son, W. Owen, T. Longman, B. Law, J. Dodsley, C. Dilly,
W. Lowndes, G. G. J. and J. Robinson, T. Cadell, Jo. Johnson, J. Robson, W. Richardson, J. Nichols,
R. Baldwin, W. Goldsmith, J. Murray, W. Stuart, P. Elmsly, W. Fox, S. Hayes,
W. Bent, T. and J. Egerton, D. Ogilvy, and E. Newbery.

M.DCC.LXXXV.

A Dictionary of
the English Language

1755

Samuel Johnson

With his *Dictionary of the English Language*, published in 1755, Samuel Johnson set the standard for English lexicography for more than a hundred years. It was the first popular and comprehensive study of the English language, and the first to use literary quotations to illustrate the meanings of words. His work provided the starting point for the extensive, complex and scholarly study of language.

The mid-18th century, at the height of the Age of Enlightenment, was a time of enthusiastic list-making, referencing, and collecting of knowledge. Between 1754 and 1762, the Scottish philosopher David Hume published his magisterial six-volume *History of England* (originally entitled *The History of Great Britain*); the first *Encyclopaedia Britannica* appeared between 1768 and 1771; and in France, the *Encyclopédie*, advertised as a systematic dictionary of the sciences, arts and crafts, was published over 21 years, starting in 1751. Johnson's *Dictionary* fed this cultural appetite too, and, at last, provided a reference point for the English language that had been sorely lacking: elsewhere in Europe, major language-dictionaries had appeared in the previous century.

The *Dictionary*, which appeared in two volumes in April 1755, was the culmination of nearly nine years' commitment by Johnson and his small team of clerks. It contained a total of 42,773 entries, supported by nearly 115,000 quotations from writers such as William Shakespeare, John Milton, John Dryden and Jonathan Swift. It also included an authoritative grammar and a history of English. While there had been other dictionaries before, there had never been anything to match Johnson's learning and meticulousness. The entry for the verb 'to take', for instance, ran to 8000 words over 5 pages, with Johnson identifying 134 different meanings of the word.

The slipperiness of language

In the Preface to his *Dictionary*, Johnson admitted that his attitude to his task had changed as he worked on it. Initially, he planned to bring order to the English language and set a permanent standard for its written form; but he was persuaded that such an undertaking was impossible. Even so, he still thundered against the 'folly, vanity, and affectation' of linguistic change.

'Those who have been persuaded to think well of my design, will require that it should fix our language, and put a stop to those alterations which time and chance have hitherto been suffered to make in it without opposition. With this consequence I will confess that I flattered myself for a while; but now begin to fear that I have indulged expectation which neither reason nor experience can justify. When we see men grow old and die at a certain time one after another, from century to century, we laugh at the elixir that promises to prolong life to a thousand years; and with equal justice may the lexicographer be derided, who being able to produce no example of a nation that has preserved their words and phrases from mutability, shall imagine that his dictionary can embalm his language, and secure it from corruption and decay, that it is in his power to change sublunary nature, and clear the world at once from folly, vanity, and affectation.'

A Dictionary of the English Language, Preface, 1755

Johnson himself was not quite joking when he described himself regretfully as 'a poet doomed at last to make a lexicographer', but the Scottish essayist Thomas Carlyle (1795–1881) later said of him: 'Had he left nothing but his *Dictionary*, one might have traced there a great intellect – a genuine man.' His life (1709–84) is almost better known than his writing, thanks to the work of James Boswell, whose *Life of Samuel Johnson* gave him a kind of immortality. During a career spent turning out essays, pamphlets and parliamentary reports, Johnson tried many literary forms. He wrote two long poems in imitation of the Roman satirist Juvenal, *London* (1738) and *The Vanity of Human Wishes* (1749), produced the journal *The Rambler* (from 1750) and the columns published as 'The Idler' (in the late 1750s), as well as a prose romance, *Rasselas* (1759), written in the evenings of a single week to provide money to pay for his mother's funeral. His play, *Irene,* was performed briefly in London, to a muted reception, and he was also responsible for a series of biographies, *The Lives of the Poets,* written in his seventies, which were originally planned as a series of prefaces to editions of each poet's works. A collected edition of Johnson's essays was published in 1781.

The *Dictionary*, occupying the middle part of his life and career, was originally commissioned in 1746 by a group of London booksellers and printers, who paid Johnson a flat fee of 1500 guineas, or £1575 (around £150,000/$300,000 today) in regular instalments to write it – a task which he optimistically estimated would take him about three years.

In fact, he took nearly three times that long. Although he employed a team of six clerks – at his own expense – the research, writing, and selection of the quotations was done single-handedly. The French Academy, by contrast, had devoted a team of 40 scholars, over some 55 years, to the completion of its *Dictionnaire* (1694) – a contrast in which Johnson took great pride.

Soon after he started work on the *magnum opus*, he approached the British statesman Lord Chesterfield for patronage. Chesterfield was less than encouraging, and did not offer any meaningful support until the work was nearly complete. At that point he hinted that he would appreciate it if the book were dedicated to him. Johnson's reply was devastating: 'The notice which you have been pleased to take of my labours, had it been early, had been kind; but it has been delayed till I am indifferent, and cannot enjoy it: till I am solitary, and cannot impart it; till I am known, and do not want it.'

The two volumes of Johnson's *Dictionary*, A–K in one and L–Z in the other, weighed around 20 pounds together – so heavy that many purchasers decided to have them bound into four volumes instead. For all its bulk, the quantity of words may seem restricted to the eyes of a modern reader; but the total of 42,773 entries was vastly more than any word-book had included before. For one thing, Johnson deliberately excluded vulgar or profane words, and he famously chided a lady who congratulated him on having done so for clearly having searched for them.

Perhaps the book's greatest and enduring triumph was its unrivalled collection of around 114,000 quotations. Over 4500 came from the Bible, and many from the *Book of Common Prayer* – Johnson intended his *Dictionary* to have both a moral and religious

JOHNSONISMS

Johnson took the work on his *Dictionary* extremely seriously, but he also included a few jokes among his definitions – this one, for instance, was at the expense of the five Scots among his six-strong team of clerical helpers: 'Oats: a grain which in England is generally given to horses, but in Scotland supports the people.' He was not, though, above an ironic dig at himself: 'Lexicographer: a writer of dictionaries; a harmless drudge that busies himself in tracing the original, and detailing the signification of words.'

In other places, his political prejudices got the better of him, as in his definitions of the two principle political parties of his time: 'Tory: one who adheres to the ancient constitution of the state, and the apostolical hierarchy of the Church of England, opposed to a Whig; Whig: the name of a faction.' Or in the following: 'Excise: a hateful tax levied upon commodities and adjudged not by the common judges of property but wretches hired by those to whom excise is paid.'

But perhaps the most pointed definition, considering Johnson's quarrel with Lord Chesterfield, is this one: 'Patron: one who countenances, supports, or protects. Commonly a wretch who supports with insolence, and is paid with flattery.'

tone – but there were others from over 500 different authors. He included several from his own work, and some, labelled 'Anonymous', which modern scholars believe he made up himself for the purpose.

Wide circulation of the *Dictionary* was inhibited by its price – at £4 10s (£4.50, or about £450/$900 today) it was beyond the reach of all but the wealthiest citizens. It was warmly received, though, in the London magazines, and its reputation continued to grow over succeeding decades. Second and third editions and an abridged version appeared quickly, and in 1762 Johnson was awarded a state pension of £300 a year by King George III.

For the fourth edition of 1773, Johnson carried out substantial revisions, and the *Dictionary* remained the most authoritative reference book about the English language until the publication of the *Oxford English Dictionary* in 1884, which clearly dwarfed Johnson's endeavour in its number of entries: over 410,000. In the United States, where Noah Webster produced his own independent *Compendious Dictionary of the English Language* in 1828, Johnson's influence remained inescapable. Webster claimed to dismiss his predecessor's book, but simply lifted many of his definitions and quotations from it.

Johnson's original aim had been to provide a lasting guide to written and spoken English – but as he worked on the *Dictionary*, he came to see that languages could not remain static. What he achieved, however, was to provide an unprecedented description of the language of his day, and he set a standard for future lexicographers. Anyone who cares about language owes an immense debt to Samuel Johnson.

The Sorrows
of Young Werther

1774

Johann Wolfgang
von Goethe

The Sorrows of Young Werther, Goethe's semi-autobiographical account of the intense love affair and suicide of a passionate young German artist, swept through Europe in the late 18th century. It became one of the first literary bestsellers, making its author an international celebrity. More than that, as one of the most influential novels of the German *Sturm und Drang* ('storm and stress') movement it played a prominent role in the cultural shift towards the new aesthetic of Romanticism.

Johann Wolfgang von Goethe (1749–1832) grew up in Frankfurt am Main with a mother who indulged his literary aspirations, and a lawyer father who favoured more sensible professions like his own. After a period studying the law in Leipzig and some time dabbling in poetry and plays, Goethe leapt to fame with *The Sorrows of Young Werther* (in German, *Die Leiden des jungen Werther*), his first novel, published when he was just 24 years old.

Altogether, Goethe produced more than 90 books – poetry, fairy tales, dramas, novels, philosophy and scientific research – as well as 50 volumes of letters. His ambitious two-part play *Faust,* on which he worked for most of his life, was undoubtedly his greatest work and is considered one of the masterpieces of world theatre. Apart from his *Theory of Colours* (the book by which he believed he would be remembered), he carried out other important scientific work in geology, botany and human anatomy.

The Sorrows of Young Werther is written mainly in the 'epistolary' form of a series of letters from its hero, Werther, to his friend Wilhelm, and tells the story of Werther's passionate, but one-sided, love affair with Lotte, a beautiful young woman whom he meets in the fictional town of Wahlheim

Fatal attraction

Werther's last words, presumably written down in a final letter to Lotte, spill over with the fevered intensity of feeling concerning the woman for whose love he is about to shoot himself. He is found by his servant the next morning, and dies a few hours later. To a modern reader, the language may appear melodramatic; but to its original readers, the psychological reality of a man *in extremis* was profoundly moving.

'"I wish to be buried in these clothes, Lotte; you touched them and they are sacred; I have made the request of your father also. My soul will be keeping watch over my coffin. I do not want anyone going through my pockets. This pink ribbon you wore at your breast the first time I saw you amongst your children – oh, give them a thousand kisses, and tell them the fate of your wretched friend. The dear creatures! I can almost feel them romping about me. Ah, how attached I have been to you! How impossible it has been to leave you since that first moment! – This ribbon is to be buried with me. You gave it to me on my birthday! I could not get enough of it all! Ah, I little thought that my path was leading me this way! – Be of peaceful heart, I implore you! Be of peaceful heart!

They are loaded! It is striking twelve! So be it! Lotte! Lotte, farewell! Farewell!"

A neighbour saw the flash of the powder and heard the shot; but, since everything remained quiet, he thought no more about it.'

The Sorrows of Young Werther, translated by Michael Hulse, 1989

(supposedly based on the town of Garbenheim, near Wetzler). She is already engaged to a man 11 years her senior, but Werther cultivates her friendship, and also that of her fiancé, Albert, whose methodical and practical character contrasts with his own fiery impulsiveness. Eventually, finding the situation too painful, he leaves to take up a diplomatic post in the nearby city of Weimar. He continues to write to Lotte, and after being humiliated by the snobbish aristocrats of Weimar, returns to Wahlheim to find that she and Albert have married.

He tries to maintain their friendship, even though she makes half-hearted efforts to reject him, and one evening he calls on her while Albert is away. After he reads to her from the poems of Ossian, they are both overcome with emotion and he kisses her passionately.

Lotte runs away and locks herself in her room, refusing to see him, and Werther returns home. Believing the only solution to his pain is to kill himself, he writes farewell letters to Wilhelm, Albert and Lotte, and sends Albert a message asking to borrow his pistols, because, he says, he is going on a journey.

Lotte is filled with foreboding when the message arrives, but the pistols are sent, and Werther shoots himself in the head, on the stroke of midnight. He is buried in a corner of the churchyard, and – the last words in the novel – 'No priest attended him.'

The events in the novel are based partly on Goethe's own life. At a ball in the German town of Wetzlar in 1772 – about 18 months before the book was written – he met a beautiful young woman called Charlotte ('Lotte') and her fiancé, an older man called Johann Christian Kestner. Goethe, who had just completed his law studies at university, fell in love with her, but she told him there was no hope of an affair, and he left her, as Werther does, without saying goodbye.

The parallels are striking: Charlotte was 19, like Lotte; like her, she looked after her younger brothers and sisters; they both share the same birthday on 28 August; Werther, like Goethe, leaves on 11 September.

But there are also clear echoes of the life of one of Goethe's acquaintances in Wetzlar, another young lawyer named Karl Wilhelm Jerusalem, who fell in love with a married woman and killed himself with a pair of pistols he had borrowed from Kestner for the purpose. Parts of Kestner's letter to Goethe describing the tragedy are incorporated into the book.

The life of Johann Wolfgang von Goethe

1749 Born in Frankfurt.

1765–8 Studies law in Leipzig, under duress.

1773 Publishes *Götz von Berlichingen*, a tragic play.

1774 Publishes *Die Leiden des jungen Werther* (*The Sorrows of Young Werther*).

1775 Arrives at the court of the Duke of Weimar, where he will remain for most of his life, holding various positions.

1790 Publishes *Römische Elegien* (*Roman Elegies*), a poetry collection.

1791 Appointed director of the Weimar court theatre.

1796 Publishes *Wilhelm Meisters Lehrjahre* (*Wilhelm Meister's Apprenticeship*), a novel.

1808 Publishes *Faust, Part One*, a tragic play.

1809 Publishes *Die Wahlverwandtschaften* (*Elective Affinities*), a novel.

1810 Publishes *Zur Farbenlehre* (*On the Theory of Colours*), a scientific study of light.

1828–9 Publishes his revised edition of *Faust, Part One*.

1832 Dies in Weimar. *Faust, Part Two* is published posthumously.

The Sorrows of Young Werther was one of Europe's first bestselling novels. The distinctive dress which Werther wears in the book – a blue coat with a yellow leather waistcoat, brown boots and a felt hat – became sought-after fashion items for young bourgeois intellectuals. There were also suggestions that the book led to a wave of suicides, with some reports saying that as many as 2000 young men shot themselves. No proper studies were carried out to establish whether there was a genuine increase in suicides after its publication, or to what extent the book could be considered responsible for any deaths, but several city and state legislatures banned it. Modern psychiatrists still refer to the 'Werther effect' to describe the phenomenon of copycat deaths after a high-profile and publicized suicide.

The most lasting effect of the novel was on the literary world of the 19th century. With its concentration on the passionate force of feeling, its exaltation of emotion above intellect, its super-sensitive artist-figure as the protagonist, and its highly charged sensitivity to Nature, it was one of the earliest shoots of the new Romantic movement that would flourish across Europe. It was a movement that would produce some of the most important English poets, including Wordsworth, Coleridge, Byron and Blake. And in the 20th century, poets as diverse as Dylan Thomas or Ted Hughes could trace their ancestry back that far as well.

Politically, the French Revolution of 1789–99 was, in some respects, an early manifestation of Romanticism's libertarian impulses and reactions against outmoded hierarchies; so were the nationalist movements in Europe in the mid-19th century. Napoleon loved Goethe's novel, and, in a more sinister direction, it is possible to see in the Romantics' fascination with the power of the individual will the beginnings of Nietzsche's *Übermensch* and the first stirrings of 20th-century fascism.

Were Goethe and *The Sorrows of Young Werther* responsible for all this? Of course not – but the book was an important part of the initial reaction against the calm rationalism of the Enlightenment. To that extent, it helped to create not just an early 19th-century literary movement, but a literary and political climate that has lasted to our own day.

GOETHE AND OSSIAN

**'All night I stood on the shore: I saw her by the faint beam of the moon.
All night I heard her cries …'**

The Sorrows of Young Werther includes lengthy extracts from Goethe's own German translations of what he believed to be the poems of the ancient Gaelic warrior-bard Ossian, or Oisin. At one point, Werther exclaims excitedly, 'Ossian has ousted Homer from my heart!' Indeed, after reading from the poems, Werther is so moved that he forces his kisses on Lotte, leading directly to his banishment and ultimately his suicide.

But the poems Goethe had translated, and about which Werther was so passionate, were almost certainly written by their editor-compiler, the contemporary Scottish poet James Macpherson. In 1762–3, Macpherson published *Fingal* and *Temora*, claiming them to be 'translations' of ancient Gaelic originals he had gathered during his Scottish researches. These books were quickly claimed as pearls of Scottish culture, though some critics at the time, notably Samuel Johnson (who made his own enquiries), suspected that the 'ancient' provenance of the poems was not what it seemed. But Goethe, and many other leading intellectuals in Germany, France and Hungary, believed implicitly that they were genuine.

By the end of the 19th century it was generally believed that Johnson was right, and that Goethe had been fooled.

The Wealth
of Nations

1776

Adam Smith

Adam Smith's *The Wealth of Nations* is widely regarded as the book that laid the foundations of modern economics. It introduced the concept of the 'invisible hand' of competition and the free market, which, Smith contended, would transform the self-seeking acts of the individual so that they eventually worked for the common good. It is an idea that was adopted enthusiastically by the *laissez-faire* economists of the 19th century, and to this day lies behind the tax-cutting policies of many centre-right governments.

Smith's book, properly titled *An Inquiry into the Nature and Causes of the Wealth of Nations,* appeared in 1776. It is composed partly of history, partly of philosophy and partly of the new science of economics – then called 'political economy'. Smith, a Scottish intellectual, describes a four-stage development of human society, from the prehistoric hunting era through nomadic agriculture and farming in a feudal society to his own world, which, at least in its ideal form, he sees as one of commerce, trade and cooperation. In this modern world, he argues, the free exercise of the will of the individual will eventually lead to an orderly and productive society. Other chapters deal with the origin of money; the price of commodities; wages, profits and rents; and the use of capital. The three main economic themes that Smith presents in studying contemporary society are the division of labour, the pursuit of self-interest and freedom of trade.

He explains his theory of the division of labour by taking the example of a pin-making factory. One man working alone, he says, might struggle to produce a single pin a day – but with the work divided among ten different workers, each of whom is responsible for a single stage of the process, the factory could produce 48,000 pins a day, or 4800 for each worker. Such specialization, he argues, makes the worker more efficient. There is no time lost in moving from job to job, and the development of new machinery is encouraged, further improving productivity.

In another part of the book, Smith makes the famous observation: 'It is not from the benevolence of the butcher,

The life of Adam Smith

c. **1723** Born in Kirkcaldy, Fife.

1737 Enters the University of Glasgow, aged 14.

1740 Goes to Oxford to study at Balliol College, but finds the teaching far inferior to that at Glasgow.

1746 Leaves Oxford.

1748 Begins giving public lectures in Edinburgh, on a variety of subjects.

1750 Meets the philosopher David Hume, another key figure in the Scottish Enlightenment.

1751 Appointed Professor of Logic at Glasgow University, and Professor of Moral Philosophy in 1752.

1759 Publishes *The Theory of Moral Sentiments.*

1762 Receives the title 'Doctor of Laws'.

1763–6 Resigns from Glasgow University to tutor the young Duke of Buccleuch: they tour Europe, meeting a number of leading intellectuals.

1773 Elected to the Royal Society.

1776 Publishes *The Wealth of Nations,* in two volumes.

1778 Appointed commissioner of customs in Scotland.

1783 Becomes a founder-member of the Royal Society of Edinburgh.

1790 Dies in Edinburgh.

the brewer, or the baker, that we can expect our dinner, but from their regard to their own interest.' Although they are working in order to make money for themselves, they are also producing something that other people value, he reasons, and thus benefiting society at large. The market, he says, has its own self-correcting mechanism – 'an invisible hand'.

He also argues strongly against the then prevalent doctrine of mercantilism – the attempt by government to maintain a trade surplus in the expectation that it will lead to prosperity. Such a policy encourages monopolies and the protection of national trading interests, but the true benefit of trade, Smith says, is in opening up new markets for surplus goods, while at the same time providing other goods more cheaply from abroad than they could be produced at home.

The Wealth of Nations appeared at a time of great social and economic change in the Western world. Four months after its publication, the American Declaration of Independence marked the start of a revolution against taxation and the birth of a new nation dedicated to the political idea of individual freedom.

THE INDUSTRIAL REVOLUTION

A common view in the early 18th century was that wealth was essentially made up of land and gold, and that the landowning aristocracy was wealthy because God willed it so. The poor, similarly, owed their plight to the divine will. *The Wealth of Nations* was an intellectual challenge to this self-serving prejudice, but it was the Industrial Revolution, with its rapid transition from an agricultural economy to one based on capitalism and urban development, that demonstrated that it was nonsense. The Industrial Revolution, just beginning when Smith published his great work, radically and permanently changed society, as people flooded from the rural areas into the towns.

The changes were caused partly by technological advances, such as Smith's imaginary pin-making machine, the real-life spinning jenny (1767) and James Watt's steam engine (1769), and these inventions made manufacturing more efficient and more profitable. With the growth of empire, there was also a huge expansion in markets and a flood of cheap raw materials.

New wealth was created year by year in the smoking mill-towns of the North of England, supported by the rapidly developing capitalist economic system that Smith described. For many workers, the immediate result was squalor, poverty and misery; but the new developments helped to encourage the growth of a new middle class. Britain was the self-proclaimed 'workshop of the world' for the next hundred years.

It also started one of the greatest economic and political arguments of the last 200 years, an argument that continues to this day. How much can or should democratic governments interfere in the actions of their citizens? Should they tax incomes and profits in order to provide services for their electorates? Should they seek to protect the poor and vulnerable from suffering? Should they plan the economy and encourage particular forms of economic activity that they believe will promote growth and prosperity? Or should they leave people to make their own way, with a minimum of interference or taxation from the state?

The impact of Smith's book on the study of economics has been compared with that of Isaac Newton's *Principia* on physics. Whether economists accept it or fight against it, the free-market capitalist model has proved to be one of the most important propositions in the whole of economic thought. In the 19th century a diverse range of economists and political philosophers, such as David Ricardo (1772–1823), Thomas Malthus (1766–1834) and John Stuart Mill (1806–73), drew on Smith's work, refining it so that it became the basis for 'classical economics' as an explanation of economic growth and development. Karl Marx (1818–83) took Smith's basic ideas and argued that the working of the

Led by an invisible hand

Smith had already used his famous image of the 'invisible hand' in his earlier book, *The Theory of Moral Sentiments*, but here, in a passage frequently quoted today by politicians of the Right, he describes how the pursuit of individual self-interest can be beneficial to society at large. Businessmen and tradesmen, he suggests, know better than politicians how their money should be spent.

'Every individual ... neither intends to promote the public interest, nor knows how much he is promoting it. By preferring the support of domestic to that of foreign industry, he intends only his own security; and by directing that industry in such a manner as its produce may be of the greatest value, he intenn gain, and he is in this, as in many other cases, led by an invisible hand to promote an end which was no part of hids only his ows intention. Nor is it always the worse for the society that it was no part of it. By pursuing his own interest he frequently promotes that of the society more effectually than when he really intends to promote it. I have never known much good done by those who affected to trade for the public good. It is an affectation, indeed, not very common among merchants, and very few words need be employed in dissuading them from it.

... The statesman who should attempt to direct private people in what manner they ought to employ their capitals would not only load himself with a most unnecessary attention, but assume an authority which could safely be trusted, not only to no single person, but to no council or senate whatever, and which would nowhere be so dangerous as in the hands of a man who had folly and presumption enough to fancy himself fit to exercise it.'

The Wealth of Nations, Book IV, Chapter 2, 1776

market was ultimately unfair to workers. In the 20th century, J.M. Keynes (1883–1946) also reacted against Smith's ideas, but right-wing economists, including Milton Friedman (1912–2006) and Friedrich Hayek (1899–1992), built on his free-market economic model. Politicians such as Margaret Thatcher and Ronald Reagan in the 1980s paid lip-service to Adam Smith in their political pursuit of free-market policies, and modern international trade negotiations remain committed, at least in theory, to Smith's belief in free trade.

But Smith was not just a proponent of unrestrained self-interest, and *The Wealth of Nations* is only part of his wider thinking in the field of social philosophy. In his earlier *The Theory of Moral Sentiments* he tried to explain why, despite the natural instinct to act in accordance with self-interest, individuals are still capable of making disinterested moral judgements about their own and others' behaviour. Where, he asked, did a sense of right and wrong come from? His argument was that self-interest was controlled by the ability to reason and feel sympathy for other people. Using the same image that he later famously employed in *The Wealth of Nations*, he said that despite their 'natural selfishness', people were 'led by an invisible hand to ... advance the interest of the society'.

But it is back to *The Wealth of Nations* that much of today's political thinking can be traced. Smith's conclusions, written more than two centuries ago – when neither 'economics' nor 'capitalism' were words that anyone would have understood – may have been developed, adapted and refined, but they remain at the heart of mainstream politics in the 21st century.

COMMON SENSE:

ADDRESSED TO THE

INHABITANTS

OF

AMERICA.

On the following interesting

SUBJECTS.

I. Of the Origin and Design of Government in general, with concise Remarks on the English Constitution.

II. Of Monarchy and Hereditary Succession.

III. Thoughts on the present State of American Affairs.

IV. Of the present Ability of America, with some miscellaneous Reflections.

Written by an ENGLISHMAN.

By Thomas Paine

Man knows no Master save creating HEAVEN,
Or those whom choice and common good ordain.

THOMSON.

PHILADELPHIA, Printed
And Sold by R. BELL, in Third-Street, 1776.

Common Sense

1776

Thomas Paine

Common Sense, a potent mixture of argument, invective and religious phraseology, swept through the American colonies in 1776 during the opening months of the American Revolutionary War. Thomas Paine's book sold more than 120,000 copies in three months and changed the whole nature of the debate among the colonists. He declared that only complete and irrevocable independence from Great Britain would bring prosperity to America. Without *Common Sense*, the American Revolution might have faltered, and the establishment of the new United States would have been postponed indefinitely.

Published anonymously, *Common Sense* began to circulate among the colonists in Philadelphia in January 1776, some nine months after the outbreak of hostilities. It soon emerged that a firebrand English freethinker named Thomas Paine had written it. He had arrived in America two years earlier and become the rabble-rousing editor of the *Pennsylvania Magazine*. Within weeks, the short book – barely 20,000 words long – was being reprinted throughout the colonies.

Paine's pamphlet, the title page of which is reproduced opposite, challenged the colonists' feelings for King George III head-on: the institution of monarchy, he said, was ridiculous, and George himself no more than a 'royal tyrant'. Independence would enable the new nation to trade with all countries, instead of selling its products only to the British, and allow America to establish itself as a free port for the whole of Europe. The outcome would be peace and prosperity, he said, and freedom from the wars between European powers that had already spread across the Atlantic.

But apart from encouraging the self-interest of his audience, Paine also appealed to their self-esteem. 'This New World hath been the asylum for the persecuted lovers of civil and religious liberty from every part of Europe,' he said. Aware that many colonists were deeply religious and

Government – a necessary evil

For Thomas Paine, government was a 'necessary evil', but its worst manifestation was the 'exceedingly ridiculous' institution of monarchy:

'Society in every state is a blessing, but Government, even in its best state, is but a necessary evil; in its worst state an intolerable one: for when we suffer, or are exposed to the same miseries by a Government, which we might expect in a country without Government, our calamity is heightened by reflecting that we furnish the means by which we suffer. Government, like dress, is the badge of lost innocence; the palaces of kings are built upon the ruins of the bowers of paradise. For were the impulses of conscience clear, uniform and irresistibly obeyed, man would need no other lawgiver; but that not being the case, he finds it necessary to surrender up a part of his property to furnish means for the protection of the rest; and this he is induced to do by the same prudence which in every other case advises him, out of two evils, to choose the least ... There is something exceedingly ridiculous in the composition of Monarchy; it first excludes a man from the means of information, yet empowers him to act in cases where the highest judgment is required. The state of a king shuts him from the World, yet the business of a king requires him to know it thoroughly; wherefore the different parts, by unnaturally opposing and destroying each other, prove the whole character to be absurd and useless.'

Common Sense: Of Origin and Design of Government in General, Chapter 1, 1776

instinctively pacifist, he stressed the justice of their cause: 'We are not insulting the world with our fleets and armies nor ravaging the globe for plunder. Beneath the shade of our own vines are we attacked; in our own houses, and on our own lands, is the violence committed against us.'

In particular, Paine hit out bitterly against the idea that the colonists' differences with the 'mother country' could be resolved by any solution short of full-scale independence. The colonists, he declared, were peace-loving folk who wanted only to be left to enjoy their freedom, but who were being forced to defend their homes by brutal British aggression. True or false, it was what many of the colonists wanted to hear.

The war that was to lead to the independence of the American colonies and the establishment of the United States of America had begun in April 1775 with skirmishes at Lexington and Concord. The British had already caused fury in the colonies by the deployment of thousands of German mercenaries, and the rebels' initial success encouraged hopes that, poorly armed and badly organized as they were, they could force King George's army to back down. More than 15,000 rebel militias converged on Boston from all over New England, besieging the 5000 British forces in the town.

But there was still no general agreement that the aim of the revolution should be complete independence, and many of the colonists still felt a lingering loyalty to King George, who would, they believed, eventually repudiate the wicked ministers who had misled him. During the winter of 1775–6, just before *Common Sense* was published, recruitment to the rebel cause had slumped so that fresh drafts of militia had to be called up to reinforce the siege of Boston. If American determination had weakened then, the movement towards independence could have been stopped in its tracks.

British officers and American loyalists were outraged by Paine's attacks on King George, and Paine's democratic republicanism caused dismay even among supporters of the revolutionary cause. Many of them argued that his proposal for a single, directly elected and unchallengeable ruling assembly would be unwieldy and unworkable – but Paine had clearly set out the options facing the colonists, and he had caught the mood of the moment over the question of independence. George Washington himself – later bitterly criticized as a slave-owner by Paine – declared that '*Common Sense* is working a powerful change in the minds of men.'

The book was a clear influence on the drafting of the Declaration of Independence, adopted by Congress on 4 July 1776, six months after the appearance of *Common Sense*. Paine had suggested that a manifesto should be produced to explain to the world why the colonists were rebelling against the British, and the Declaration was the result. It was also Paine who suggested the name 'United States of America' for the new nation. In Europe, editions of *Common Sense* were printed in Germany, France and the Low Countries, and also in London, where the more outspoken attacks on King George had to be cut out before it could be sold.

Paine was never at ease in the practicalities and compromises of active politics, and took no part in the actual setting up of the government that emerged from the Revolutionary War. He returned to England in 1787, and then, shortly after the French Revolution, travelled to France, where he was elected to the National Assembly. His book *The Rights of Man* aimed to set out the libertarian basis of his revolutionary ideas – but he remained as outspoken in Europe as he had been in America. He was outlawed in Britain as an anti-monarchist, and imprisoned in France after refusing to endorse the execution of Louis XVI. Napoleon, he declared as the French leader's personal power increased, was 'the completest charlatan that ever existed'.

Paine returned to America in 1802 at the invitation of the new president, Thomas Jefferson, where he remained a forceful, tactless and controversial figure, particularly because of his attacks on organized religion. In his old age he sank into poverty and alcoholism, and when he died the influential *New York Citizen* sourly declared: 'He lived long, did some good, and much harm.' It seems an ungenerous verdict on the man who provided the impetus for America's War of Independence.

A TALE OF TWO REVOLUTIONS

From the beginning of the American Revolutionary War, the French secretly supplied the colonists with military equipment, and individual officers such as the Marquis de Lafayette travelled to America to fight for the patriot cause. The French hoped to regain some of the disastrous losses they had sustained during the French and Indian War (1754–63, the North American component of the Seven Years War with Britain); but it was not until 1778 that they signed a formal alliance. French troops were with Washington when he besieged the British at Yorktown, and a French fleet prevented the British navy from re-supplying the beleaguered British army. When General Cornwallis surrendered to the Americans at Yorktown in 1781, it effectively brought the war to an end.

Eight years later, in 1789, there were hopes in America that the French Revolution would provide a democratic ally in Europe, but as violence took hold in France, President George Washington's government was split, with Secretary of State Thomas Jefferson leading a pro-French faction, and Treasury Secretary Alexander Hamilton at the head of a Federalist group that supported Britain.

The spread of war, as the European monarchies and empires tried to crush the French Revolutionary government, led Washington, anxious about the economic consequences of being drawn into hostilities, to insist on a policy of neutrality, but many Americans – including Thomas Paine – went to France to support the Revolution.

The Revolution, though, was witnessing its bloodiest phase under Robespierre, and Paine, along with several other leading US citizens, was arrested and only narrowly avoided execution. This increased American suspicion of the French, and in 1794 the US government signed a peace treaty with Great Britain. In fact, for all the radical fervour of Jefferson, Paine and the Democrat-Republicans, the two revolutions were fundamentally different from the start, with the Americans concerned in their Constitution to limit the power of the state, while the French established a state that would in theory represent the people while remaining effectively above the law.

Lyrical Ballads

1798

William Wordsworth
and Samuel Taylor Coleridge

Lyrical Ballads, which was written by William Wordsworth and Samuel Taylor Coleridge at the end of the 18th century, is one of the most influential books of English poetry. Its aim, set out explicitly by Wordsworth, was to bring 'the language of conversation' and the individual experience of daily life to poetry. Its achievement, as the first great statement of English Romanticism, was to make a lasting change in the whole direction of English poetry, prose and the wider artistic sensibility.

Lyrical Ballads was a slim volume of just 23 poems, published anonymously in England in 1798. Wordsworth described the poems as 'experiments', although the collection, starting with *The Rime of the Ancient Mariner* by Samuel Taylor Coleridge (1772–1834), and ending with 'Lines composed a few miles above Tintern Abbey' by William Wordsworth (1770–1850), included poems that would rank among their best-known work.

The book represented an attempt to drag poetry away from what the two young poets – still in their twenties – saw as the 'gaudiness and inane phraseology' of 18th-century literature, and to open it up to the words and rhythms of everyday conversation. Rather than the restraint, reason and formality of the 18th century, their poetry would be founded on feeling and imagination. Where earlier poets, such as Spenser, Donne, Milton and Pope, had written about religion, mythology and events of high national importance, they would focus on individual experience. The poems avoided sophisticated, metropolitan subjects or studied classical allusions. They concentrated instead on 'natural' man. As such, they opened the way for the success of the English Romantic aesthetic in the early 19th century, and the durable influence it was to exert.

The poems of *Lyrical Ballads*, nineteen of them by Wordsworth and just four by Coleridge, were preceded in the first edition by a brief 'Advertisement', or Introduction, which Wordsworth wrote to explain the thinking behind them. The proper subject for poetry, he said, was to be found 'in every subject which can interest the human mind'. For the second edition, published with additional poems two years later, he expanded this introductory essay into a Preface, and set out his famous exposition of the new Romantic vision. Above all, poetry should be based on the honest expression of deep

The lives of the poets

1770 William Wordsworth is born in Cockermouth, Cumbria.

1772 Samuel Taylor Coleridge is born in Ottery St Mary, Devon.

1795 Wordsworth and Coleridge meet.

*c.***1796** Coleridge starts taking laudanum (opium) as pain relief.

1797 Wordsworth and Coleridge, living near each other in Somerset, start work on *Lyrical Ballads*.

1798 They publish *Lyrical Ballads*.

1799 Wordsworth starts work on *The Prelude* (published posthumously 1850).

1800 A second, expanded edition of *Lyrical Ballads* appears.

early 1800s Coleridge is, by now, addicted to opium.

1807 Wordsworth publishes *Poems in Two Volumes*.

1816 Coleridge publishes 'Kubla Khan' (written 1797).

1817 Coleridge publishes *Biographia Literaria*.

1834 Coleridge dies in London.

1843 Wordsworth is appointed Poet Laureate.

1850 Wordsworth dies in Grasmere, Cumbria.

From the South Pole to Tintern Abbey

Coleridge's *The Rime of the Ancient Mariner* consciously imitates the language, metre and style of traditional ballads. In it, the mariner narrates the supernatural events of his voyage near the South Pole, in which the appearance of an albatross accompanies a renewed wind, rescuing his becalmed ship. Unaccountably, he shoots and kills the bird and the wind dies, for which crime his fellow sailors hang its body around his neck. Eventually, they too die, but ascend to heaven, while the mariner, the sole survivor, is condemned to an itinerant life narrating his tale. Guilt, punishment and the proper relationship of man to Nature are all important themes in this startling and symbolic poem.

> *'Water, water, everywhere*
> *And all the boards did shrink;*
> *Water, water, everywhere,*
> *Nor any drop to drink.*
>
> *The very deeps did rot: O Christ!*
> *That ever this should be!*
> *Yea, slimy things did crawl with legs*
> *Upon the slimy sea.*
>
> *About, about, in reel and rout*
> *The Death-fires danc'd at night;*
> *The water, like a witch's oils,*
> *Burnt green and blue and white.'*

In Wordsworth's 'Lines composed a few miles above Tintern Abbey', the natural world takes on a religious quality. He describes the beauty of the Wye Valley landscape, but his real subject is not simply Nature itself, but rather the inspirational effect he feels that it has upon his own soul.

> *'Though absent long,*
> *These forms of beauty have not been to me*
> *As is a landscape to a blind man's eye:*
> *But oft, in lonely rooms, and mid the din*
> *Of towns and cities, I have owed to them,*
> *In hours of weariness, sensations sweet,*
> *Felt in the blood, and felt along the heart,*
> *And passing even into my purer mind*
> *With tranquil restoration:—feelings too*
> *Of unremembered pleasure: such, perhaps,*
> *As may have had no trivial influence*
> *On that best portion of a good man's life;*
> *His little, nameless, unremembered acts*
> *Of kindness and of love.'*

From *Lyrical Ballads*, 1798

emotion. 'All good poetry is the spontaneous overflow of powerful feelings,' he said. 'It takes its origin from emotion recollected in tranquillity.'

The poems come from different sources – some, such as Wordsworth's 'Goody Blake and Harry Gill', were said to be based on actual incidents; 'The Thorn' by Wordsworth, and Coleridge's 'The Foster-Mother's Tale' and *The Rime of the Ancient Mariner* are each in their different ways dramatic pieces, spoken by imagined characters; Wordsworth's 'Expostulation and Reply', according to its author, sprang from a conversation he had with a friend about philosophy.

Like the *Sturm und Drang* ('storm and stress') writers in Germany, such as Goethe (1749–1832) and Schiller (1759–1805), Wordsworth and Coleridge focused on the awe-inspiring and inspirational beauty of Nature, and on powerful and emotional personal responses to it. Nature took on a religious, inspirational quality. They were also drawing on the ideas of the French philosopher Jean-Jacques Rousseau (1712–78), who had argued more than 50 years earlier that man was at his best when at his most primitive.

The Rime of the Ancient Mariner, which is still one of the most widely quoted English poems, attracted immediate attention: in their division of labour, Coleridge took on the more 'supernatural' themes, most expansively in this, his 600-line-long masterpiece.

The rest of the poems in the book were widely ridiculed by

critics because of the simplicity of the diction, the informality of their style and the lowly nature of most of their characters – exactly the features that Wordsworth and Coleridge had been aiming at.

When they wrote *Lyrical Ballads,* Wordsworth and Coleridge were not just two idealistic poets seeking to free literature from the stultifying formality of the 18th century – they were also political radicals writing passionately in an atmosphere of reaction and repression. The fear of political upheaval was in the air in Britain: first the American colonies had achieved their independence in 1776, then, in 1789, the French Revolution had brought the end of France's hereditary monarchy and ushered in a period of bloodshed and mayhem across the Channel. Wordsworth, in particular, was known as a revolutionary sympathizer who had marched in a demonstration in Paris, while Coleridge had his own reputation as a fiery radical thinker. At one point, as they discussed their new book in Somerset, where they were living, a government spy was sent to investigate them.

The alliance between Wordsworth and Coleridge did not last. As early as 1800, biographers see tensions developing between them, caused partly by Coleridge's mounting addiction to opium. Their growing literary differences can be seen in the contrast between Wordsworth's long autobiographical poem *The Prelude* (completed 1805, published posthumously 1850), in which he describes the development of his own mind under the influences of his rural Cumbrian upbringing, and Coleridge's prose work *Biographia Literaria* (published 1817), where he looks at his literary influences. By 1815, Wordsworth had lost both his poetic inspiration and his passionate political radicalism, and his reputation over the final 35 years of his life was that of a bitter, disillusioned reactionary. Coleridge, meanwhile, sank further into opium addiction and depression, dying in 1834.

But the *Lyrical Ballads* inspired a generation of poets, including Lord Byron (1788–1824), Percy Bysshe Shelley (1792–1822) and John Keats (1795–1821). None of them would have recognized the description 'Romantic', which was not used in its literary sense until about 20 years after the publication of the book, but they each, in their individual ways, continued the original philosophy of poetry based upon intense personal experience.

TWO MODERN ROMANTICS

The poetry of Ted Hughes (1930–98) and Seamus Heaney (b.1939) shows how the attitudes and passions of the Romantics are still being developed and reworked two centuries on.

Both poets – Hughes from the North of England, Heaney a Northern Irish Catholic – have produced poems that are, in different ways, deeply rooted in Nature and packed with closely observed, intimate details of daily life. Both of them have been fascinated by the transformations of Nature – frogspawn into tadpoles and frogs, or the fall of leaves in the autumn – and they are also intensely aware of the uniqueness of the individual. Like their 19th-century predecessors, they have focused closely on their own personal responses, as well as having a lively sense of the historical, pre-historical and mythical context of their poems.

But behind the awareness of the natural world and their own reactions to it lies a sense, particularly for Hughes, of the ever-present, random and unexceptional horror that is tied up with Nature. Hughes's *Crow* character has a strain of pure savagery running through his soul, while his Hawk declares 'My manners are tearing off heads' (in 'Hawk Roosting', 1957). It is a modern twist on the 19th-century Romantics' more abstract sense of Nature's amorality: this is the meaningless cruelty of the everyday, in which natural descriptions reflect the psychological cruelty the poet finds within himself.

Pride and Prejudice

1813

Jane Austen

Jane Austen, the quiet unmarried daughter of a Hampshire clergyman, was certainly no revolutionary – but *Pride and Prejudice*, the most popular of her six books, brought a new realism to the English novel. Her ironic detachment and minute concentration on character, personality and provincial society make *Pride and Prejudice* one of the first novels to feel truly modern in tone.

When Jane Austen (1775–1817) was writing, novels were considered barely respectable. Partly for that reason, her books were published anonymously. But *Pride and Prejudice* helped to bring novel-writing within the socially acceptable mainstream of early 19th-century literary activity.

When it appeared in 1813, Austen had been writing plays, verses and stories for more than 20 years. A novel, *Sense and Sensibility*, had been published two years earlier, while another, *Mansfield Park*, appeared in 1814. By the time *Emma* was published in 1815, Austen had acquired a devoted following, and the book was dedicated to the Prince Regent (later George IV), who had let it be known that he was a great admirer of the books. *Northanger Abbey* (an early work, completed in 1803) and *Persuasion* were published in 1817, shortly after her death.

Like all her novels, *Pride and Prejudice* is the story of how a young woman navigates pitfalls and misunderstandings on the way to marriage, and how she gains deeper self-knowledge and a wider understanding of other people as she does so. At the same time, Austen provides subtly implied but incisive critiques of her characters and their attitudes and actions.

On the face of it, her novels are remarkable for how little the outside world impinges on them. As she was writing, Europe was convulsed by the Napoleonic Wars, Britain was undergoing a period of political repression, and the Industrial Revolution was beginning to change daily life across vast areas of the country almost beyond recognition. Why, then, are they regarded as triumphs of realism or

'An object of some interest'

In this extract, Jane Austen describes how Mr Darcy's initial poor opinion of Elizabeth Bennet gradually changes. Elizabeth, however, still finds him pompous and objectionable, and will shortly reject his proposal of marriage with contempt. It is only later in the novel, when her own prejudices about Darcy are proved to be mistaken, that she changes her mind.

'Occupied in observing Mr Bingley's attentions to her sister, Elizabeth was far from suspecting that she was herself becoming an object of some interest in the eyes of his friend. Mr Darcy had at first scarcely allowed her to be pretty; he had looked at her without admiration at the ball; and when they next met, he looked at her only to criticize. But no sooner had he made it clear to himself and his friends that she had hardly a good feature in her face, than he began to find it was rendered uncommonly intelligent by the beautiful expression of her dark eyes. To this discovery succeeded some others equally mortifying. Though he had detected with a critical eye more than one failure of perfect symmetry in her form, he was forced to acknowledge her figure to be light and pleasing; and in spite of his asserting that her manners were not those of the fashionable world, he was caught by their easy playfulness. Of this she was perfectly unaware; – to her he was only the man who made himself agreeable no where, and who had not thought her handsome enough to dance with.'

Pride and Prejudice, Chapter VI, 1813

TWO LITERARY TRADITIONS

The quiet realism of Jane Austen's literary world is in marked contrast to the macabre plots of the then popular Gothic novels. Writers such as Horace Walpole (1717–97) and Ann Radcliffe (1764–1823) seized enthusiastically on the Romantic fascination with horror, passion and the supernatural. Mary Shelley's *Frankenstein* (1818) was perhaps the most famous example.

Jane Austen wrote a parody of the Gothic novel in *Northanger Abbey* and was reacting against this fashion with *Pride and Prejudice*. 'Three or four families in a country village is the very thing to work on,' she famously said about novel-writing, and the stability of the world she describes contrasts strikingly with the menacing fury and emotional intensity of the Gothic novels.

Later in the century, books like Elizabeth Gaskell's *Cranford* (1851) and George Eliot's *Middlemarch* (1874) developed Jane Austen's realism and restraint. But the Gothic tradition also endured, in such works as Edgar Allen Poe's *The Fall of the House of Usher* (1839) and Emily Brontë's *Wuthering Heights* (1847).

held up as examples of early feminist writing? Because, at the level of society Austen wrote about, she illuminated the complex social and economic rituals and constraints that determined people's lives, and in particular women's lives. And she did it in her own quiet but forensic way.

The heroine of *Pride and Prejudice,* Elizabeth Bennet, is the intelligent and spirited daughter of a wry country gentleman. He has no sons, and by virtue of the legalities of inheritance the family home and the income from it will pass on his death to a distant male relative rather than to his daughters. It is the principal reason why Elizabeth's mother is desperate for her daughters to make a 'good marriage', and the novel starts with the author's own famous sideways comment on such ambition: 'It is a truth universally acknowledged, that a single man in possession of a good fortune must be in want of a wife.'

Just such a single man comes into the Bennets' neighbourhood in the person of Mr Bingley, a well-born and wealthy landowner, and Mrs Bennet claims him as the 'rightful property' of her own family. However, her plans for Bingley to marry her eldest daughter, Jane, are thwarted by Bingley's friend, the also wealthy Fitzwilliam Darcy, who advises him that the marriage would be unsuitable.

It transpires, however, that Darcy has fallen in love with Elizabeth. The pride and prejudice of the title apply to both of them – Darcy is proud of his rank and fortune, and prejudiced against Elizabeth's family and her foolish mother, while Elizabeth takes a prickly pride in her own independence, and is prejudiced against what she sees as Darcy's self-importance and snobbery.

Set against the Elizabeth–Darcy two-step are the lives of Elizabeth's sisters and their own aspirations and options, which range from giddy obsession with a glamorous, feckless military officer (resulting in an ill-advised marriage) to an inevitable drift towards self-effacing spinsterhood and a life at the piano.

Eventually, Elizabeth and Darcy come to understand each other, and marriage ensues. Elizabeth is installed as chatelaine of Pemberley, Darcy's country mansion, and those characters who tried to keep them apart have been discomfited. Importantly, in their own ways both of them reject the conformities attached to their class; but, Austen implies, not everyone is so lucky.

It is a slight and simple plot, which it is impossible to imagine being written by Daniel Defoe (*c.*1660–1731) or Henry Fielding (1707–54) during the years before her, or even by her contemporary, Sir Walter Scott (1771–1832). Scott made much the same point in his diary shortly after her death. 'The big Bow-wow strain I can do myself like any now going, but the exquisite touch which renders ordinary commonplace things and characters interesting from the truth of the description and the sentiment is denied to me.'

Where Romantic novelists such as Scott and, later, the Brontës shouted, Jane Austen whispered. Scott realized that Austen was a notable literary talent, but some 30 years after her death, Charlotte Brontë (1816–55) still dismissed her work contemptuously: 'Her business is not half so much with the human heart,' she wrote, 'as with the human eyes, mouth, hands and feet.' But an important part of Austen's achievement was that she took ordinary people in everyday circumstances – and examined how they reacted to their small triumphs and disasters. The *point* about her characters is that within that world, they are generally unexceptional.

Pride and Prejudice then, like Austen's other novels, is classically simple in its construction, but Jane Austen was a genuine innovator. The originality lies not just in the way that her books revolve around the ordinary and the everyday, but also in the way her acute representation of apparently unremarkable conversations helps to reveal the hidden meanings and motives in what is said. In addition, her narrative technique broke new ground. One of the most important 'characters' in all her novels is that of the narrator herself – a detached commentator who plays no part in the action. The raised eyebrow of 'It is a truth universally acknowledged' is echoed repeatedly and concentrates the reader's attention on the novel as moral and social critique.

Austen received little critical attention while she was alive, although her novels rapidly enjoyed fashionable success. Later in the century, the mass of the reading public began to agree with Charlotte Bronte's criticism of the lack of passionate emotion in her novels. But if Wordsworth and Coleridge's *Lyrical Ballads* prepared the way for Romantic poetry in England, Jane Austen's work performed a similar service for the realist novel that dominated the 19th century.

In the modern age, a revived appreciation of Jane Austen has led to burgeoning academic interest – in technique, Austen's 'feminist' status, her social concerns, and the degree to which the books reflected her life. It has also produced an enormous mass readership, particularly among women, who have appreciated the irony, perceptiveness and the sheer satisfaction of these 'comedies of manners'. It is no wonder that the novels, and pre-eminently *Pride and Prejudice*, have spawned many film and television adaptations.

The life of Jane Austen

1775 Born in Steventon, Hampshire.

1783–6 Attends boarding school.

1787 Begins to write to amuse herself and her family.

*c.***1795** Starts work on *Sense and Sensibility*.

1797 Completes *First Impressions* (an early version of *Pride and Prejudice*).

*c.***1798** Completes an early version of *Northanger Abbey*.

1802 Receives her only proposal of marriage, from a wealthy but unattractive acquaintance, and turns it down.

1803 Sells *Northanger Abbey* to a London publisher for £10, but he fails to print it.

1811 Publishes the novel *Sense and Sensibility*.

1813 Publishes *Pride and Prejudice*.

1814 Publishes another novel, *Mansfield Park*.

1815 Publishes *Emma*.

1816 Re-acquires the copyright of *Northanger Abbey*.

1817 Dies at Chawton, Hampshire in July. Her identity as an author becomes more widely known. *Northanger Abbey* and *Persuasion* are published in December.

A Christmas Carol

1843

by Charles Dickens

Charles Dickens is probably Britain's most influential and popular novelist, and *A Christmas Carol*, the novella written over a period of two months in 1843, became one of his best-loved books. Although it develops many of the themes that run through his novels, such as poverty, philanthropy, the role of the family and the social evils of Victorian Britain, it is far from typical of his work. But this short book laid the foundations for the traditional Christmas celebration and, in *A Christmas Carol*, Dickens himself became the continuing Spirit of Christmas Present.

Charles Dickens (1812–70) wrote well over a dozen full-length novels that are still widely read today. *A Christmas Carol* is uncharacteristic of his output in that it is less than 30,000 words long – under a tenth of the length of *Bleak House* or *David Copperfield*. It was written at a time when Dickens urgently needed money: with great novels like *Oliver Twist*, *Nicholas Nickleby* and *The Old Curiosity Shop* behind him, he was already a popular and successful author, but he had high living expenses, and his latest full-length novel, *Martin Chuzzlewit*, was not making him as much money in its serialized form as he had hoped.

With its intimate tone, pantomime good humour and unashamed sentimentality, *A Christmas Carol* was a runaway success from the start. It appeared on 17 December 1843, and 6000 copies of the initial print run were sold out by Christmas – although Dickens's insistence that it should be priced at an affordable five shillings (25 pence) meant that it never made him much money. It was also almost immediately pirated by unscrupulous publishers, further cutting Dickens's own income from his work. But *A Christmas Carol* was the first of Dickens's novels to be presented to audiences at his hugely popular public readings over the next few years, and it was followed by four more short seasonal works (*The Chimes*, *The Cricket on the Hearth*, *The Battle of Life* and *The Haunted Man*), all aimed specifically at the Christmas market.

A Christmas Carol introduces one of Dickens's most successful characters, the miserly Ebenezer Scrooge, 'a squeezing, wrenching, grasping, scraping, clutching, covetous old sinner'. As the story opens it is Christmas Eve, and Scrooge, failing to enter into the Christmas spirit, bullies his poverty-stricken young clerk, Bob Cratchit, snarls at his young nephew who has called to wish him Merry

The novels of Charles Dickens

Several of Dickens's novels first appeared in serial form, published over a couple of years.

1836–7 *Pickwick Papers*

1837–9 *Oliver Twist*

1838–9 *Nicholas Nickleby*

1840–1 *The Old Curiosity Shop* and *Barnaby Rudge*

1843 *A Christmas Carol*

1843–4 *Martin Chuzzlewit*

1848 *Dombey and Son*

1849–50 *David Copperfield*

1852–3 *Bleak House*

1854 *Hard Times*

1857 *Little Dorrit*

1859 *A Tale of Two Cities*

1861 *Great Expectations*

1864–5 *Our Mutual Friend*

1870 *The Mystery of Edwin Drood* (unfinished on Dickens's death)

Christmas, spurns appeals from two gentlemen collecting for charity, and chases away a carol singer. It is all humbug, he grumbles.

But then during the night, after a visitation from the ghost of his long-dead business partner, Jacob Marley, three spirits appear to him in turn, representing Christmas Past, Christmas Present and Christmas Yet to Come. The spirits show him his own childhood and youth, and then force him to see the sufferings of the poor in the present – including Cratchit's family, and their crippled child Tiny Tim. Finally they present Scrooge with a vision of the future, in which Tiny Tim dies a sad death, and his own death goes unmourned. Scrooge is chastened, and transformed.

The next day – Christmas morning – Scrooge gives money to the men who were collecting for the poor, sends a huge turkey to the Cratchits, and presents himself for lunch with his nephew's family. On Boxing Day, he suddenly announces to Bob Cratchit that he is giving him a pay rise. Tiny Tim, we are told, does not die, the Ghost of Christmas Yet to Come having made clear that what he saw in the future was what might happen, not what would happen. Scrooge's reformation has redeemed him, and for the rest of his life 'it was always said of him, that he knew how to keep Christmas well, if any man alive possessed the knowledge'.

A Christmas Carol touches on many of the themes that recur in Dickens's longer novels. Sin and redemption are central concerns; the law is berated as a heartless and flawed; and the better-off are encouraged to use their wealth to mitigate the poverty and suffering experienced by many in Victorian England. 'Are there no prisons?' the old Scrooge asks, the two gentlemen collecting for the poor. 'I don't make merry myself at Christmas and I can't afford to make idle people merry.'

Marley's ghost

In this extract, from the first chapter, Scrooge has just arrived home to see his door-knocker miraculously transformed into the face of his long-dead partner, Jacob Marley. Unsettled, Scrooge tries to dismiss it as humbug, but as he sits by his dying fire, all the bells in the house begin to ring …

'The bells ceased as they had begun, together. They were succeeded by a clanking noise, deep down below; as if some person were dragging a heavy chain over the casks in the wine merchant's cellar. Scrooge then remembered to have heard that ghosts in haunted houses were described as dragging chains.

The cellar-door flew open with a booming sound, and then he heard the noise much louder, on the floors below; then coming up the stairs; then coming straight towards his door.

"It's humbug still!" said Scrooge. "I won't believe it."

His colour changed though, when, without a pause, it came on through the heavy door, and passed into the room before his eyes. Upon its coming in, the dying flame leaped up, as though it cried, "I know him; Marley's Ghost!" and fell again.

The same face: the very same. Marley in his pigtail, usual waistcoat, tights and boots; the tassels on the latter bristling, like his pigtail, and his coat-skirts, and the hair upon his head. The chain he drew was clasped about his middle. It was long, and wound about him like a tail; and it was made (for Scrooge observed it closely) of cash-boxes, keys, padlocks, ledgers, deeds, and heavy purses wrought in steel. His body was transparent, so that Scrooge, observing him, and looking through his waistcoat, could see the two buttons on his coat behind.'

A Christmas Carol, 'Stave One – Marley's Ghost', 1843

RESCUING CHRISTMAS

The spirit of Scrooge was nothing new in either Britain or America. Under Oliver Cromwell, after the defeat of King Charles I, the celebration of Christmas was banned in Britain from 1645 until the Restoration of Charles II in 1660, and in Boston in the Massachusetts Bay Colony it was outlawed under the ruling Puritans for more than 20 years from 1659. In both cases, the authorities were worried about 'ungodly' celebrations, drunkenness and the pagan associations of many of the Christmas traditions. By Dickens's day, the mass movement to the cities caused by the Industrial Revolution meant that Christmas was losing popularity again, and there were worries that the practice might die out altogether.

Efforts were already being made to revive it by the 1840s. In 1841 Queen Victoria's consort, Prince Albert, had a large Christmas tree erected at Windsor Castle, introducing a custom that was popular in his native Germany. Two years later the first specially designed Christmas cards were commissioned and printed in London, encouraged by the invention of the penny post.

So *A Christmas Carol* caught the mood of the times in presenting a joyful family celebration, and bringing together the Victorians' fascination with ghost stories, philanthropy and the possibilities of redemption. It also, incidentally, introduced the idea of a 'white Christmas', possibly as a result of Dickens remembering a succession of unusually snowy winters from his childhood.

The huge popularity of *A Christmas Carol* – first as a book, then as the most popular item in Dickens's famous public readings, and also as a stage play – helped to create the popular image of Christmas that has survived to this day.

Like many of Dickens's books, *A Christmas Carol* also highlights specific contemporary issues, in this case proposals to force bakeries to close on Sundays in honour of the Sabbath. Poor families like the Cratchits would get their dinners cooked at the bakery on Sundays and Christmas Day, when no bread was baked, and the change would have denied them the chance of a hot meal. Scrooge questions the Spirit of Christmas Present about the policy, and is told it springs from 'passion, pride, ill-will, hatred, envy, bigotry, and selfishness'.

The description of Bob Cratchit's family enjoying their Christmas exemplifies Dickens's concern for the 'deserving' poor and the almost holy quality of family life. 'They were not a handsome family; they were not well dressed; their shoes were far from being water-proof; their clothes were scanty; and Peter might have known, and very likely did, the inside of a pawnbroker's. But, they were happy, grateful, pleased with one another, and contented with the time.'

For all its popularity, *A Christmas Carol* also highlights some of Dickens's weaknesses as a writer for a modern audience. Some of the puns in which he delights seem infantile – doubting whether the appearance of the ghost of Jacob Marley may not be due to indigestion, Scrooge observes: 'There's more of gravy than of grave about you.' At the end of the book, Dickens declares that he 'had no further intercourse with Spirits, but lived upon the Total Abstinence Principle, ever afterwards'.

And apart from the bad puns, there is Dickens's occasionally cloying sentimentality. When Bob Cratchit tells how Tiny Tim said after going to church 'that he hoped the people saw him in the church, because he was a cripple, and it might be pleasant to them to remember upon Christmas Day, who made lame beggars walk, and blind men see', one might need, as Oscar Wilde said about the death of Little Nell in *The Old Curiosity Shop*, a heart of stone not to laugh. But in the end, once one has circumvented the sentimentality, there is something about Dickens's avuncular optimism that survives even the most cynical of onslaughts.

*The Communist
Manifesto*

1848

Karl Marx

The Communist Manifesto, which first appeared in German in London in 1848, became, over the next hundred years, one of the most widely read and controversial political documents in the world. Its initial impact was slight, although the year of its publication coincided with a wave of largely unsuccessful uprisings that swept across France, Germany, the Italian states, the Habsburg Empire and elsewhere in Europe, in a wave of revolutionary and nationalist fervour. But on the foundations laid by Marx, later generations would build the Russian Revolution of 1917 and a whole family of different communist ideologies. The struggle between communism and the Western nations (whether democratic or fascist) became one of the defining features of the 20th century.

The *Manifest der Kommunistischen Partei* (*The Communist Manifesto*) is a brief document of 23 pages, divided into an Introduction and four short chapters – a marked contrast with Marx's other famous work, the massive three-volume *Das Kapital* (*Capital*), the first volume of which was published nearly 20 years later. But *The Communist Manifesto* – it was translated into English in 1850 – contained within it the bones both of Marx's analysis of the past and his predictions for the future. Communism and the rise of the proletariat, he says, are historically inevitable – but the *Manifesto*, with its famous closing words, 'Working men of all countries, unite!', remains a rallying call for left-wing radicals and revolutionaries. *The Communist Manifesto* was first published anonymously, but in later editions the name of Friedrich Engels (1820–95), Marx's collaborator in developing and defining communist thought, appears alongside his on the title page. Engels, however, confirmed later that both the writing of the book and the thought behind it were almost entirely down to Marx.

In the brief Introduction to the *Manifesto* Marx talks of communism as 'a spectre … haunting Europe'. The spectre,

The life of Karl Marx

1818 Born in Trier, Germany.

1842 Becomes editor of a radical paper, *Rheinische Zeitung*, which is suppressed.

1843 Moves to Paris, then the centre of socialist thought.

1844 Meets Friedrich Engels, his longtime friend and collaborator.

1845 Writes *Theses on Feuerbach* (not published until 1888), which includes the famous conclusion: 'Philosophers have hitherto only interpreted the world in various ways; the point is to change it.'

1847 Publishes *Misère de la philosophie* (*The Poverty of Philosophy*).

1848 Publishes *Manifest der Kommunistichen Partei* (*The Communist Manifesto*). The year witnesses nationalist revolutionary uprisings across Europe.

1849 Moves to London, where he spends the rest of his life in research, writing and journalism.

1859 Publishes *Zur Kritik der politischen Ökonomie* (*A Contribution to the Critique of Political Economy*); the *Grundrisse* ('Preparations') for this are published in 1939–41.

1864 The International Working Men's Association (the First International) is established, of which Marx soon assumes the leadership.

1867 Publishes Volume I of *Das Kapital*.

1883 Dies in London, and is buried in Highgate Cemetery.

1893–4 Volumes II (dealing with land ownership) and III (dealing with the production process in industry) of *Das Kapital* appear.

he claims, was created by governments across Europe, which implicitly acknowledged the power of the communists by accusing opposition groups of being part of a wider communist movement – although the fact that Europe's revolutions of 1848 were largely nationalistic in character suggests that both the governments and Marx himself may have been exaggerating the communist influence at the time. The point of the *Manifesto*, Marx says, is to counter the 'nursery tale of the spectre of communism' by setting out the beliefs and ambitions of the movement clearly and unambiguously.

Over the next 22 pages, he does exactly that. The first chapter sketches out his historical analysis, which suggests that class warfare, the struggle between oppressor and oppressed, has been central to the development of society. The unavoidable conflict in his own time he says, is between the bourgeoisie, who own the means of production, and those whom they pay to work for them, the proletariat. Writing in the shadow of the Industrial Revolution, which was forcing millions of families off the land and into factories and city slums, he declares that 'modern industry' has left workers enslaved by machines, by overseers and by bourgeois manufacturers.

The second chapter, entitled 'Proletarians and Communists', seeks to extend support for communism beyond those who would describe themselves as communists. The communists are not opposed to other working-class parties, Marx says, but 'always and everywhere, represent the interests of the movement as a whole'. He also sets out ten key elements of the manifesto (see opposite). In the third chapter, despite his declaration earlier in the document that communism is not 'a separate party opposed to other working-class parties', Marx attempts to demolish all the other socialist theories

Class struggle since the Roman Empire

The opening of *The Communist Manifesto* introduces the Marxist interpretation of history as a power struggle between the workers and those who would exploit them. But, as the final paragraphs make clear, the *Manifesto* was more than an academic view of history. It was also a call to arms that would reverberate around the world for a hundred years or more.

'The history of all hitherto existing society is the history of class struggles. Freeman and slave, patrician and plebeian, lord and serf, guild-master and journeyman, in a word, oppressor and oppressed, stood in constant opposition to one another, carried on an uninterrupted, now hidden, now open fight, a fight that each time ended, either in a revolutionary reconstitution of society at large, or in the common ruin of the contending classes.

In the earlier epochs of history, we find almost everywhere a complicated arrangement of society into various orders, a manifold gradation of social rank. In ancient Rome we have patricians, knights, plebeians, slaves; in the Middle Ages, feudal lords, vassals, guild-masters, journeymen, apprentices, serfs; in almost all of these classes, again, subordinate gradations.

The modern bourgeois society that has sprouted from the ruins of feudal society has not done away with class antagonisms. It has but established new classes, new conditions of oppression, new forms of struggle in place of the old ones ...'

'... Communists everywhere support every revolutionary movement against the existing social and political order of things.

In all these movements, they bring to the front, as the leading question in each, the property question, no matter what its degree of development at the time.

Finally, they labour everywhere for the union and agreement of the democratic parties of all countries.

The communists disdain to conceal their views and aims. They openly declare that their ends can be attained only by the forcible overthrow of all existing social conditions. Let the ruling classes tremble at a communist revolution. The proletarians have nothing to lose but their chains. They have a world to win.

Proletarians of all countries, unite!'

The Communist Manifesto, Chapters I and IV, translated by Samuel Moore, 1888

that were common across Europe at that time. They all, in different ways, propose to reform the system rather than overturn it, he says. The *Manifesto* ends with the famous call for international unity and with a clear statement of intent: 'The communists disdain to conceal their views and aims. They openly declare that their ends can be attained only by the forcible overthrow of all existing social conditions.'

Marx went on to elaborate his theories in far greater depth in his other well-known work, *Das Kapital*, a detailed and analytical study of the workings of a capitalist economy. The first volume appeared in 1867, and two more volumes appeared posthumously in 1893 and 1894. His other books on economics and philosophy included *Theses on Feuerbach* (1845), a study of the German materialist philosopher Ludwig Feuerbach (1804–72), *The Poverty of Philosophy* (1847) and *A Contribution to the Critique of Political Economy* (1859).

The Communist Manifesto, aimed at a wider readership than the other works, was effectively the birth certificate of international communism. Although it had little immediate impact on revolutionary movements, it spread through European socialist groups, with copies of the original German edition being taken back from London to Germany, where the individual state governments were facing revolutions demanding freedom, democracy and the establishment of a unified German state.

Despite the collapse of the German revolutions, the initial printing was sold out within a few months, and several thousand copies were bought within a year. Translations into Swedish (1848), English (1850 and 1888), Russian (1869) and French (1872) followed. Marx's thinking, set out in the *Manifesto*, was one of the driving forces behind the Russian Revolution of 1917. In their different ways, such leaders as Vladimir Ilyich Lenin (1870–1924), Josef Stalin (1878–1953), and, in China, Mao Zedong (1893–1976) claimed to be developing Marx's thinking, so the immense human suffering that took place under Stalin's Five Year Plans of the late 1920s and 1930s and Mao's Great Leap Forward 20 years later can be traced back to *The Communist Manifesto*.

A TEN-POINT PLAN

In *The Communist Manifesto*, Marx says that different measures will be needed to establish communism in different countries. But he sets out ten basic and immediate demands that he says will generally be necessary in advanced countries.

1. Abolition of property and application of all rents to public purposes.
2. A heavily progressive or graduated income tax.
3. Abolition of all right of inheritance.
4. Confiscation of the property of all emigrants and rebels.
5. Centralization of credit in the hands of the state, by means of a national bank with state capital and an exclusive monopoly.
6. Centralization of the means of communication and transport in the hands of the state.
7. Extension of factories and instruments of production owned by the state, the bringing into cultivation of waste lands, and the improvement of the soil generally in accordance with a common plan.
8. Equal liability of all to labour. Establishment of industrial armies, especially for agriculture.
9. Combination of agriculture with manufacturing industries; gradual abolition of the distinction between town and country, by a more equable distribution of the population over the country.
10. Free education for all children in public schools. Abolition of children's factory labour in its present form. Combination of education with industrial production.

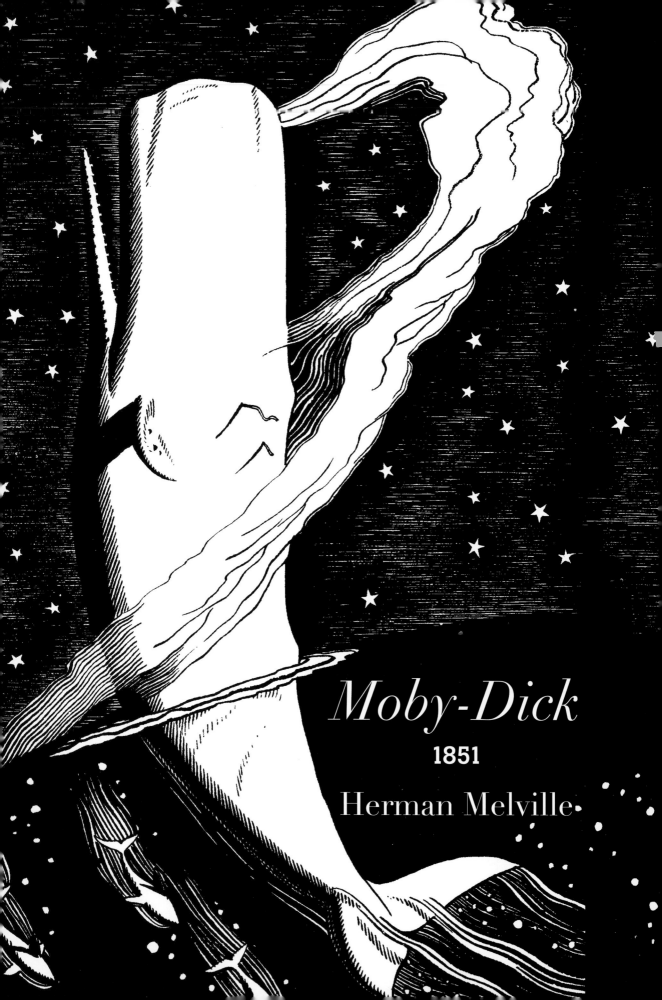

Moby-Dick

1851

Herman Melville

Herman Melville's meandering but highly original epic of the hunt for a great white whale was a major landmark in the emergence of a distinctive American literature. *Moby-Dick* demonstrated in 1851 that the young nation of the United States had its own unique literary voice, capable of dealing with the heights and depths of human experience. It is widely regarded today as the first great American novel, and some would say that it has never been surpassed.

Moby-Dick appeared first in October 1851 in London, under the title *The Whale*; a month later it appeared in New York City under the title by which it is now known. It was not an immediate success, and even half a century later the great novelist Joseph Conrad (himself a man of the sea) complained: 'It struck me as a rather strained rhapsody with whaling for a subject and not a single sincere line in the 3 vols of it.' It was not until the 1920s that critics such as Carl Van Doren (1885–1950) and D.H. Lawrence (1885–1930) began to rescue Melville, pointing to him as a precursor of the new 'modernism' in literature.

At around 220,000 words in 135 chapters, *Moby-Dick* is a long book that tells, on the surface, a very simple story. An eccentric and obsessive whaling captain called Ahab has lost his leg in an encounter with a great white whale called Moby Dick (oddly, in the book the whale is spelled without its hyphen), and sets sail from Nantucket aboard the *Pequod* to take his revenge. After a voyage that takes him almost around the world, Ahab finds the leviathan, and dies in the fight as he tries to kill it.

Intent on annihilation

In this excerpt, Ahab at last comes face to face with the whale that, in an earlier encounter, has cost him his leg. He brings all his skill and experience as a whaling captain into play – but the whale shows a malevolent and almost supernatural cunning that will eventually destroy the boats that seek to kill him.

'As if to strike a quick terror into them, by this time being the first assailant himself, Moby Dick had turned, and was now coming for the three crews. Ahab's boat was central; and cheering his men, he told them he would take the whale head-and-head – that is, pull straight up to his forehead – a not uncommon thing; for when within a certain limit, such a course excludes the coming onset from the whale's sidelong vision. But ere that close limit was gained, and while yet all three boats were plain as the ship's three masts to his eye; the White Whale churning himself into furious speed, almost in an instant as it were, rushing among the boats with open jaws, and a lashing tail, offered appalling battle on every side; and heedless of the irons darted at him from every boat, seemed only intent on annihilating each separate plank of which those boats were made. But skilfully manoeuvred, incessantly wheeling like trained chargers in the field; the boats for a while eluded him; though, at times, but by a plank's breadth; while all the time, Ahab's unearthly slogan tore every other cry but his to shreds.'

Moby-Dick, Chapter 134, 'The Chase – Second Day', 1851

The life of Herman Melville

1819 Born in New York City.

1830–2 Attends Albany Academy.

1839 Crew member for several months on the *St Lawrence*, a packet (mail) ship sailing to Liverpool.

1841–4 Sailor, first with the whaler *Acushnet* in the South Seas, spending time on Marquesas Islands (with cannibals) and later Tahiti and Hawaii; accused of mutiny on the *Lucy Ann*.

1846 Publishes fictionalized account of his voyages in *Typee*.

1847 Publishes *Omoo*, a sequel to *Typee*.

1849 Publishes *Mardi and a Voyage Thither*, a third South Seas novel.

1851 Publishes *Moby-Dick*, to moderately positive if baffled reviews.

1856 Publishes *The Piazza Tales*, including the widely admired 'Bartleby the Scrivener'.

1857 Publishes *The Confidence-Man, His Masquerade*, a darkly comic novel, and his last: they have not earned him much money.

1866 Publishes the civil war poems *Battle-Pieces*. Acquires position as deputy customs inspector, Port of New York (until 1885).

1891 Dies in New York City.

Melville drew on his own experiences at sea. Born in 1819, his formal education ended when he was 15, and after a variety of jobs, in 1839 he shipped as a cabin boy on a voyage to Liverpool. In 1841 he sailed aboard the whaler *Acushnet* for the South Seas, where he jumped ship, spending time in the Marquesas Islands and Tahiti, before enlisting with the US navy in Honolulu. He eventually returned to America in 1844, having thus completed his education at what he said was the only Harvard and Yale that were open to him.

As well as using his own experience of whaling, Melville was also inspired by Owen Chase's narrative of the sinking of a real-life Nantucket whaler, the *Essex*, published some 30 years earlier. Another important source was J.N. Reynolds's account of a cunning and lethally aggressive white sperm whale in the Pacific, published in 1839. Whalers had dubbed the beast 'Mocha Dick', after a small island off the coast of Chile where it was first sighted.

These antecedents help to make Melville's story an authentic account of the lucrative but dangerous business of whaling, as well as an epic adventure story. But *Moby-Dick* is much more than either. Freighted with literary allusion and philosophical speculation, and written in often highly poetic language with strong echoes of Shakespeare and the King James Bible, it is one of the most richly symbolic novels ever written, whose ambition is to encompass nothing less than the whole of human experience – albeit from a very male perspective.

The crew of the *Pequod* is drawn from all parts of the world: there is Queequeg from the South Seas, the Native American Tashtego, Daggoo from Africa, the Indian Parsi Fedallah. There is also a range of personalities, from the monomaniac Ahab to the earnest and prudent first mate, Starbuck; from the devil-may-care second mate Stubb to the third mate, Flask, whose imagination does not extend beyond the business of catching whales.

The *Pequod* thus becomes a microcosm of the world, and its voyage across the oceans becomes also a voyage through time and space, through myth and metaphysics. 'All visible objects are but as pasteboard masks,' declares Ahab, and it seems at times that his quest is to pierce the veil of appearances to find some ultimate reality beyond. This imagined higher reality may or may not be there, just as the hieroglyphic markings on a whale's back may signify a greater truth – or nothing at all.

The half-crazed Ahab, set on his quest, embodies both the dignity and the folly of human aspiration, of struggle for its own sake, even where there is no hope of victory, in the Romantic tradition of Prometheus and Faust. The great whale itself symbolizes almost anything a man wishes it to symbolize, yoking together opposites. The 'white-headed whale with a wrinkled brow and a crooked jaw' is both hunted and hunter, both the apotheosis of evil – as Ahab sees him – and the god that man seeks to destroy. Moby Dick is also untameable nature and the unknowable, indifferent cosmos, the goal of human ambitions and man's unavoidable fate, his fatal flaw, against which he struggles in vain.

As Ahab and his crew find themselves 'in tormented chase of that demon phantom that, some time or other, swims before all human hearts', the atmosphere of mystery and madness intensifies. From the beginning, there are dark portents of what is to come. The narrator himself, an outcast youth, tells us in his opening words, 'Call me Ishmael' – referring to the Old Testament Abraham's eldest son, overlooked in favour of Isaac. Feeling 'a damp drizzly November' in his soul, he and his roommate Queequeg sign on with Captain Ahab, after which they are buttonholed by the character Elijah (the name of a prophet who in the Old Testament condemns Ahab, King of Israel, for building a temple in honour of Baal, the god of his Phoenician wife Jezebel). Elijah suggests that in signing on with Ahab they may have let themselves in for more than they bargained for: 'Anything down there about your souls?' he asks. Elijah is equivocal, however, about what is to come: 'What's to be, will be,' he says, 'and then again, perhaps it won't be, after all.'

After sailing across the Atlantic, through the Indian Ocean and into the Pacific, the *Pequod* at last encounters the great white whale. An epic battle ensues. On the first day Moby Dick smashes up a whaleboat; on the second day he destroys another, and snaps off Ahab's ivory leg; on the third day, Ahab succeeds in striking the whale with a harpoon that he has had the ship's blacksmith temper in blood. But Ahab becomes caught up in the line, and ends up pinioned to Moby Dick, who rams the *Pequod*, sending it and all its crew to the bottom – except for Ishmael, who survives by clinging to – of all things – a coffin.

With whaling – even symbolic whaling – now deeply unfashionable, recent criticism has described *Moby-Dick* as patriarchal, capitalist, imperialist and even 'ecocidal'. Tastes change. But *Moby-Dick* marked the start of a characteristic strand in American literature (of which Ernest Hemingway and William Faulkner were perhaps the greatest exponents) in which men – for it is usually men – do what men have to do, making myths as they battle against nature and fate.

'THE GREAT AMERICAN NOVEL'

In January 1868 the American novelist John William DeForest published an essay in *The Nation* magazine entitled 'The Great American Novel', and started an argument that has lasted ever since. The phrase was seized upon to describe a novel that would focus on the unique character of the United States and act as an acknowledged masterpiece of American literary art. *Moby-Dick* is one of several books that have been suggested as fulfilling that goal. Among others are *The Last of the Mohicans* by James Fenimore Cooper (1789–1851), *The Adventures of Huckleberry Finn* by Mark Twain (1835–1910), *The Great Gatsby* by F. Scott Fitzgerald (1896–1940) and *The Grapes of Wrath*, by John Steinbeck (1902–68).

The novelist Frank Norris – whose own book *McTeague* is also cited – said in 1903 that the Great American Novel was 'not extinct like the dodo, but mythical like the hippogriff'. Perhaps he was right; but if there are any truly great American novels, *Moby-Dick* must be numbered among them.

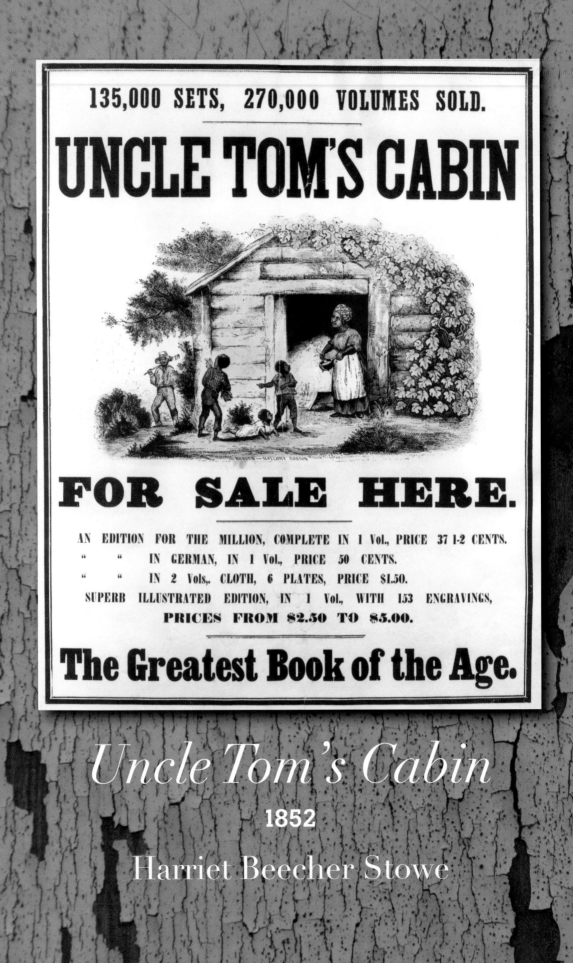

Uncle Tom's Cabin

1852

Harriet Beecher Stowe

Harriet Beecher Stowe's 1852 story of a patient and long-suffering African-American slave swept around the world to become, by far, the bestselling novel of its day: only the Bible sold more copies in the 19th century. Its immediate influence was huge, reinforcing abolitionist feeling in the Northern US states, and causing bitterness and resentment among Southern whites. It galvanized American and international opinion against the institution of slavery, and also established stereotypes of people of African origin that were to last for generations.

Uncle Tom's Cabin, or, Life Among the Lowly gives an uncompromising insight into the appalling cruelty of slavery in the mid-19th century, through the intertwining stories of several African-American slaves in the South who are bought, sold, beaten and killed. A highly sentimental novel with a heavy Christian message, it highlights the brutal way in which families were broken up and children taken from their mothers on the Southern plantations. It also demonstrates the involvement of the Northern states in the slave trade and stresses the redemptive power of Christianity.

Harriet Beecher Stowe (1811–96), a teacher and the daughter of a leading Calvinist preacher, originally wrote the story as a weekly serial in response to the passing of the Fugitive Slave Act of 1850, which required runaway slaves anywhere in the United States to be returned to their 'owners' in the South on pain of penalties for those who did not assist. It appeared in the anti-slavery magazine *National Era* in 1851, and was an instant success when it was published in book form a year later. In its first year, 300,000 copies were sold in America, and another 200,000 in Britain, while scores of dramatizations further increased its popularity. Since then, it has been translated into almost every language in the world.

The eponymous hero is an African-American slave who is parted from his wife and sold to a slave-trader by Arthur Shelby, a debt-ridden Kentucky plantation owner. Tom is shipped down the Mississippi River to New Orleans, and on the way he rescues a young White girl, Eva St Clare, who has fallen into the river. Her grateful father buys Tom and installs him as a driver at his home.

Tom and Eva are pious Christians, and over the next two years they become friends. When

A vicious slave-owner

Among the slave-owners depicted in *Uncle Tom's Cabin* are some who are well-meaning but weak, like Arthur Shelby and Eva's father, Augustine St Clare. But in Simon Legree, the novel presents an image of unmitigated brutality and irredeemable wickedness. Here, having bought Tom and other slaves in New Orleans, he warns them as they are shipped back to his plantation what is in store for them.

' "Now," said he, doubling his great, heavy fist into something resembling a blacksmith's hammer, "d'ye see this fist? Heft it!" he said, bringing it down on Tom's hand. "Look at these yer bones! Well, I tell ye this yer fist has got as hard as iron knocking down niggers. I never see the nigger, yet, I couldn't bring down with one crack," said he, bringing his fist down so near to the face of Tom that he winked and drew back.

"I don't keep none o' yer cussed overseers; I does my own overseeing; and I tell you things is seen to. You's every one on ye got to toe the mark, I tell ye; quick, – straight, – the moment I speak. That's the way to keep in with me. Ye won't find no soft spot in me, nowhere. So, now, mind yerselves; for I don't show no mercy." '

Uncle Tom's Cabin, **Chapter 31, 1852**

The life of Harriet Beecher Stowe

1811 Born Harriet Elizabeth Beecher in Litchfield, Connecticut, and displays precocious talent at school.

1826 Moves to Boston, then to Cincinnati (1832).

1836 Marries a widowed professor of biblical studies, Calvin Ellis Stowe.

1843 Publishes her first book, *The Mayflower*, containing sketches.

1851 *Uncle Tom's Cabin* is serialized, and appears in book form in 1852.

1853 Visits Europe to promote her book and her cause. Defends the novel's integrity in *A Key to Uncle Tom's Cabin*.

1854 *Uncle Tom's Cabin* has been translated into 60 languages.

1856 Publishes *Dred: A Tale of the Great Dismal Swamp*, about White slave-owners.

1861 Civil War breaks out.

1862 Meets President Lincoln, who reportedly says: 'So you're the little lady who started this great war.'

1865 End of Civil War: Thirteenth Amendment to US Constitution abolishes slavery.

1896 Dies in Hartford, Connecticut.

Eva becomes ill and dies, after experiencing a vision of heaven, her father is consumed by grief and promises to give Tom his freedom. However, Eva's father is killed after intervening in a fight, and his wife, ignoring his promise, sells Tom to the violent plantation owner Simon Legree.

The novel describes the degradation of the slave warehouse, the horror of the auction, and the unmitigated misery of life on Legree's plantation, which culminates in a savage beating given to Tom after he refuses to whip one of the other slaves. Legree is incensed by Tom's piety and courage, and when Tom refuses to give information about two women who have escaped, he orders another brutal beating for him. Tom forgives the slaves who are carrying it out, and they are so impressed by his courage that they repent and convert, but too late to save his life. George Shelby, the son of Tom's original 'owner' in Kentucky, arrives to buy his freedom, but he is just in time to hear Tom's dying words: 'Who, – who, – who shall separate us from the love of Christ?'

Around this central story are woven the stories of other slaves. There is Eliza, for instance, who runs away from Mr Shelby's plantation with her young son after she hears that the boy is to be taken from her and sold. With her husband, who has run away previously, they finally make their way to Canada, meeting up later in their journey with the two women whose escape from Legree led to Tom's beating and death. Eliza, it transpires, is the long-lost daughter of one of the women, and the little group travels on to Europe and finally to freedom in Liberia, the nation that had been set up for former slaves in Africa.

Other characters include Topsy, a young girl bought by Eva's father in New Orleans, who is asked if she knows about God, or about who made her, and who famously replies: 'I spect I grow'd. Don't think nobody never made me.' Then there is Cassie, Eliza's mother, who escapes from Legree's plantation, and who tries unsuccessfully to persuade Tom to kill Legree; and Eliza's husband George Harris, who shoots and nearly kills a slave hunter who is tracking them, and then takes him to a Quaker settlement to be treated.

At the end of the book, George Shelby returns to his plantation in Kentucky to give all his slaves their

THE SLAVES' OWN STORIES

Alongside *Uncle Tom's Cabin* and other works by White abolitionists, a significant body of literature was produced by slaves or former slaves. These 'slave narratives', which first appeared in England during the 18th century, include scores of graphic accounts of the conditions of slavery. Sometimes they were 'as told to' works, mediated through White authors, such as *The Confessions of Nat Turner* (1831), which was based on dictations by the leader of a slave uprising. But many were written by former slaves themselves, of which the best known are by Frederick Douglass (*Narrative of the Life of Frederick Douglass*, 1845) and Harriet Jacobs (*Incidents in the Life of a Slave Girl*, 1861), the latter exceptional as a woman's account. Many focused on the steadfast Christian faith of the slaves, and although none achieved the massive sales of *Uncle Tom's Cabin*, they provided convincing support for the authenticity of the conditions Stowe described.

freedom. But there is no optimism expressed about the future of slavery in the United States; on the contrary, in a final chapter addressed to the reader, Stowe emphasizes that the conditions she has described are based on reality. The book, she says, is 'only a faint shadow, a dim picture, of the anguish and despair that are, at this very moment, riving thousands of hearts, shattering thousands of families, and driving a helpless and sensitive race to frenzy and despair'.

At the time that Stowe was writing, there were around 4 million slaves in the United States, most of them engaged in agricultural production on Southern plantations. There had been widespread pressure for abolition ever since the birth of the United States in 1776, but although all the Northern states had outlawed slavery by 1804, there was still widespread investment in slavery coming from the North, as manifested by the Fugitive Slave Act.

Although Stowe, a passionate abolitionist, had never seen a plantation when she wrote *Uncle Tom's Cabin*, she was living in Cincinnati, just over the Ohio River from the slave-owning state of Kentucky, and claimed that much of the novel was based on meetings with escaped slaves, who were trying to make their way north to Canada.

Suggestions that the book could have been responsible for the Civil War nine years later may be exaggerated, but it certainly inflamed passions on both sides of the argument. Abolitionists, both in the United States and abroad, said that it revealed the horrifying truth about slavery, while Southern slave-owners were incensed at what they believed was a biased and inaccurate portrait.

In 1853, anxious to stress her book's foundation in fact, Stowe brought out *A Key to Uncle Tom's Cabin*, which claimed to present people in real life whose sufferings and experiences paralleled those of her characters. In a later book, *Dred: A Tale of the Great Dismal Swamp*, she describes the collapse of a society that depends on slave labour. She not only wrote about slavery, but also published local-colour novels, travel books, manuals of home economics and even a defence of the poet Lord Byron's much-criticized widow (famously accusing Byron of incestuous relations with his half-sister). But it was *Uncle Tom's Cabin* that defined her.

The suggestion that *Uncle Tom's Cabin* was responsible for the Civil War and the end of slavery certainly ignores many other factors, including the efforts of many African-American slaves themselves. But its impact on public opinion both at home and in Europe was unparalleled, and Stowe had amply demonstrated how fiction could stir millions of people and whip up support for a political cause.

Madame Bovary

1857

Gustave Flaubert

Madame Bovary, subtitled 'Customs of the Provinces', was a controversial novel from the start. A highly publicized trial for alleged obscenity in 1857 helped to make the book a bestseller. But the public prosecutors missed the truly innovative nature of the book, in which the Romantic aesthetic that had swept through Europe in the early 19th century finally came of age, encountering a new, penetrating and merciless realism.

Gustave Flaubert (1821–80), like the early Romantics, was fascinated by the innermost motivations for human action. Like them, he saw the potentially far-reaching and tragic consequences of passion, but in *Madame Bovary* he brought those consequences into the everyday world of the provincial northern France he knew so well.

The story of a doctor's wife in northern France, *Madame Bovary* tells how her self-destructive deceit and adultery drive her to suicide and her husband to bankruptcy. It first appeared as a serial in *La Revue de Paris*, late in 1856. Flaubert's undisguised contempt for bourgeois manners and morality and his determinedly non-judgemental attitude towards his heroine led to charges that he was encouraging or condoning adultery, and when the story appeared in book form, it immediately faced a public prosecution. The case was dismissed, but *Madame Bovary* continued to remain bitterly controversial.

Flaubert's meticulous attention to realistic detail and the presentation of immediately recognizable scenes and exchanges made the novel appear shockingly like an objective depiction of provincial life – which was exactly what he wanted. But where the passions of Jane Austen's similarly provincial characters, in her ironic social novels 40 years before, smouldered respectably below the surface, those of Emma Bovary burst out in flame. It was this combination of passion and realism that made the book truly revolutionary.

In the novel, Charles Bovary, a doctor with a second-rate medical degree, is dragooned by his overbearing mother (the first Madame Bovary of the novel) into a respectable marriage with a 45-year-old widow, 'ugly … as thin as a lathe, and with a face as spotted as a meadow in springtime'. Visiting one of his patients, he meets the young and beautiful Emma Rouault, and on the death of his first wife persuades Emma to marry him.

The life of Gustave Flaubert

1821 Born in Rouen, northern France.

1831–9 Studies at the Collège Royal, obtaining his *baccalauréat*.

1841–5 Studies law at the Ecole de Droit, Paris; in poor health from 1844, returning to live at Croissart, near Rouen.

1849–51 Travels to Egypt and the Middle East.

1856 *Madame Bovary*, begun in 1850, is serialized in *Revue de Paris*, which is prosecuted (unsuccessfully) for obscenity.

1857 Publishes *Madame Bovary* in book form; it becomes a *succès de scandale*.

1858 Visits North Africa.

1862 Publishes the novel *Salammbô*.

1863 Starts work on *Bouvard et Pécuchet* (published posthumously, though unfinished, in 1881).

1869 Publishes the novel *L'Education sentimentale* (*Sentimental Education*).

1874 Publishes his final, third version of the novel *La Tentation de Saint Antoine* (*The Temptation of St Anthony*), begun in the 1840s.

1877 Publishes *Trois Contes* (*Three Tales*), including the much-admired 'Un coeur simple' ('A Simple Heart').

1880 Dies at Croisset.

1881 The unfinished novel *Bouvard et Pécuchet* appears posthumously.

From then on, Emma – the Madame Bovary of the title – is at the centre of the novel. From her reading of sentimental literature, Emma has developed a romantic yearning for luxury and passion, and rapidly grows bored with her dull and uninspiring husband, with married life in general, and soon afterwards with motherhood when she has her daughter, Berthe. Two love affairs follow: the first, a seemingly unrevealed longing for a young student, Leon, ends when he moves away; the second is an ardent three-year relationship with a rich and cynical local landowner, Rodolphe, with whom she plans to run away.

Rodolphe lets Emma down callously at the last minute, and she is grief-stricken and falls ill. As she recovers, the unsuspecting Charles insists on taking her to the opera in Rouen, a few miles away (and Flaubert's birthplace). There, they meet Leon again by chance, and a passionate affair ensues, as Emma pretends to take piano lessons in the city in order to be with him. Gradually, their affair fizzles out, and Emma begins to compare Leon unfavourably with the dashing, romantic, and entirely selfish Rodolphe.

By now, Emma is in financial thrall to the trader Lheureux in her home town, from whom she has been buying goods on credit to maintain her taste for luxury. When he demands payment, neither Leon nor Rodolphe help her. In despair, she steals arsenic from the pharmacy opposite her house and poisons herself, dying a slow and painful death. Charles Bovary is distraught. He stops working, and starts selling his possessions to pay his bills, but more debts incurred by Emma keep appearing. Even when he finds love letters sent to Emma by Rodolphe, he remains desperately in love with the wife who has betrayed and destroyed him. In a painful interview, he tells Rodolphe

'Absinthe, cigars and oysters'

In this extract, from the third part of the novel, Emma has travelled to Rouen by coach ('Hirondelle'), supposedly for a piano lesson, but actually to meet her lover, Leon. At this stage, they are still passionate about each other, but already, Emma's excitement comes almost as much from the thrill of their illicit rendezvous as from the anticipation of seeing her lover. Flaubert ensures we appreciate realities, with the 'perspiring' heroine navigating the alleys of 'bars and prostitutes'.

'There was a stop at the city gate. Emma took off her overshoes, changed her gloves, arranged her shawl, and twenty paces farther on, she left the Hirondelle.

The city was coming to life. Clerks in caps were polishing shop windows, and women with baskets on their hips stood on street corners, uttering loud, regular cries. She walked on, her eyes lowered, keeping close to the house walls and smiling happily under her lowered black veil.

For fear of being seen, she usually didn't take the shortest way. She would plunge into a maze of dark alleys, and emerge, hot and perspiring, close to the fountain at the lower end of the Rue Nationale. This is the part of town near the theatre, full of bars and prostitutes. Often a van rumbled by, laden with shaky stage-sets. Aproned waiters were sanding the pavement between the tubs of green bushes, There was a smell of absinthe, cigars, and oysters.

Then she turned a corner. She recognized him from afar by the way his curly hair hung down below his hat.

He walked ahead on the sidewalk. She followed him to the hotel; he went upstairs, opened the door of the room, went in – what an embrace!'

Madame Bovary, Part III, Chapter 5, translated by Francis Steegmuller, 1993

that he blames no-one for the affair, which was, he says 'decreed by fate'; shortly afterwards, Charles is found dead in the garden by his young daughter.

It is a simple, even trite plot; what makes it exceptional is the depth of Flaubert's understanding of the motives and emotions of his characters. Flaubert takes many of the clichés of Romantic fiction and presents them with an icy realism – Rodolphe, for instance, is clearly well aware how shallow and self-centred his passionate declarations are, and the grand Romantic gesture of Emma's eventual suicide is described in all its agonizing and undignified physical detail.

The contempt in the novel for the hypocrisy and self-seeking of the peripheral characters such as Lheureux is complete, but there are no simple moral judgements about Emma – which angered some critics. On the contrary, Flaubert observed after the book had been published: 'Madame Bovary, c'est moi' ('Madame Bovary is me').

'The author, in his work,' Flaubert commented, 'must be like God in the universe, present everywhere and visible nowhere.' He was a meticulous stylist, obsessively working and reworking each page that he completed. The 120,000 words of *Madame Bovary* took him more than five years to write, and *The Temptation of St Anthony*, which he started sometime during the 1840s, appeared in three versions over a period of nearly three decades. He spent the four years after the publication of *Madame Bovary* writing *Salammbô*, a historical novel about the city of Carthage in the 3rd century BC, and then immediately started work on *Bouvard and Pécuchet*, a satirical novel about a junior clerk who inherits a fortune. This occupied him until his death 17 years later, and it was still unfinished when it was published posthumously.

While he was working on *Bouvard and Pécuchet*, he completed his other masterpiece, *Sentimental Education*, centring on the love of a young man for an older woman amid the social, moral and political vicissitudes of mid 19th-century Paris. It is at once a *Bildungsroman*, charting a young man's induction into dizzy obsession and the unprincipled ways of the world, and an ambitious panoramic novel about the life of a city. Here, too, grand ideals fail to be lived up to, and aspirations are undercut, by characters' own failings and by the self-interest of others. Some have called Flaubert a pessimist about human nature. Many would say that Flaubert's skill, here as in *Madame Bovary*, was to tell it like it is.

ROMANTICISM, REALISM AND NATURALISM

More than 20 years before *Madame Bovary*, Honoré de Balzac applied a similar close research and meticulous detail to give his own stories an air of realism. But within that superficially realistic world, Balzac's plots were often as contrived, sensational, and improbable as those of the Romantics. The plot of *Madame Bovary*, by contrast, might almost have come from the daily newspapers of the time.

By the time Flaubert died in 1880, Emile Zola (1840–1902) had developed this realistic technique into what he termed 'naturalism'. His series of twenty *Rougon-Macquart* novels, tracing the story of the two branches of a single extended family under France's Second Empire, had a similarly realistic setting, but Zola claimed that his characters responded to their environment in accordance with their social background and with scientific ideas of inherited behaviour. Where Flaubert studies the intimate details of Emma's individual personality and motivations, Zola's characters are each part of a larger pattern, driven and often destroyed by forces they can neither control nor understand.

Zola's naturalistic influence is often particularly seen in the writing of American novelists such as Frank Norris (1870–1902), Theodore Dreiser (1871–1945), and John Steinbeck (1902–68).

On the Origin
of Species
1859

Charles Darwin

Charles Darwin's *On the Origin of Species*, containing his theory of evolution by natural selection, is incontestably the most important biological book ever written; it is probably also the book that has affected most radically humanity's conception of itself. It forced a reappraisal of the assumption that humans had been specially created by God in his own image, and made them instead subject to the evolutionary laws of Nature.

On the Origin of Species spelled out what Charles Darwin (1809–82) called his 'theory of natural selection'. Chapters 1 and 2 compare the variation within living domesticated animals with that of animals in the wild, which he later described as the most beautiful part of his theory. Chapter 3 describes the 'struggle for existence'. From reading Thomas Malthus's *Essay on the Principle of Population* (1798), Darwin realized in 1838 that individuals of almost all species had more offspring than could possibly survive to become adults. Darwin's argument was that they competed for limited resources, such as food or a mate. Small differences that existed naturally between individual members of a species might prove advantageous in the competition for resources. Many of these differences could be inherited, and the descendants of particularly successful individuals would be more likely to survive, find mates and breed.

He called this process 'natural selection', because it was analogous to how breeders select crops or animals with desirable characteristics for breeding together. (Darwin also described how natural selection of unfavourable characteristics could lead to extinction.) Evolution by natural selection would take many generations, but the accumulating changes would produce first variations within the species, and ultimately new species.

Darwin's ideas on species change were formulated during a five-year voyage around the world as a naturalist on board the Royal Navy survey ship *Beagle*, between 1831 and 1836. Having just graduated in divinity from Cambridge, Darwin had intended to become a clergyman. However as an undergraduate his interest in natural history had blossomed: he attended botany lectures and field trips and became determined to make a contribution to science.

Darwin spent more than three years of the expedition on land in South America and – most famously – in the Galapagos Islands, New Zealand and Australia. On the Galapagos he collected many specimens of small birds, which varied from island to island. Darwin also collected many fossils during his journey.

The similarities between the fossil mammals Darwin collected and modern mammals led him to believe that the species, though related, had changed, and he set out these initial observations in his *Journal and Remarks* (1839). Experts showed him that the Galapagos birds were similar but separate species of finch, and all were different from the related species on mainland South America. Darwin discussed the finches in a revised second edition (1845). 'Seeing this gradation and diversity of structure in one small, intimately related group of birds,' he wrote, 'one might really fancy that from an original paucity of birds in this archipelago, one species had been taken and modified for different ends.'

Darwin was not the first to propose that species could change over time. Theories had been put forward earlier, notably by Robert Hooke (1635–1703), that fossils could be the remains of vanished ancient species. Darwin had studied the ideas of Jean-Baptiste de Lamarck (1744–1829), who held that species could evolve through the inheritance of acquired characteristics. Darwin's own

The 'recurring struggle for existence'

Darwin realized from the start that natural selection was 'not the exclusive means of modification' and he acknowledged other mechanisms for how species change. But in this extract from the Introduction to the first edition of *On the Origin of Species*, he set out the bones of a theory that would revolutionize scientific thought.

'As many more individuals of each species are born than can possibly survive; and as, consequently, there is a frequently recurring struggle for existence, it follows that any being, if it vary however slightly in any manner profitable to itself, under the complex and sometimes varying conditions of life, will have a better chance of surviving, and thus be naturally selected. From the strong principle of inheritance, any selected variety will tend to propagate its new and modified form ... I am fully convinced that species are not immutable; but that those belonging to what are called the same genera are lineal descendants of some other and generally extinct species, in the same manner as the acknowledged varieties of any one species are the descendants of that species.

Furthermore, I am convinced that Natural Selection has been the main but not exclusive means of modification.'

On the Origin of Species, Introduction, 1859

grandfather, Erasmus Darwin (1731–1802), had suggested that species might develop over time by passing changes on through reproduction. On the *Beagle* voyage, Darwin had with him a copy of the first volume of *Principles of Geology* by Charles Lyell (1797–1875). Published in 1830, this described how continual gradual change over an immense period of time had formed the landmasses and landscapes of what had previously been believed to be an unchanging world.

It took Darwin more than 20 years after returning from his voyages to develop the explanation for how species could change that he outlined in *On the Origin of Species*. During this time, other scientists came close to spelling out their own versions of evolution by natural selection. In 1858, Darwin received a manuscript from Alfred Russel Wallace, a naturalist working in the Malayan archipelago, whom he had previously corresponded with. Wallace had independently proposed the principle on which Darwin had been working. A composite paper containing work by both scientists was presented in London later that year, with excerpts highlighting Darwin's priority.

In 1859 Darwin finally published *On the Origin of Species by Means of Natural Selection, or the Preservation of Favoured Races in the Struggle for Life* – though in the Introduction he said he still needed 'two or three more years' to complete his work. He had expected the response to the book to be animated, and it was. In his private notebooks, he expressed the fear that abandoning the idea that man had been uniquely created in the image of God might deal a crushing blow to Christianity and organized religion. 'What a book a Devil's Chaplain might write on the clumsy, wasteful, blundering, low and horridly cruel works of Nature,' he wrote in one entry.

Darwin's aim was to describe descent of species without reference to the origin of life itself or the origin or descent of humans, but it was easy to see the unstated implication. He tried to preserve the idea that God might have been the moving force behind the whole evolutionary process. Evolution, he wrote in the first edition, was part of 'the laws impressed on matter by the Creator'. But the argument between the evolutionists and those who held to the biblical account that each species had been separately created raged savagely in impassioned sermons, lengthy reviews and

The life of Charles Darwin

1809 Born in Shrewsbury, Shropshire.

1825–7 Studies medicine at Edinburgh University.

1827–31 Studies divinity at Christ's College, Cambridge, earning degree, but his interests turn to natural history.

1831–6 Accompanies HMS *Beagle* as a naturalist, on the ship's scientific survey in the southern Atlantic and Pacific oceans.

1838–41 Secretary of the Geological Society.

1839 Publishes *Journal and Remarks 1832–1836* as the third volume of *Narrative of the Surveying Voyages of His Majesty's Ships Adventure and Beagle*; many editions published with different titles, the best known being *Voyage of the Beagle*.

1842 Having married, settles in Downe, Kent.

1858 A joint paper with Alfred Russel Wallace is read at the Linnean Society, London.

1859 Publishes *On the Origin of Species by Means of Natural Selection, or the Preservation of Favoured Races in the Struggle for Life*.

1868 Publishes *The Variation of Animals and Plants under Domestication*.

1871 Publishes *The Descent of Man, and Selection in Relation to Sex*.

1882 Dies in Downe, and is buried in Westminster Abbey.

public meetings. In one famous exchange in Oxford in 1860, Samuel Wilberforce, the Bishop of Oxford, asked the biologist and evolutionist T.H. Huxley (1825–95) contemptuously: 'Is it on your grandfather's or your grandmother's side that you claim descent from a monkey?' Huxley's calm and collected demolishing of his opponent's arguments garnered him the nickname of 'Darwin's bulldog'.

But while the scientists and clerics argued, the public bought the book in huge numbers. The first printing, of 1250 copies, sold out within days of its issue, and almost immediately Darwin was working on revisions and corrections for a second edition of another 3000 copies, printed less than a month later. He continued to work on his theories and refine them over six subsequent editions, giving a new Introduction in the third edition to acknowledge writers whose ideas anticipated parts of his theory. It was not until the fifth edition of 1869 that Darwin used the phrase 'survival of the fittest', which had been coined by the philosopher Herbert Spencer (1820–1903) in writing about Darwin's theories. The sixth edition in 1872 included extensive revisions, including Darwin's reply to scientific objections to his theory.

He had intended from the start to write a longer version, explaining and cataloguing his theories more thoroughly, which he referred to as his 'big book'. In 1868 *The Variation of Animals and Plants under Domestication* was published, followed three years later by *The Descent of Man, and Selection in Relation to Sex*.

Darwin's theory is today more famous than ever. Nearly 150 different editions of the book were published during the 20th century alone. The book's popularity was due not just to the originality of its ideas, but also to Darwin's lucid and straightforward explanations. 'Every line of Darwin, you know he really wanted to be understood,' says Richard Dawkins, Oxford University Professor for the Public Understanding of Science, and a lifelong admirer of Darwin. 'There was no pretentious showing off about him.' Although some Christians and Muslims still do not accept his arguments, and instead take the scriptural account of the Creation to be revealed and literal truth, Darwin's theories have been refined and built on by biologists. Today, the vast majority of educated opinion accepts that the principle of natural selection describes how species change and new species may form.

On Liberty

1859

John Stuart Mill

It is a mark of the influence of John Stuart Mill that many of his ideas are accepted, at least in theory, in most modern democracies. Today, the need to protect individual liberty against the dominance of society at large is part of the general consensus, as are equal rights for women and universal education. But when *On Liberty* was written in the mid-19th century, Mill's proposals were deeply controversial, and the book itself was seen as a radical, even dangerous tract.

On Liberty is a short work of fewer than 50,000 words, divided into five chapters. The first chapter sets out the basic principle that lies behind the whole book, that there can be no justification for society to interfere with the freedom of action of any individual, except where that freedom causes harm to someone else. This is followed by three chapters that deal with liberty of thought and discussion, individuality as one of the elements of well-being, and the limits that should be set to the authority of society over the individual. A final section looks at practical ways in which Mill's ideas can be applied in society. *On Liberty* became the most widely read defence of individual freedom in the English-speaking world, and it remains a template for the maintenance of human and civil rights in a free society.

In his Introduction, Mill takes a historical perspective on the concept of liberty, starting with the Ancient Greeks and Romans, and concluding with the English parliamentary system of his own day. His theory is that as society tends to progress over time, ultimately attaining a level of representative democracy, so liberty in the past generally meant the protection of society from over-powerful individuals.

The sovereignty of the individual

In Mill's view, expressed in *On Liberty*, justice for individuals is inextricable from civil and social liberty. Individuals should not be prevented from doing anything that they choose, as long as they do not harm other people: his book, he says, is based on this 'one very simple principle'.

'That principle is, that the sole end for which mankind are warranted, individually or collectively, in interfering with the liberty of action of any of their number, is self-protection. That the only purpose for which power can be rightfully exercised over any member of a civilized community, against his will, is to prevent harm to others. His own good, either physical or moral, is not a sufficient warrant. He cannot rightfully be compelled to do or forbear because it will be better for him to do so, because it will make him happier, because, in the opinions of others, to do so would be wise, or even right. These are good reasons for remonstrating with him, or reasoning with him, or persuading him, or entreating him, but not for compelling him, or visiting him with any evil in case he do otherwise. To justify that, the conduct from which it is desired to deter him, must be calculated to produce evil to some one else. The only part of the conduct of any one, for which he is amenable to society, is that which concerns others. In the part which merely concerns himself, his independence is, of right, absolute. Over himself, over his own body and mind, the individual is sovereign.'

On Liberty, Introduction, 1859

Modern society, he suggests, reverses the problem: it is the individual that is threatened by the possibility that a democratic majority might force its will on a minority. Mill declares that this is likely to be 'the vital question of the future'. Three distinct forms of liberty need to be jealously guarded – freedom of thought, freedom of action and freedom to join together with other like-minded individuals. Unless these three freedoms are preserved, Mill says, society itself can become the tyrant – 'a social tyranny more formidable than many kinds of political oppression'.

In the second chapter, Mill defends the idea of freedom of speech: the censorship of any opinion, however repugnant, he says, is morally wrong – much the same point of view as Voltaire expressed nearly a century earlier, when he reputedly said: 'I disagree with what you say, but I will defend to the death your right to say it.' Mill suggests that dissent and argument are the only way to prevent truth from being confused with prejudice and dogma. 'Wrong opinions and practices gradually yield to fact and argument: but facts and arguments, to produce any effect on the mind, must be brought before it,' he says. It is in the interests of society, in short, to defend the right of unpopular people to hold unpopular views.

In the third chapter, Mill concedes that there have to be more limits on actions than on thought and opinions: you may hold unpopular views, but still not be permitted to put them into effect. One route towards progress in society, he suggests, is through experimentation with different and possibly unpopular ways of living, but actions that damage the interests of other people may be forbidden by law, and those that may be hurtful to other people, without actually violating their rights, may be punished by society at large.

The fourth chapter considers the exceptions – the areas in which society can legitimately limit the freedom of the individual. If people expect to be protected by society, they have to accept the responsibility to protect each other from harm. Society, in fact, must be able to put a stop to behaviour that harms other people. This, the so-called principle of harm, marks the limit of legitimate state power.

In the fifth and final chapter, Mill sums up his argument: individuals can do what they like as long as their actions affect no one but themselves, and society has the right and duty to prevent or punish action that causes harm. He also looks at the implications of these general principles – that women, for instance, should enjoy the same rights as men, and that children should enjoy a universal right to education.

In an age of what Mill called 'the almost despotic power of husbands over wives' and the 'absolute and exclusive control' allowed to a father over his children, these were bold and controversial suggestions.

As a Member of Parliament from 1865 to 1868, Mill was able in more practical terms to espouse many liberal causes, including opposition to English repression in Ireland. He was the first MP to demand votes for women, and in 1869 he published *The Subjection of Women*, specifically aimed at setting out the case for giving women equal political rights.

Elements in the political establishment were already moving towards some of the policies that Mill encouraged, but it was a slow process. Compulsory education, for instance, was introduced in Britain in 1888, but it was 1928 before women in Britain were granted the vote on the same terms as men. (In the United States, national women's suffrage was granted in 1920.) The real influence of *On Liberty* was not so much on particular political issues as on the general tenor of political debate.

Some more recent critics have questioned Mill's commitment to liberalism, suggesting that he was interested only in defending liberty for intellectuals or 'persons of decided mental superiority' by protecting them against the mass of the people. But at the time *On Liberty* appeared there was general acceptance that Mill was propounding and codifying political ideas that would extend individual rights across society. Many of these had already been expressed in the American Declaration of Independence, although the French historian and philosopher Alexis de Tocqueville (1805–59), a friend of Mill, had warned that the power of the state in the new American nation was threatening to swamp that of the individual.

Mill's achievement was to bring these ideas on individual liberty into mainstream political discussion, and to establish as a benchmark of political maturity the idea that 'If all mankind minus one were of one opinion, and only one person were of the contrary opinion, mankind would be no more justified in silencing that one person, than he, if he had the power, would be justified in silencing mankind.' It remains a defining principle of a properly functioning democracy that it defends the rights of minorities rather than simply exerting the will of a majority.

UTILITARIANISM

The Utilitarian movement of the 19th century was largely founded by the radical philosopher and social reformer Jeremy Bentham (1748–1832), who said that law and personal morality ought to be based on a pragmatic desire to increase people's happiness. The policy that should be followed, he said, was always that which would bring about 'the greatest good of the greatest number'.

Bentham's leading disciples included the economist David Ricardo (1772–1823) and the philosopher and journalist James Mill (1773–1836). Mill – the father of John Stuart Mill – wrote at length about Utilitarianism, stressing that, since people would naturally make choices that would result in their own happiness, the best form of government according to Utilitarian principles would be a representative democracy based on wide suffrage.

The young John Stuart Mill was educated according to Benthamite ideas, spending much of his youth copying out his father's philosophical and political works. Utilitarian principles lay behind much of his work in *On Liberty*, and also encouraged his defence of free-market economics in *Principles of Political Economy* (1848). In his book *Utilitarianism* (1863), however, he departs from Benthamite ideas in the distinctions he makes between different forms of happiness, proposing a hierarchy in which intellectual and moral pleasures are superior to 'lower' physical pleasures: 'It is better to be a human being dissatisfied than a pig satisfied,' he writes, 'better to be Socrates dissatisfied than a fool satisfied.'

War and Peace

1869

Leo Tolstoy

War and Peace by Leo Tolstoy was one of the first great novels to show the reality of warfare, depicting not only the generals and commanders, but also the civilians under threat from invading troops and, most crucially, the soldiers on the battlefield. Tolstoy's vastly ambitious historical epic did not succeed in destroying the myths of 'great men' and noble conflicts – but *War and Peace* amply evoked the reality of war's confusion, desperation and futility.

The novelist Henry James (1843–1916) famously described *War and Peace* – *Voyna i mir* in the original Russian – as a 'large loose baggy monster', and Tolstoy himself denied that it was a novel at all. It mixes fiction, history and philosophy in a work of around half a million words, with a very sprawling structure, deploying many hundreds of characters. Philosophical essays on the nature of history are incorporated in a series of long, rambling, interwoven stories. These study the period of Russia's struggle with Napoleon (1805–14) in forensic detail, focusing not just on the actual conflict, but on its effect on the whole of society, and the way that it transforms the lives of the central characters.

Leo Tolstoy, a landed aristocrat, inherited his western Russian estate of Yasnaya Polyana in the 1840s, but in 1851 he joined up with the Russian army as a non-commissioned officer. In 1854–5 he saw action at Sevastopol, during its Crimean War siege by the combined Anglo-French and Turkish forces, so he had personal experience to draw on for *War and Peace*. His early writing included autobiographies, and in 1855–6 he wrote his *Sevastopol Sketches*, grimly detailed deconstructions of war, presenting it as little other than futile, pointless, and destructive of lives and values.

Almost 40 chapters of *War and Peace* had appeared in 1865, under the title *1805*, before Tolstoy had completed his first draft of the whole. After that, there were several redraftings, rewritings and title changes over the next few years before the book as we know it today was finally published in 1869. Even then, it lacked much in the way of formal structure; one reason for its lengthy rewriting was Tolstoy's unhappiness with the ending, and his final version has no real conclusion.

TOLSTOY THE SOLDIER

The understanding of the soldier's view of warfare in *War and Peace* came partly from Tolstoy's own experience of battle as a young soldier in the Caucasus and in the siege of Sevastopol in the Crimean War, more than ten years earlier.

He originally joined the army as a *junker*, or gentleman-volunteer in 1851, at the age of 23, disillusioned with his 'completely brutish life' of drinking, gambling and partying in Moscow. He served with his brother Nikolai in the Cossack region of the Caucasus in campaigns against irregular Muslim guerrillas who were trying to resist the encroachment of the Russians. Tolstoy was posted to the Terek River with an artillery unit, but soon after the start of the Crimean War in 1853, he transferred to Wallachia as a second lieutenant in an artillery battery in the defence of Sevastopol against British, French and Ottoman forces.

He had already started writing – the first two books of his autobiographical trilogy, *Childhood* (1852) and *Boyhood* (1854), were both published while he was a serving soldier – and he left the army shortly after the surrender of the city in 1855. His descriptions of the suffering and futility of the siege had already been published in a St Petersburg magazine, and brought him to the notice of Tsar Alexander II and the Russian literary elite, marking the start of his literary career.

War and Peace traces the interactions of five aristo-cratic families, concentrating particularly on the Bezukhovs, the Bolkonskys, and the Rostovs, during the war against Napoleon and the French invasion of Russia in 1812. It also sets out Tolstoy's theory of history, which suggests that even the most powerful leaders have only a marginal effect on the progress of great events, which are much more radically affected by chance or fate.

The book opens at a party in St Petersburg, with the aristocratic guests expressing their anxieties about Napoleon's increasing power. Among them are the wealthy Pierre Bezukhov, the hard-living, hard-drinking illegitimate son of a wealthy aristocrat, and his patriotic friend Prince Andrey Bolkonsky. Bezukhov is a constant critic of the government, but Bolkonsky is on the point of leaving St Petersburg and his pregnant wife to join the army to fight against Napoleon.

Other crucial characters are the members of the Kuragin family, including the socially ambitious fortune-hunting Anatole Kuragin and his beautiful sister Helene, and the Rostovs, a leading family in Moscow.

Tolstoy's fictional world concentrates on the social strata he knew best – the aristocracy and the peasants – and in *War and Peace* especially the former. They are depicted from imperial ballrooms to battlefields, to country life on grand estates. This does not mean that the characters are remote, however, for in the course of the intertwined plots that follow, readers are drawn into Tolstoy's crowded canvas, to witness love affairs, marriages, duels, infidelities, inheritances won, finances ruined, suicides attempted – the highs and lows of life set against the background of a dramatic historical conflict. As one critic, A.V. Knowles, has commented: 'the reader lives with Tolstoy's characters as with those of no other writer'.

Added to this saga of leading families are the glimpses of names from the historical record, including not only a pompously ineffectual Napoleon but also Tsar Alexander I, the Emperor of Austria and other leading politicians and military men. Tolstoy stresses his anti-Romantic view that history has its own momentum, and is not dominated by the actions of supposedly 'great men'. In one of the most powerful sections of the novel, Bezukhov, now convinced that

The life of Count Leo Tolstoy

1828 Born on the family estate of Yasnaya Polyana, near Tula, western Russia.

1837 After a home education, studies in Moscow (until 1841) and then at Kazan, but leaves university without a degree (1847) and then occupies himself as estate owner and playboy.

1851 Begins military service, in the Caucasus.

1852–7 Publishes the autobio-graphical trilogy *Childhood, Boyhood and Youth*.

1854–5 Commands an artillery battery during the siege of Sevastopol, 1854–5, in the Crimean War.

1855–6 Publishes *Sevastopol Sketches*, his first works of fiction, and begins his European travels.

1863 Publishes *The Cossacks* and the first version of *War and Peace*, entitled *1805*. Now married, settles on his estate.

1869 Publishes the full version of *War and Peace*.

1875–7 Publishes the novel *Anna Karenina*.

1879 Publishes his autobio-graphical-religious *A Confession*, and in the last decades of his life his beliefs and writings turn to a personal, ascetic form of Christianity, resulting in a rejection of Jesus and excommunication by the Orthodox Church.

1910 Falls ill while travelling, and dies at Astapovo, in western Russia.

Humanity and history

War and Peace intertwines close personal observation with a wide-ranging, overarching historical standpoint, and so the author's voice correspondingly moves from the touching and the individuated to a sometimes coruscating commentary on the times.

The first extract introduces Natasha Rostova as a young girl. As the plot develops, she will fall in love with a series of men, and then marry – but her liveliness, her impetuosity, and her naïve simplicity are all evident in this first glimpse:

'This black-eyed, wide-mouthed girl, not pretty but full of life – with childish bare shoulders which after her run heaved and shook her bodice, with black curls tossed backward, thin bare arms, little legs in lace-frilled drawers, and feet in low slippers – was just at that charming age when a girl is no longer a child, though the child is not yet a young woman. Escaping from her father she ran to hide her flushed face in the lace of her mother's mantilla – not paying the least attention to her severe remark – and began to laugh. She laughed, and in fragmentary sentences tried to explain about a doll which she produced from the folds of her frock ...'

Tolstoy's Introduction to Napoleon's invasion of Russia is utterly different:

'... On the twelfth of June, 1812, the forces of Western Europe crossed the Russian frontier and war began, that is, an event took place opposed to human reason and to human nature. Millions of men perpetrated against one another such innumerable crimes, frauds, treacheries, thefts, forgeries, issues of false money, burglaries, incendiarisms, and murders as in whole centuries are not recorded in the annals of all the law courts of the world, but which those who committed them did not at the time regard as being crimes.'

War and Peace, Book 1, Chapter XI, and Book 9, Chapter I,
translated by Louise and Aylmer Maude, 1922

he has a divine mission to assassinate Napoleon, watches from a hilltop as Russian forces try to halt Napoleon's advance at the Battle of Borodino. Joining in by carrying ammunition for the Russian forces, he experiences the slaughter, devastation and futility of the inconclusive struggle. In their different ways, Napoleon and the Russian General Kutuzov are revealed as equally deluded about the effect of strategies and tactics on the outcome of events.

Such episodes, though, intermingle with others more remote from the theatre of war, to provide the epic, often generous-hearted, sense of humanity on display, in all its complexity and muddle, which suffuses *War and Peace*. Tolstoy was a man whose life and writing were characterized by the breadth of his attempts to bridge contrasts and contradictions in himself and in his world. In his writings, the nobility, the generals, the Orthodox Church and the sophisticated cities vie with peasants, the country and unofficial religion; and the values of Russia contrast with those of the West (i.e. Western Europe). Tolstoy himself was an aristocrat who grew to idealize the peasant class eventually striving to become one of them; he was a Slavophile and lover of Russia's rural vastness who was yet a cosmopolitan traveller. *War and Peace* exudes a sense of the totality and variety of life, and it is ultimately perhaps this quality that ranks it among the world's greatest novels.

THE

TELEPHONE

DIRECTORY.

NOVEMBER, 1878.

NEW HAVEN, CONN.:
PUBLISHED BY THE CONN. DISTRICT TELEPHONE CO.

The Telephone Directory

1878

New Haven District
Telephone Company

On 10 March 1876, with the words, 'Mr Watson – come here, I want to see you,' the world was changed for ever. Alexander Graham Bell's invention of the telephone ushered in an era of instant long-distance communication that revolutionized commerce, industry, politics and personal relationships. The telegraph had already been invented, in 1837, but it required a specialist operator to put the (usually terse) message into Morse code, another operator at the receiving end to decode it, and then someone to deliver it to the recipient. The telephone, by contrast, put people directly and vocally in touch with each other.

The telephone also created an occasion for the new technology of telecommunications to join with a much old technology – print. Subscribers to the new telephone services needed to know how to contact other subscribers – otherwise the new invention would be little more than a toy. Hence the publication of the first telephone directory, called simply *The Telephone Directory*. It was issued in Connecticut in 1878 by the New Haven District Telephone Company, the world's first, and comprised a single-sheet list of 50 subscribers. Most of the entries were for businesses or public services such as the police and the post office. Only 11 were for private residences, 4 of those for individuals connected to the company. The directory did not actually give the subscribers' telephone numbers – callers had to ring the New Haven exchange to be put through.

The idea of a directory was not new in itself. All kinds of specialist directories had been published since at least the 18th century, a notorious example being *Harris's List of Covent Garden Ladies*, a bestselling annual directory of prostitutes in London's West End that began life in the 1740s. Other examples include *Debrett's Peerage and Baronetage*, a genealogical guide to the British aristocracy first published in 1769, and *Crockford's Clerical Directory*, founded in 1858, which gives details of thousands of Anglican clergy in the UK. All these, in one way or another, helped to put people in touch with each other – but it was the telephone directory that eventually enabled virtually everybody to get in touch with virtually everybody else.

The development of telephone technology was driven partly by governments, who recognized its military potential – the Anglo-Boer War (1899–1902) was the first major conflict in which field telephones were used to maintain communications between military units. But it was the mass

THE FIRST TELEPHONE

There have been bitter arguments as to who was the true inventor of the telephone. In the late 1850s the Italian-born inventor Antonio Meucci created a device to send voice messages between different rooms of his home on Staten Island, New York; another Italian, Innocento Manzetti, was reported to have transmitted his voice down a telegraph wire in 1864; and Elisha Grey, an electrical engineer from Chicago, attempted to register a similar device around the same time as Alexander Graham Bell.

However, it was Bell's invention that was officially patented on 7 March 1876. And it was the Bell Telephone Company (later to grow into the modern telecommunications giant AT&T) that in 1878 licensed the construction of the first telephone exchange in New Haven, Connecticut. It was the success of that exchange that led to the first telephone directory.

market of increasingly affluent consumers that provided the main impetus; they wanted individual communication in just the same way that they wanted individual transport in the form of the motor car.

From its tiny beginning in 1878 in New Haven, the telephone directory grew into the most popular printed work in the history of publishing. Later in the same year, directories were issued in San Francisco and also in Chicago, and these, for the first time, gave individual telephone numbers alongside the names of subscribers. The first directory in Britain, containing 248 personal and business names in the London area, was issued in 1880.

The more widely the telephone spread, and the more numbers there were for subscribers to remember, the more important was the role of the telephone directory. Businesses rapidly realized the marketing potential of the new means of communication, and alongside the growing circulation of ordinary telephone directories, a new version of the phone book also made its mark. In 1886, only eight years after the first New Haven directory, an enterprising 21-year-old businessman in Chicago named Reuben Donnelley issued the first classified directory, with companies listed according to the type of business in which they were engaged. Legend has it that the printer producing the first edition ran out of ordinary paper, and had to complete the job with yellow pages.

It was in Britain, in 1896, that the first telephone directory listing numbers for an entire country appeared, a thick volume of 1350 pages with over 80,000 separate entries. By 1914 the telephone directory was Britain's single biggest printing contract, with 1.5 million copies produced every year, while in the United States, the directory for New York's Manhattan district alone was printing a million copies a year by the 1920s. That trend continued for much of the century, replicated in every industrialized country in the world.

No one would claim that the telephone directory has influenced the development of thought and literature in the way that Shakespeare's First Folio or Tolstoy's *War and Peace* have; but by releasing the potential of the telephone, it has radically changed the daily lives and expectations of billions of people all over the world.

Today, as more and more communication is conducted via email on the internet, users build up their own individualized directories – in much the same way as people tend to keep their own personal, handwritten telephone books beside the big printed volume. Communication via landlines is being superseded by cell/mobile phone calls and by texting, and users of mobile phones have resisted attempts to gather their numbers into publicly available lists. And, in the 'Information Age', fears over privacy have seen the size of printed directories shrink, as thousands opt to become 'ex-directory'. The glory days of the telephone directory may well be over.

The Thousand and One Nights

1885

translated by
Sir Richard Burton

Some of the stories of *The Thousand and One Nights* cycle, also known as *The Arabian Nights*, date back at least as far as the 9th or 10th centuries, and they had certainly been gathered together into a collection by the 15th century. Most of them originated in Arab, Egyptian, Persian and Indian folk tales, and their initial influence was to reinforce the cosmopolitan nature of life in the Abbasid Empire, in which Persians and other non-Arabs gradually acquired influence within what had been the Arab Umayyad Empire.

There were several European translations from the 18th century onwards, but the stories began to acquire an international audience with the version produced in 1885 by the British Arabist, diplomat, explorer – and *provocateur* against Victorian decorum – Sir Richard Burton. They encouraged a view of the Middle East as mystical, exotic and dangerously immoral, a view that has persisted to this day, helping to cause distrust and misunderstanding between the West and the Islamic world.

Sir Richard Burton's original version of *The Thousand and One Nights* contained hundreds of stories, published in ten volumes, along with a series of essays on their history, style and provenance. More than 150 additional stories were published in six further volumes over the next three years.

The stories include several, such as 'Sinbad the Sailor', 'Aladdin' and 'Ali Baba and the Forty Thieves', which have become famous in the West as children's fairy tales or the plots of Christmas pantomimes – although many of the original stories contain much material not considered at all suitable for children.

The stories, like similar European collections from the same period, include fairy tales, romances, legends, fables, parables and adventures. They are told simply and directly, although there are also many short verse sections and several lengthy philosophical, historical or scientific digressions. Some of the stories are entirely imaginary, while others are woven around historical characters, such as the 8th-century Abbasid caliph, Haroun al-Rashid.

The structure of the cycle is a complicated and many-layered one, containing stories-within-stories. The whole cycle, however, is framed by the story of King Shahryar, who has his wife put to death when he discovers that she has been unfaithful, and swears that he will take a new wife each night and execute her the next morning. Eventually his vizier cannot find any more virgins in the kingdom, until his own daughter, Scheherazade, eventually volunteers herself. As she lies in bed with her new husband that night, she begins a story, which is still unfinished when the morning comes. The only way the king can find out how the story ends is by allowing his wife to live. Each night, Scheherazade begins another story, and each morning the king postpones her execution so that he can hear the conclusion. After a thousand and one such nights, Scheherazade begs the king to allow her to live. He bursts into tears, and declares that he has pardoned her long ago.

Burton's translation did not avoid the sexual and erotic aspects of the stories, including those that deal with homosexuality. 'It does not enter into my plan to ignore any theme which is interesting to the Orientalist and the Anthropologist,' he wrote in one of the essays in his final volume. He expected to be prosecuted when the work was published, and even made his own wife promise not to read it, because, he said, it was intended only for scholars. In fact, sold by private subscription, it was by far the most successful of his books, and made him a handsome profit of around £11,000.

The exuberance of Burton's language, and the way he concentrates on the quaint and exotic qualities of the stories, was a major contribution to the 'Orientalist' tendency in European culture.

This trend had begun in the mid-18th century, and it found in the deserts, souks, palaces and harems of the Middle East ideal settings for the fantasies of the Romantic imagination. William Beckford's novel *Vathek* (1786) and Lord Byron's poem *The Giaour* (1813) are just two of many literary works to revel in their imaginary Middle Eastern settings, while painters such as Delacroix and Ingres titillated their audiences with fantasies of fleshy harem girls, slaves to their masters' wishes.

All this helped to encourage a growing European perception of the Arab world as a bizarre and foreign place, ruled by cruel and debauched tyrants, where the people hide their true identities behind screens or veils, where nothing is as it seems and nobody is to be trusted, where men and women live only for sensual gratification, and liberty is sacrificed on the altar of luxury.

For many Westerners, their first childhood view of the Middle East is through various stories from *The Thousand and One Nights*, largely culled and bowdlerized from Burton's translation, and transposed into nursery tales or onto the pantomime stage. This make-believe, infantilized version of the Arab world still lingers on, and has been interpreted as an aspect of Western imperialism, for example in the Palestinian scholar Edward Said's ground-breaking work *Orientalism* (1978). It is ironic that the lasting effect of a work that Burton declared was supposed to improve European understanding of Islamic culture may actually have played a part in creating the gulf between East and West that exists to this day.

Whiling away the waking hours

In this extract Scheherazade, who has agreed to become the king's latest wife, although she knows she will be executed the morning after their wedding night, begins to spin her tales to put off the moment of her death.

'When it was midnight Scheherazade awoke and signalled to her sister Dunyazade, who sat up and said, "Allah upon thee, O my sister, recite to us some new story, delightsome and delectable, wherewith to while away the waking hours of our latter night." "With joy and goodly gree [satisfaction]," answered Scheherazade, "if this pious and auspicious King permit me." "Tell on," quoth the King, who chanced to be sleepless and restless and therefore was pleased with the prospect of hearing her story. So Scheherazade rejoiced, and thus, on the first night of the Thousand Nights and a Night, she began her recitations ...'

The Book of the Thousand Nights and a Night, Book I, translated Richard Burton, 1885

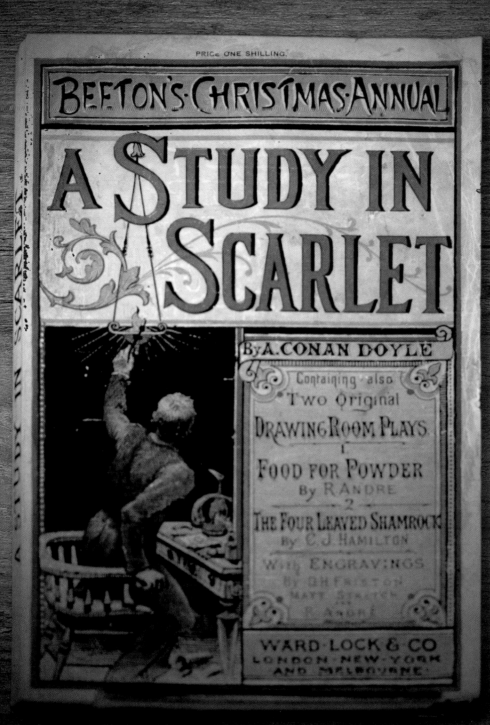

A Study in Scarlet

1888

Arthur Conan Doyle

Sherlock Holmes, the iconic detective from 221b Baker Street, in Victorian London, lies behind the whole genre of modern detective fiction. He was not the first imaginary character to outdo the police in the solving of crimes, but he was by far the best known and the most influential. *A Study in Scarlet* was the first of four full-length novels and 56 short stories written about Holmes by Sir Arthur Conan Doyle, introducing him both to the public and to his long-serving assistant, Dr Watson.

Much of *A Study in Scarlet* is supposedly taken from the diaries of John Watson, an army surgeon invalided out of the forces after being wounded in Afghanistan. It first appeared as one of three full-length stories in the magazine *Beeton's Christmas Annual* in 1887 (depicted opposite). Its author, Arthur Conan Doyle, had been working on it for two years or more, under the title *A Tangled Skein*, and had suffered a series of rejections from other publications. The story received little attention at the time, but the magazine, which appeared in November and was sold out by Christmas, is now one of the most sought-after in the world, with only 31 copies known to survive. The following summer, the 44,000-word story was published as a standalone book and, along with the other Sherlock Holmes stories, it has never been out of print since.

Its author, (Sir) Arthur Conan Doyle, was a late-Victorian polymath, who in some ways embodied the age in the breadth of his industry and endeavours. By the end of his life he had been a successful doctor, had saved soldiers' lives in the Anglo-Boer War (1899–1902), had stood as a parliamentary

The importance of reasoning backwards

At the end of *A Study in Scarlet*, with the murderer arrested and the case solved, Holmes explains to Watson – who is reporting the conversation in his journal – the difference between 'synthetic' and 'analytic' reasoning, which is, he says, the basic theory behind his method of investigation.

' *"I have already explained to you that what is out of the common is usually a guide rather than a hindrance. In solving a problem of this sort, the grand thing is to be able to reason backward. That is a very useful accomplishment, and a very easy one, but people do not practise it much. In the everyday affairs of life it is more useful to reason forward, and so the other comes to be neglected. There are fifty who can reason synthetically for one who can reason analytically."*

"I confess," said I, "that I do not quite follow you."

"I hardly expected that you would. Let me see if I can make it clearer. Most people, if you describe a train of events to them will tell you what the result would be. They can put those events together in their minds, and argue from them that something will come to pass. There are few people, however, who, if you told them a result, would be able to evolve from their own inner consciousness what the steps were which led up to that result. This power is what I mean when I talk of reasoning backward, or analytically."'

***A Study in Scarlet*, Chapter VII, 1888**

HOLMES'S PREDECESSORS

For all his claims in *A Study in Scarlet* to be the world's only 'consulting detective', Sherlock Holmes had several literary antecedents as a master detective. He even criticizes two of them, Edgar Allen Poe's Auguste Dupin and Emile Gaboriau's Monsieur Lecoq, as 'a very inferior fellow' and 'a bungler' respectively.

Poe (1809–49) created the amateur detective Dupin in his short story 'The Murders in the Rue Morgue' of 1841, and featured him in two further stories. The young Parisian police officer M. Lecoq appeared in the first detective story by Gaboriau (1832–73), *L'Affaire Lerouge* (1866). Despite Holmes's contempt, both of these characters employed much the same detailed observation and logical deduction as he did.

Several writers have been credited with the first English detective novel, including Charles Dickens (1812–70), who includes the investigation of a murder as one strand in his massive novel *Bleak House* (1853). Another claimant is Wilkie Collins (1824–89), whose novel *The Moonstone* (1868) features the detective Sergeant Cuff, who is called in to solve the mystery of an enormous Indian diamond stolen from Rachel Verinder on the night of her eighteenth birthday.

candidate on several occasions, had written and campaigned on a raft of issues from divorce-law reform to imperialism in Africa, had become one of the leading advocates of the power of spiritualism, and had become a knight of the realm. He had also tried to make his literary mark as a writer of historical romances. But posterity ignored almost all of that, in favour of one enduring creation: Sherlock Holmes. And *A Study in Scarlet* began it all.

The book starts with Dr Watson searching for cheap lodgings in London and being introduced to his roommate, the mysterious Sherlock Holmes, who is working in the chemical laboratory of a nearby hospital. Holmes is said to have beaten the bodies in the morgue with a stick to find out how much bruising takes place after death; he has an immensely detailed and wide-ranging knowledge of crime, poisons and chemistry, and an astonishing ability to deduce facts about strangers from observing their appearance. It is only after Watson has puzzled for days about his new roommate that Holmes casually tells him, 'I have a profession of my own. I suppose I am the only one in the world. I'm a consulting detective.'

Holmes is called in when a body is discovered in a deserted London house. He uses his techniques of observation and deduction, and eventually contrives to arrest the guilty man in the presence of Watson and Scotland Yard detectives. Holmes promises to explain how he has solved the case – but at that point, half way through the book, the scene suddenly shifts.

Most of the second half of *A Study in Scarlet* takes place in the Mormon settlement in Utah, United States. Conan Doyle had no direct personal knowledge of the Mormons, but he depicts the community they established in Utah as one of repression, intolerance and violence. A settler is murdered when he tries to take his daughter away in order to protect her from a forced polygamous marriage. The girl dies shortly after her wedding, and the story describes the obsessive quest for revenge mounted by the man she had wanted to marry. He follows the two men responsible when they leave Utah, and finally tracks them down and kills them in London.

The culprit dies of natural causes before he can be brought to trial. Holmes explains how he solved the case, and shrugs resignedly when all the credit for the success goes to the detectives rather than to him.

The importance of *A Study in Scarlet* does not lie in any influence it may have had on the handling of criminal investigations. There was little revolutionary or new in Holmes's belief in the importance of close observation, and his use of deductive reasoning is frequently flawed;

many of the supposedly brilliant deductions, here and throughout the stories, are capable of alternative explanations. It would be hard to argue that forensic science would not have developed without the prompting of Conan Doyle. In any case, Holmes's cavalier treatment of evidence would have got him sacked from the most junior role in any police force: in *A Study in Scarlet*, he demonstrates the potency of a poison pill left at the scene of a crime by feeding it to a dog.

The significance of the Sherlock Holmes stories is, of course, literary, not forensic. When the stories began serial publication in 1891, in *Strand Magazine*, a complete story in each monthly issue, the public's voracious appetite for the detective was truly awakened – and it has never died.

In Holmes, Conan Doyle created something of a literary archetype. Here was the gentleman detective, socially and intellectually superior to the plodding, lower-class, almost comically rendered policemen. ('I am afraid, Rance, that you will never rise in the force,' he condescends to one.) Here too is the solver of crimes as a type of remote clinician, whose ability to perceive motives, extract evidence and assess behavioural traits is ill-matched by any wider sense of empathy with his fellow human beings. It is Dr Watson, the 'everyman' and reader's representative in the stories, to whom we look for ordinary human feelings.

For Conan Doyle, the popular success of Holmes was a mixed blessing. His real literary ambition was to be lauded as a writer of historical novels, such as *Micah Clarke* (1889), *The White Company* (1891) and *The Exploits of Brigadier Gerard* (1896), but the fame of Holmes was pushing his other work into the shadows. Conan Doyle was provoked to kill off his hero in the 1893 story 'The Adventure of the Final Problem', but, appropriately enough for this believer in the spirit life, the author could not prevent Holmes beckoning from beyond the grave. In the 1903 'Adventure of the Empty House' Conan Doyle appeased the reading public, explaining how Holmes had, in fact, survived. Another 32 Holmes stories and one full-length novel followed.

The 20th century would see over 200 film versions, and an explosion in 'detective fiction' as one of the world's most popular forms of literary escapism. In no small part, this was due to the eccentric sleuth first revealed in *A Study in Scarlet*.

The life of Arthur Conan Doyle

1859 Born in Edinburgh, and educated at schools in Lancashire.

1876–81 Studies medicine at Edinburgh University, obtaining MB (MD in 1885).

1882 Works as doctor in Southsea, Hampshire (until 1890).

1887 *A Study in Scarlet*, published in *Beeton's Christmas Annual*, introduces the character of Sherlock Holmes; it appears as a separate book in 1888.

1889 Publishes *Micah Clarke*, the first of several historical novels.

1891 Begins issuing monthly Holmes stories in *Strand Magazine*, garnering immense popularity and fame.

1893 Publishes *The Sign of Four*, a Sherlock Holmes adventure in book form, but attempts to kill off Holmes in 'The Adventure of the Final Problem'.

1899–1902 Acts as a senior medical officer during the Anglo-Boer War.

1900 The first Sherlock Holmes film is made, *Sherlock Holmes Baffled*.

1902 Receives a knighthood.

1903 Revives Holmes in the story 'The Adventure of the Empty House'.

1927 Publishes the final Holmes story, 'The Adventure of Shoscombe Old Place', in *The Casebook of Sherlock Holmes*.

1930 Dies in Crowborough, Sussex.

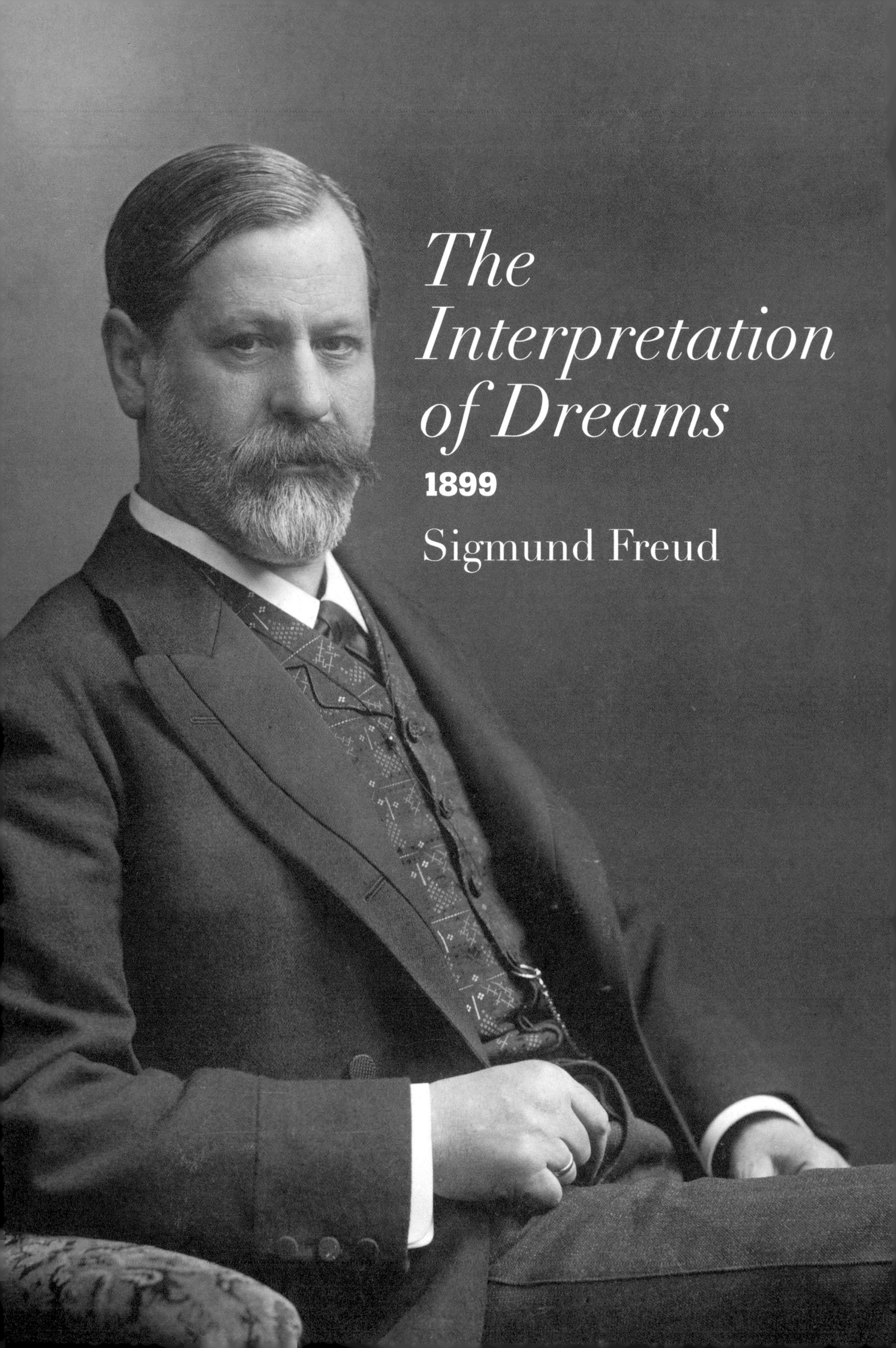
The Interpretation of Dreams
1899
Sigmund Freud

Sigmund Freud declared that humanity had suffered three historic humiliations – Galileo's discovery that the earth was not at the centre of the universe, Darwin's that mankind was not qualitatively different from the animal kingdom, and his own that we are not in control of our own minds. Modern specialists reject many of his theories about the healing powers of psychoanalysis, but his revelation that the unconscious retains many thoughts and emotions that the conscious mind appears to have forgotten has radically changed the way that people think about themselves.

Freud's fundamental insight has influenced much of our detailed understanding of the importance of childhood experiences in shaping the character of an individual. In *The Interpretation of Dreams*, he suggests that the study of dreams offers a 'royal road to a knowledge of the unconscious' – and a new way to understand our fears, ambitions and motivations.

The Interpretation of Dreams was first published in German in 1899 under the title *Die Traumdeutung* ('dream meanings'). Freud had spent about two years writing it, after starting a course of self-analysis alongside his examination of patients at his consulting rooms in Vienna. Both his own experiences and those related to him by his clients had convinced him of the importance of dreams as a way of understanding the unconscious mind. The book focuses in particular on his theory that dreams represent a way of fulfilling unconscious wishes or resolving conflicts that the conscious mind may not acknowledge or approve. These might relate to recent experiences or to memories of the distant past, but through the interpretation of the dreams, Freud suggests, these deeply buried feelings can be brought out into the open. The problem is that such desires, experiences or memories are disguised twice over – once by the unconscious, which presents them in symbols and images that might be more acceptable

The life of Sigmund Freud

1856 Born into a Jewish family in Freiberg, Moravia, then part of the Austrian Empire (now Pribor in the Czech Republic).

1882 Having studied medicine, starts work at a psychiatric clinic in Vienna.

1885 Studies in Paris with the distinguished neurologist Jean Martin Charcot.

1895 Publishes, with the neurologist Joseph Breuer, *Studien über Hysterie* (*Studies of Hysteria*).

1899 Publishes *Die Traumdeutung* (*The Interpretation of Dreams*).

1904 Publishes *Zur Psychopathologie des Alltagslebens* (*The Psychopathology of Everyday Life*) in book form.

1905 Publishes *Drei Abhandlungen zur Sexualtheorie* (*Three Essays on the Theory of Sexuality*).

1912 Breaks with his former colleague Carl Jung.

1913 Publishes *Totem und Tabu* (*Totem and Taboo*).

1920 Publishes *Jenseits des Lustprinzips* (*Beyond the Pleasure Principle*).

1923 Publishes *Das Ich und das Es* (*The Ego and the Id*).

1930 Publishes *Das Unbehagen in der Kultur* (*Civilization and Its Discontents*). Receives Germany's Goethe Prize.

1933 The German Nazi regime publicly burns his books.

1938 Leaves Vienna for London.

1939 Having suffered mouth cancer for many years, persuades his doctor to give him a fatal dose of morphine.

'Every dream will reveal itself'

Freud's book is both a theoretical and practical guide to the analysis of dreams, which Freud saw as a direct route into the subject's unconscious mind. Many of the dreams to which he referred were his own, but other examples came from patients he had treated in his practice. In this extract, he describes how a patient can be prepared for analysis.

'In the following pages I shall demonstrate that there is a psychological technique which makes it possible to interpret dreams, and that on the application of this technique every dream will reveal itself as a psychological structure, full of significance, and one which may be assigned to a specific place in the psychic activities of the waking state.'

'… A certain psychic preparation on the part of the patient is necessary. A twofold effort is made, to stimulate his attentiveness in respect of his psychic perceptions, and to eliminate the critical spirit in which he is ordinarily in the habit of viewing such thoughts as come to the surface. For the purpose of self-observation with concentrated attention it is advantageous that the patient should take up a restful position and close his eyes; he must be explicitly instructed to renounce all criticism of the thought-formations which he may perceive. He must also be told that the success of the psycho-analysis depends upon his noting and communicating everything that passes through his mind, and that he must not allow himself to suppress one idea because it seems to him unimportant or irrelevant to the subject, or another because it seems nonsensical. He must preserve an absolute impartiality in respect to his ideas; for if he is unsuccessful in finding the desired solution of the dream, the obsessional idea, or the like, it will be because he permits himself to be critical of them.'

The Interpretation of Dreams, Chapters 1 and 2, translated by A.A. Brill, 1911

to the conscious mind, and once by the patient, who might distort or misrepresent them in recounting the dreams to the analyst.

The dream's disguise, which Freud calls the 'dreamwork', may defy day-to-day logic, cause and effect, or narrative sequence. Deeply felt anxiety might turn the dreams into nightmares; images might give place one to another apparently at random; and recent memories may be mixed with experiences or wishes from childhood. It is the job of the analyst first to enable the client to recall and recount the dreams accurately, and then to disentangle this confusion. *The Interpretation of Dreams* aims both to explain Freud's theories and to offer practical suggestions as to how to undertake dream analysis.

The Interpretation of Dreams introduces the theory that sexuality is an intrinsic part of childhood, and that sexual desires and anxieties felt early in life may be reflected in neuroses in later life. It also sketches out the basic framework that Freud would eventually refine into his description of the Oedipus complex – the idea (named after the legendary Greek figure who unknowingly killed his father and married his mother) that children as young as three feel an instinctive sexual desire for the parent of the opposite sex, and a wish for the death of the parent of the same sex. These ideas, an intrinsic part of his thinking, were profoundly shocking at the time.

The book was largely ignored when it first appeared, with no reviews in the important scientific journals. It took eight years to sell the 600 copies that were initially printed. Ten years later, however, Freud produced a second edition, which was followed by six more during his lifetime.

Freud himself never had any doubts about the importance of his work. 'Insight such as this falls to one's lot but once in a lifetime,' he wrote – and the impact of his book over succeeding decades suggests that he was right. *The Interpretation of Dreams* is now considered to be his most important and most original work, even though much of the detail of his theories of the workings of dreams has been superseded. The first English translation from its original German was made in 1911, and a Russian version appeared in the same year.

In 1920 Freud published an essay, 'Beyond the Pleasure Principle', in which he expands on his suggestion that unconscious sexual urges are the impetus to much human activity, and proposes that a similarly unconscious 'death instinct' is constantly at work, urging the individual towards aggression and self-destruction. Other important developments in his thought are contained in *The Ego and the Id* (1923) and *Civilization and Its Discontents* (1930).

Later psychologists and philosophers have criticized Freud. Karl Popper (1902–94), the noted philosopher of science, suggested that Freud's theories were not scientific as they could not be proved to be false, while the psychologist Hans Eysenck (1916–97), in a critical study, declared: 'What is true in Freud is not new, and what is new in Freud is not true.'

But Freud, particularly in *The Interpretation of Dreams*, was responsible for the huge growth in interest in the workings of the unconscious mind in the first half of the 20th century – an interest that spread beyond the scientific community into the worlds of art, literature and even advertising. Despite the disagreement over his conclusions, and despite the continuing lack of certainty about the workings of the human mind, Freud inspired important research into the effects of the experiences of childhood on the adult individual. In establishing the significance of the unconscious mind, and the crucial role that sex plays in our motivations, he completely changed the way that people think about themselves.

FREUD AND SURREALISM

The Surrealist movement, which sprang up in Paris in 1924 and rapidly spread through Europe and America, is often seen as an expression in art of Freud's ideas about dreams and the unconscious.

Many of the Surrealist painters, among them Salvador Dalí (1904–89), René Magritte (1898–1967) and Joan Miró (1893–1983), sought to reflect the arbitrary and nonsensical quality of dreams within their work, often juxtaposing objects and images in unusual, shocking and irrational ways. Paintings might show objects metamorphosing from one state into another, like Dalí's famous melting watches. Film makers, among them Luis Buñuel (1900–83) and Man Ray (1890–1976), also attempted to express the irrational unconscious in art. Buñuel's *L'Age d'or* ('The Golden Age'; 1930), which he directed and co-wrote with Dalí, depicts a couple who are in love, but who are kept apart by the church, their families and society in general, and includes a Christ-like figure, a scientific insert about the scorpion, and shots of four bishops sitting in state on a rocky headland and gradually decomposing.

There were, though, important differences between Freud and the Surrealists: while Freud's aim was to understand the human psyche, they were dedicated to revolutionizing the arts and overthrowing bourgeois convention. Freud saw himself as an objective, scientific scholar, and he made the point that the works of the Surrealists were actually carefully thought through rather than genuine products of the unconscious.

The Jewish Peril

PROTOCOLS

OF THE

Learned   Elders

of   Zion.

SECOND EDITION.

Published by "THE BRITONS," 62 Oxford Street, London, W.

1920

Price, 3/- Net.

The Protocols of the
Elders of Zion

1905

The Protocols of the Elders of Zion first circulated in Russia in the early years of the 20th century as a mysterious, anonymous document, which claimed to give details of a vast Jewish plot for world domination. Eventually published in book form in Russia and then around the world, it purported to be the minutes of a secret meeting of Jewish leaders during the first Zionist Conference in Basle (Basel), Switzerland, in 1897. Today, it is generally accepted that the document, a fake, was produced at the behest of Russia's tsarist secret police, that the so-called 'Elders' never even existed, and that the secret meeting in Basle never took place.

The product of the fevered Russian anti-Semitism of the late 19th and early 20th century, the protocols continued to provide a focal point for the anti-Semitic organizations in Europe and beyond, and they lay at the heart of Germany's Third Reich and the Nazis' devastating racial policies. They have been exploited as a potent force for evil for a hundred years, demonstrating how successfully malice can play upon gullibility.

The book's authorship is still debated, though a Russian journalist and agent in late 19th-century Paris, Matvei Golovinski, remains a strong contender. Passages were serialized in a Moscow newspaper, *Znamya* ('The Banner'), during 1903, and two years later the full text appeared as a chapter in a book by Sergei Nilus, an eccentric Russian religious mystic. His book, which translates as *The Great in the Small: The Coming of the Anti-Christ and the Rule of Satan on Earth*, greatly impressed the credulous Tsar Nicholas II with its warnings of the dangers posed to Russia by Jews and Freemasons, and it provided Nilus with an entrée to the Russian court.

The 24 separate protocols, or minutes, spell out different ways in which world domination can be achieved, by gaining control of the press and of financial

The history of a forgery

1903 *The Protocols of the Elders of Zion* are published, in part, in the Moscow newspaper *Znamya* ('The Banner').

1905 The *Protocols* appear in book form in Moscow.

1920–1 The *Protocols* are translated into German and English, but a backlash begins.

1921 The London *Times* exposes the similarities between the *Protocols* and Maurice Joly's 1864 satire *Dialogue in Hell*, under the headline 'Truth at last', and books in Britain and the USA condemn the *Protocols* as a fabrication.

1925 Undeterred by the revelations, Hitler praises the *Protocols* in *Mein Kampf*. Both books become pillars of Nazi race ideology.

1927 US Industrialist Henry Ford is forced into a public apology for publishing the *Protocols* in 1920 (under the title *The International Jew*).

1935 A judge in Bern (Berne), Switzerland, dismisses the *Protocols* as a fake.

1964 The Judiciary Committee of the US Senate publishes a report on the *Protocols*, subtitled *A 'Fabricated' Historic Document*.

2002 An Egyptian television channel produces a drama series, *Knight Without a Horse*, based on the *Protocols*.

2005 New editions of the *Protocols* are published in countries as far apart as Mexico and Syria.

Plagiarism as propaganda

The Protocols of the Elders of Zion starts with an overview of the basic doctrine that lies behind the supposed Jewish plot for world domination. By using their wealth, and playing upon the degeneracy, disunity, and weakness of the *Goyim* (non-Jews), the Elders will seize power from existing governments.

This extract sets out a cynical justification for the use of force, and an explanation for its effectiveness. But the passage was later shown to bear strong similarities to words that the Frenchman Maurice Joly put into the mouth of the 16th-century political theorist Niccolò Machiavelli in his satire *Dialogue in Hell*, published more than 30 years earlier. Indeed, read as satire, the intent and effect would be very different from that which the *Protocols* purported to convey.

> *'It must be noted that men with bad instincts are more in number than the good, and therefore the best results in governing them are attained by violence and terrorisation, and not by academic discussions. Every man aims at power, everyone would like to become a dictator if only he could, and rare indeed are the men who would not be willing to sacrifice the welfare of all for the sake of securing their own welfare.*
>
> *What has restrained the beasts of prey who are called men? What has served for their guidance hitherto?*
>
> *In the beginnings of the structure of society, they were subjected to brutal and blind force; afterwards – to Law, which is the same force, only disguised. I draw the conclusion that by the Law of Nature, right lies in force.'*
>
> **The Protocols of the Elders of Zion**, Protocol 1, 3–5, translated by Victor E. Marsden, 1922

and political institutions. Religions will be replaced with 'arithmetical calculations and material needs'; wars will be fomented among the European powers; and the plotters will use the immense wealth at their disposal to seize control. 'In our hands is the greatest power of our day – gold; in two days, we can procure from our storehouses any quantity we may please,' the *Protocols* say.

After the fall of the tsar in the Russian Revolution of 1917, White Russian émigrés brought copies of the *Protocols* to the West and pointed to the Jewish Bolshevik leader Leon Trotsky as evidence that the Revolution was part of the Jewish conspiracy that the *Protocols* described. In 1920, translations into German and English appeared, while in the United States, the industrialist Henry Ford (1863–1947) sponsored the printing of hundreds of thousands of copies under the title *The International Jew*.

But 1920 also marked the beginning of the deconstruction of the *Protocols'* dubious legitimacy, when an English journalist published *The Jewish Bogey and the Forged Protocols of the Elders of Zion*. A year later, the London *Times* ran articles pointing out the *Protocols'* many instances of plagiarism. The newspaper's Constantinople (Istanbul) correspondent, Philip Graves, had spoken to a Russian émigré who had demonstrated the similarities between the *Protocols* and an obscure 1864 political satire by the French writer Maurice Joly. Joly's book, *Dialogue in Hell between Machiavelli and Montesquieu*, was an attack on the French emperor Napoleon III, and it made no mention of Jews.

Even though many passages of the *Protocols* were clearly copied from Joly (and others), the book stubbornly persisted in selling briskly throughout Europe and spread around the world.

In the United States, a reporter for the *New York Herald* wrote *The History of a Lie* to puncture its credibility in the eyes of the US public. But elsewhere, the first Arabic translation reached the streets of Jerusalem and Cairo in the mid-1920s. And, ominously, the Nazi 'intellectual' Alfred Rosenberg published *'The Protocols of the Elders of Zion' and Jewish World Policy* in 1923.

In 1935, a Swiss trial of some Nazis who were disseminating the *Protocols* ended with the judge declaring the book to be 'nothing but laughable nonsense' – but by now its popularity in right-wing and anti-Semitic circles was so great that truth or falsehood was immaterial. Even if the book was fake, ran the argument, it still conveyed the essential truth about the Jews and their malign ambitions. Adolf Hitler dismissed claims that the *Protocols* were based on a forgery. 'The important thing is that, with positively terrifying certainty, they reveal the nature and activity of the Jewish people and expose their inner contexts as well as their ultimate final aims,' he wrote in his autobiography, *Mein Kampf*.

The *Protocols*, naturally, became a key part of anti-Semitic propaganda in Nazi Germany, where Joseph Goebbels, Hitler's propaganda supremo, shared the cynical view that their authenticity (which he doubted) was beside the point. But with the end of the Second World War the book was finally discredited in Europe, except among fringe right-wing groups.

In the Middle East, however, the creation of Israel in 1948 gave a new boost to anti-Semitic feelings, and several Arab governments funded the printing of Arabic editions. Today, with most of the world accepting that the book is a crude and unsophisticated piece of propaganda, it remains popular throughout much of the Middle East. Within the last five years, leading newspapers such as *al-Akhbar* in Egypt and the Palestinian *al-Jadida* have declared that the *Protocols* is genuine, and they have been endorsed by television series in Egypt and Iran and in schoolbooks in Saudi Arabia.

MEIN KAMPF

The two volumes of *Mein Kampf* (*My Struggle*), Adolf Hitler's personal and political autobiography, setting out his ideology and his hatred of Jews, were published in 1925 and 1926. The author was serving a prison sentence for his involvement in the Munich Beer Hall Putsch the previous year. Much of it was ghostwritten on Hitler's behalf by his comrade and future deputy Rudolf Hess. Together with *The Protocols of the Elders of Zion*, it helped to foster a climate of race hatred that ultimately manifested itself in the murder of 6 million European Jews in 1939–45.

Mein Kampf's initial print run was just 500 copies, but the mixture of invective, prejudice and hectoring caught the mood of the time, and more than 300,000 copies were sold over the next ten years. As the handbook of the Nazi Party, it was instrumental in spreading Hitler's ideas through the German people in the years leading up to the Second World War, and by the time Hitler became German chancellor in 1933, royalties from the book had made him a wealthy man. Subsequently, the Nazi policy of presenting every newly married couple with a copy of the book took sales to more than 10 million by 1945, with translations into 16 languages.

After the war, however, copyright passed to the state of Bavaria, which banned its publication. The only editions published since have been in Hebrew, for which special permission was granted, and in English, because of an agreement made in 1933. Royalties from the English edition are paid to Jewish charities.

Dulce et Decorum est.

21

Bent double, like old beggars under sacks,
Knock-kneed, coughing like hags, we cursed through sludge,
Till on the haunting flares we turned our backs
And towards our distant rest began the trudge.
Men marched asleep. ~~Some~~ ~~Many~~ had lost their boots
But limped on, blood-shod. All went lame; all blind;
~~Deaf even~~ Drunk with fatigue; deaf even to the hoots
Of ~~tired, outstripped~~ Five-Nines that dropped behind.
gas shells dropping softly

Then somewhere near in front: Whew... fup, fop, fup,
Gas shells? Or duds? We loosened masks in case,—
And listened. ~~Nothing.~~ Far ~~rumouring~~ of Krupp.
~~sudden~~ Then poisons ~~but~~ us in the face.

Gas! GAS! Quick, boys! — An ecstasy of fumbling,
Fitting the clumsy helmets just in time;
But someone still was yelling out and stumbling,
And flound'ring like a man in fire or lime...
Dim, through the misty panes and thick green light,
As under a green sea, I saw him drowning.

In all my dreams, before my helpless sight,
He plunges at me, guttering, choking, drowning.

Poems

1920

Wilfred Owen

Wilfred Owen was the authentic voice of the British soldiers who fought, suffered and died on the Western Front during the First World War. When he was killed in action, just a week before the Armistice, only a few of his poems had been published in magazines, but his reputation was already beginning to grow. His only volume, *Poems*, was published in 1920, two years after his death. It contains some of the most forceful and moving poetry to come out of the Great War, a war that shattered for ever the myth of martial glory.

Before Wilfred Owen, old poets – far from the fighting on the front – could write sentimental and jingoistic verses about suffering and sacrifice; after Owen, it was hard to take them seriously. Owen looked the horror of war in the face, and the CND protesters of the 1950s, the Vietnam marchers of the 1960s and the anti-war demonstrators of our own time all came to see war through his eyes.

Although Owen had only ever seen five of his poems in print, he was preparing many more for publication when he died. His friend, the poet Siegfried Sassoon (1886–1967), going through Owen's papers after his death, found among them the unfinished fragment of a preface, in which Owen had written: 'Above all, this book is not concerned with Poetry. The subject of it is War, and the pity of War. The Poetry is in the pity.'

Another famous young soldier-poet of the time, Rupert Brooke (1887–1915), died before he saw the reality of combat, but Owen, shattered and mauled by the experience of battle, was one of a number of poets, including Sassoon, Isaac Rosenberg (1890–1918) and Charles Sorley (1895–1915), who were responsible for a new, uncompromising and brutal style of war poetry. In trying to reflect

THE SOMME

The first day of the Battle of the Somme, 1 July 1916, saw nearly 20,000 British soldiers killed, and another 37,000 either wounded or taken prisoner.

The British and French offensive aimed to break through the German lines in a sustained infantry assault, following a seven-day artillery bombardment. The plan was for soldiers to advance at walking pace, about five yards apart. Commanders had hoped that the German defenders would have been virtually wiped out by artillery before the infantry advanced, but in fact thousands of men were cut down by machine-gun fire from three lines of heavily defended trenches. The day proved to be the most costly of human life in the history of the British army.

By the time Wilfred Owen arrived on the Somme in January 1917, the British and French had achieved an advance of some five miles, at a price of more than 1.5 million casualties. But the fighting continued, with Owen and his men facing a near-constant German artillery barrage. In a letter to his mother, he described a near miss by a German shell as he sheltered by a railway embankment: 'Before I awoke, I was blown in the air right away from the bank! I passed most of the following days in a railway cutting, in a hole just big enough to lie in, and covered with corrugated iron.'

It was from the Somme that Owen was invalided home with shell shock. He returned to the front in September 1918, winning the Military Cross after an attack on a German machine-gun post. He was killed leading a crossing of the Sambre and Oise Canal on 4 November, during the final Allied advance.

'Dulce et Decorum Est'

This poem, the manuscript of which is shown on page 152, was written while Owen was recovering from shell shock at Craiglockart War Hospital in Scotland. One of the most famous poems of the First World War, it was originally dedicated in manuscript to 'Jessie Pope etc' – a savagely ironic dedication, as Pope, one of several writers of jingoistic poems published in British newspapers to encourage young men to sign up, had described war as 'the game, the biggest that's played, / The red crashing game of a fight'. The title of Owen's poem refers to the lines of the Roman poet Horace, much beloved by old colonels and headmasters of the time: *Dulce et decorum est pro patria mori* ('It is sweet and fitting to die for one's country'). Owen, having witnessed what it is like for a man, poisoned by gas, to die slowly and painfully for his country, will have none of it.

> 'Bent double, like old beggars under sacks,
> Knock-kneed, coughing like hags, we cursed
>   through sludge,
> Till on the haunting flares we turned our backs,
> And towards our distant rest began to trudge.
> Men marched asleep. Many had lost their boots,
> But limped on, blood-shod. All went lame, all blind;
> Drunk with fatigue; deaf even to the hoots
> Of gas-shells dropping softly behind.
>
> Gas! Gas! Quick, boys! – an ecstasy of fumbling,
> Fitting the clumsy helmets just in time,
> But someone still was yelling out and stumbling
> And flound'ring like a man in fire or lime.
> Dim through the misty panes and thick green light,
> As under a green sea, I saw him drowning.
> In all my dreams before my helpless sight
> He plunges at me, guttering, choking, drowning.
>
> If in some smothering dreams, you too could pace
> Behind the wagon that we flung him in,
> And watch the white eyes writhing in his face,
> His hanging face, like a devil's sick of sin,
> If you could hear, at every jolt, the blood
> Come gargling from the froth-corrupted lungs
> Obscene as cancer, bitter as the cud
> Of vile, incurable sores on innocent tongues, –
> My friend, you would not tell with such high zest
> To children ardent for some desperate glory,
> The old lie: Dulce et decorum est
> Pro patria mori.'

'Dulce et Decorum Est', from *Poems*, 1920

the enormity of their experiences, they found the poetry in the pity – and the pity was shot through with sorrow, anger and bitterness.

Owen started the war as a talented but conventional Georgian poet, writing about throstles and bees, 'merry England' and 'gay fairyland', in verses that were consciously modelled on those of John Keats (1795–1821) a hundred years earlier. It was the experience of the Somme – where Owen found himself blasted by German artillery and trapped in forward positions with his men – that put the steel into his poetry.

But his work goes further than simply expressing the immediate physical horror of war. There is anger at the unthinking jingoism at home, and also sadness, regret and an ineffable sense of loss, when Owen considers a future beyond the war.

A poem such as 'Strange Meeting', describing an encounter between dead soldiers from the opposing sides, can be seen as a war poem, an elegy or a dream poem, and it shows Owen's astonishingly mature command of the technicalities of verse. The poem demonstrates the haunting, troubled quality of 'para-rhyme', where the consonants are the same, but the vowels differ. In the same poem, Owen is aware of the sound of words as well as their meaning in the evocative contrast between the 'thump' and the 'moan' of the guns; in 'the wildest beauty in the world', he takes a consciously romantic image that might have been culled from Rupert Brooke or his own pre-war writing, and puts it in an ominous, prophetic setting.

> … no guns thumped, or down the flues made
>   moan.
> 'Strange friend,' I said, 'Here is no cause to
>   mourn.'
> 'None,' said the other, 'Save the undone years,
> The hopelessness. Whatever hope is yours,
> Was my life also; I went hunting wild
> After the wildest beauty in the world,
> Which lies not calm in eyes, or braided hair,
> But mocks the steady running of the hour,
> And if it grieves, grieves richlier than here.'

Other well-known titles from the collection include 'Anthem for Doomed Youth', 'Exposure', 'Arms and the Boy' and 'Dulce et Decorum Est' (see opposite).

In his Introduction to Owen's *Poems*, Siegfried Sassoon deliberately avoids any critical assessment of him as a poet: the poems and the Preface, he says, can speak for themselves. In 1931 the poet Edmund Blunden – another First World War veteran – produced a new collection of Owen's work, with additional material and a critical Introduction that focused largely on the Keatsian echoes in the poems. Owen's reputation grew steadily through the 20th century, with nine reprints of the Blunden edition up to 1963, when Cecil Day Lewis, with his own memories of the Second World War, edited another critical collection. 'It is Owen, I believe, whose poetry came home deepest to my own generation,' he writes, 'so that we could never again think of war as anything but a vile, if necessary evil.'

Later editions, such as that by Jon Stallworthy in 1983, have confirmed Owen's place as the foremost poet of war in English literature. It was with the first publication of his *Poems* more than 60 years before that the voice of the frontline soldier became as loud, as insistent, and as memorable as that of the flag-waving patriot at home.

The life and afterlife of Wilfred Owen

1893 Born in Oswestry, Shropshire, England.

*c.***1903–4** Begins to write poetry.

1911 Leaves school, but fails to win scholarship to University of London; goes on to work as a lay assistant in a country parish while attending classes as University College, Reading.

1913 Goes to teach English in Bordeaux, France.

1915 Returns to England to enlist in the Artists' Rifles.

1916 Commissioned into the Manchester Regiment.

1917 Leads his men into the trenches of the Somme (January). In May is diagnosed with shell shock and sent to Craiglockhart War Hospital, near Edinburgh, to recuperate.

1918 Returns to the Western Front (September), and wins the Military Cross (October). Is killed one week before the Armistice; news of his death reaches his home town just as the church bells are rung to celebrate peace.

1920 *Poems* published.

1931 A new edition of *Poems* is published, edited by Edmund Blunden.

1962 Benjamin Britten composes *War Requiem*, featuring Owen's poetry.

1963 Another new edition of *Poems*, edited by Cecil Day Lewis, is published.

1983 Jon Stallworthy edits a new edition.

Relativity:
The Special and
the General Theory

1920

Albert Einstein

Einstein's 'special theory of relativity', published in 1905, and the 'general theory of relativity' that followed ten years later, provide a remarkable tool for understanding cosmology and astrophysics, from the bending of light near black holes to tracing the universe backwards in time. Einstein published *Relativity: The Special and the General Theory* in 1920, shortly after observations of a solar eclipse appeared to have confirmed his predictions of the effect of gravity on starlight. The book's influence on both cosmology and the philosophy of science was profound: it even seemed to allow for the possibility of time travel to the past.

Galileo Galilei and Isaac Newton in the 17th century both discussed the principle of 'relativity', or the relative nature of motion as perceived by two observers. Einstein modified Newton's laws of motion to take account of observers moving at speeds close to the speed of light, 300 million metres per second. In *Relativity*, Einstein aimed to describe the complex ideas of relativity in lucid, everyday language so that a non-specialist should be able to understand his description of the two theories. 'The work presumes a standard of education corresponding to that of a university matriculation examination, and … a fair amount of patience and force of will on the part of the reader,' he says in the Preface.

The crucial date in Einstein's development of his theories of special and general relativity was 1905, when he submitted a paper to the prestigious German scientific journal *Annalen der Physik* (*Annals of Physics*) on the mathematical theory of special relativity. The journal also published three other papers by Einstein that year, often referred to as his 'miracle year', including one that ultimately earned him a Nobel prize and one which extended the 'special' theory to describe the relationship between the mass and the energy of a body – the famous equation $E=mc^2$.

The life of Albert Einstein

1879 Born into a Jewish family in Ulm, Württemberg, Germany.

1896–1901 Trains in Zurich as a teacher of mathematics and physics.

1902 Now a Swiss citizen, begins working at the Swiss Patent Office, but undertakes amateur research.

1905 The journal *Annalen der Physik* publishes his 'theory of special relativity'.

1908 Begins his professional research life at the University of Bern (Berne).

1909–14 Holds professorships at universities of Zurich and Prague.

1914 Becomes director of the Kaiser Wilhelm Physical Institute and a professor at the University of Berlin (until 1933), taking German citizenship.

1915 Publishes his 'general theory of relativity' as a series of papers.

1919 British observations of a solar eclipse appear to confirm predictions of general relativity.

1920 Publishes his work as a book, *Über die spezielle und die allgemeine Relativitätstheorie* (*Relativity: The Special and the General Theory*).

1921 Awarded the Nobel Prize for Physics, for discovery of the photo-electric effect (one of his 1905 papers).

1933 With the Nazi regime now in power, renounces German citizenship and emigrates to the United States, becoming Professor of Theoretical Physics at Princeton University (until 1945).

1955 Dies in Princeton, New Jersey.

A fourth dimension

In this extract from *Relativity*, Einstein spells out how space and time are considered as part of a single 'continuum'. The extract also shows Einstein's determination to make his ideas as clear to the layman as he can.

'The non-mathematician is seized by a mysterious shuddering when he hears of "four dimensional" things, by a feeling not unlike that awakened by thoughts of the occult. And yet there is no more commonplace statement than that the world in which we live is a four-dimensional space-time continuum.

Space is a three-dimensional continuum. By this we mean that it is possible to describe the position of a point (at rest) by means of three numbers (co-ordinates), x, y, z, and that there is an indefinite number of points in the neighbourhood of this one, the positions of which can be described by co-ordinates such as x_1, y_1, z_1, which may be as near as we choose to the respective values of the co-ordinates x, y, z of the first point. In virtue of this latter property we speak of a 'continuum', and owing to the fact that there are three co-ordinates, we speak of it as being 'three-dimensional'.

Similarly, the world of physical phenomena ... is naturally four-dimensional in the space-time sense. For it is composed on individual events, each of which is described by four numbers, named three space co-ordinates, x, y, z, and a time-co-ordinate, the time value t ...

... That we have not been accustomed to regard the world in this sense as a four-dimensional continuum is due to the fact that in physics, before the advent of the theory of relativity, time played a different and more independent role, as compared with the space co-ordinates ...

... The four-dimensional mode of consideration of the "world" is natural in the theory of relativity, since according to this theory, time is robbed of its independence.'

Relativity: The Special and the General Theory, translated by Robert W. Lawson, 1920

In 1905 Einstein was an unknown amateur and his papers would have been virtually ignored had not the leading physicist Max Planck (1858–1947), the founder of quantum theory, drawn attention to them. Hermann Minkowski, Einstein's former mathematics professor, also took up his ideas. Following accolades for his work, Einstein was offered academic posts that enabled him to give up his job at the patent office in Bern (Berne) and develop his research full-time.

The special theory of relativity begins with two assumptions: that the laws of science should appear the same to all observers and that the speed of light is unchanged for all observers, no matter how fast they or the source are moving. Among the startling provisions of the theory are the predictions that observers who are moving relative to each other might disagree about whether two events occur simultaneously or at different times (thus shattering the idea of an 'absolute time'), and that time appears to pass more slowly, and distance appears to be correspondingly reduced, on a moving body. These effects only become important when the speeds involved are a significant proportion of the speed of light; at everyday speeds the effect is negligible and the equations of motion reduce to the level of Newtonian, or classical physics. Numerous experiments since the 1940s have confirmed Einstein's counter-intuitive predictions. Indeed it is necessary to include relativistic time corrections in the position calculations for GPS navigation systems.

Minkowski saw that since, in special relativity, time is not absolute, time is itself a fourth dimension – to add to the usual three spatial dimensions of length, breadth and height. Thus, special relativity can be represented geometrically in space-time diagrams, effectively showing the time and space 'coordinates' for observers moving relative to each other.

The special theory of relativity was 'special' in that it treated the case of bodies in 'inertial frames of reference' – that were either stationary or moving in a straight line without accelerating – as different from accelerating frames of reference, such as for objects falling under gravity. From 1905 to 1915, Einstein tried to extend the principles of special relativity more generally to make them compatible with Newton's theory of gravity.

The general theory of relativity, first announced in a paper by Einstein in 1915, suggested that the geometry of space-time was curved in the presence of a gravitational field, such as that caused by a massive body. The equations were complex, but they provided predictions, such as for the bending of light in the presence of a gravitational field, that could be tested with astronomical observations. Observations of a solar eclipse carried out by a British astronomical expedition in 1919 appeared to confirm Einstein's theories, showing that starlight was deflected by the massive gravitational pull of the sun. This confirmation brought Einstein international fame. The London *Times* printed a headline that read 'Revolution in Science – New theory of the universe – Newtonian ideas overthrown'. The following year, in response to huge demand, Einstein published *Relativity: The Special and the General Theory*.

In fact, the 1919 observations later proved to be unsatisfactory, but subsequent tests and experiments have all confirmed Einstein's propositions to a high degree of accuracy. Einstein devoted the rest of his life to the unsuccessful search for what he called a 'unified field theory', a single explanation for all the fundamental physical forces in the universe. Such a 'theory of everything', evocatively described by the British theoretical physicist Stephen Hawking (b.1942) as 'seeing inside the mind of God', remains the Holy Grail of science. If it is ever achieved, it will be largely because of the discoveries of Albert Einstein.

EINSTEIN AND THE BOMB

Einstein's theory of special relativity requires that if an object is moving at a 'relativistic' speed, the speed cannot keep increasing if we increase its energy. Instead, as we increase the energy the object's mass must increase. This line of thought led Einstein to the conclusion that energy and mass are but different manifestations of the same thing, the 'E' and 'm' in the equation $E=mc^2$ (c^2 being the speed of light squared).

The implication of this was that a huge amount of energy could be released from a very small change in mass: the principle underlying nuclear fission, which was achieved in 1938 by the German scientists Otto Frisch and Lise Meitner. With Europe on the brink of war, there were fears that German scientists might be working towards an atomic bomb.

Einstein was a pacifist by conviction, but, as a Jewish intellectual who had rejected Nazi Germany in 1933 and watched with horror Hitler's ascendancy, he signed a personal letter to President Roosevelt warning that construction of a weapon was possible and urging that experimental research into atomic energy should be funded by the government. While Einstein took little part in the work, the result was the Briggs Committee to study chain reactions in uranium, which evolved into the Manhattan Project. The further result was the US atomic bombs dropped on Hiroshima and Nagasaki in 1945, events that horrified Einstein. Shortly before his death he described his signing of the letter to Roosevelt as the one great mistake of his life.

Ulysses

1922

James Joyce

Ulysses is generally regarded as the world's first great modernist novel. With its multiple perspectives, stylistic experimentation and innovative use of stream-of-consciousness techniques, it marks the overthrow of the traditional realist novel that had dominated the literature of the 19th century. Gone is conventional narrative and the conventional hero; gone too the polite avoidance of matters sexual and scatological. Above all, the traditional distinction between the self and an objective external world is almost entirely obliterated: reality here is constantly in flux, existing only in the flow of words with which the individual apprehends it.

The idea that eventually grew into *Ulysses* was originally to have been one of a collection of stories that the Irish expatriate writer James Joyce (1882–1941) published in 1914 as *Dubliners*. Instead, he worked on it for a further eight years, while living in Trieste, Zurich and Paris. The appearance of extracts in the American journal *The Little Review* between 1918 and 1920 led to a prosecution for obscenity in the United States, and publishers in Britain refused to take the book. The laws on obscenity were more relaxed in France, and *Ulysses* was published in Paris, in 1922, by Sylvia Beach's English-language bookshop Shakespeare and Co. (depicted opposite). Eventually, in 1934, the book came out in the United States, the judge who cleared it observing: 'Whilst in many places the effect of *Ulysses* on the reader undoubtedly is somewhat emetic, nowhere does it tend to be aphrodisiac.' Publication in Britain followed in 1936.

Although written while Joyce was in self-imposed exile from Ireland, the action of *Ulysses* is firmly located in Dublin, and Joyce was so keen to get details of the place right – such as street names and the wording on shop fronts – that he would bombard his friends back home with queries. It was later said that if Dublin were ever destroyed, it could be rebuilt from the descriptions in *Ulysses*.

The first of the principal characters we meet is Stephen Dedalus, who had earlier appeared as the hero of the author's autobiographical novel *A Portrait of the Artist as a Young Man*. We then

'A fine tang of faintly scented urine'

Leopold Bloom, the Odysseus-figure in *Ulysses*, is introduced in this scene, making breakfast for his wife.

'Mr Leopold Bloom ate with relish the inner organs of beasts and fowls. He liked thick giblet soup, nutty gizzards, a stuffed roast heart, liver slices fried with crustcrumbs, fried hencod's roes. Most of all he liked grilled mutton kidneys which gave to his palate a fine tang of faintly scented urine.

Kidneys were in his mind as he moved about the kitchen softly, righting her breakfast things on the humpy tray. Gelid light and air were in the kitchen but out of doors gentle summer morning everywhere. Made him feel a bit peckish.

The coals were reddening.

Another slice of bread and butter: three, four: right. She didn't like her plate full. Right. He turned from the tray, lifted the kettle off the hob and set it sideways on the fire. It sat there, dull and squat, its spout stuck out. Cup of tea soon. Good. Mouth dry.'

Ulysses, Episode iv, 'Calypso', 1922

The life of James Joyce

1882 Born in Dublin, and receives a Jesuit education before attending University College.

1904 First goes out with Nora Barnacle, his future partner and (from 1931) wife, on 16 June, when the action of *Ulysses* will take place.

1905 Moves to Trieste, then to Rome in 1906.

1912 Returns to Ireland for the last time.

1914 Publishes the short-story collection *Dubliners*.

1915 Moves to Zurich.

1916 Publishes *A Portrait of the Artist as a Young Man*, a type of *Bildungsroman*.

1918 Publishes *Exiles*.

1920 Settles in Paris.

1922 Publishes *Ulysses* in Paris.

1934 *Ulysses* is finally published in the United States, and in Britain two years later.

1939 Publishes his last novel, *Finnegans Wake*.

1941 Dies in Zurich.

encounter Leopold Bloom and his unfaithful wife Molly, a professional singer. Bloom is a middle-aged seller of advertising space in a local paper, at once an outsider because of his Jewishness and an 'everyman' figure. This small, weak, vulgar, inadequate but highly sympathetic figure becomes an unlikely, unglamorous hero for the 20th century, the 'century of the common man'. No fictional character before Bloom was pictured as intimately and unblinkingly – we even know what goes through his mind as he sits on the lavatory.

The novel is confined to a single day – 16 June 1904, the day Joyce first took out his future wife, Nora Barnacle (every year 'Bloomsday' is celebrated in Dublin with walks around some of the locations in the novel). The plot, if one can call it that, is closely tied, often ironically, to various episodes in Homer's *Odyssey*, the epic of the wanderings of Odysseus (whom the Romans called Ulysses) before his eventual return home to Ithaca, and his faithful wife Penelope and son Telemachus. In Joyce's novel Bloom is a modern, un-heroic Odysseus; the intellectual, guilt-ridden, self-obsessed Dedalus is Odysseus's son Telemachus; and Molly is an unchaste, luxuriantly fleshy Penelope.

Bloom and Dedalus separately wander through Dublin – there are scenes in a Martello tower, a public bathhouse, a funeral chapel, the office of a newspaper, a library, a number of pubs, a maternity hospital, a brothel and innumerable streets – until they eventually meet up. Bloom, who refuses to join in the noisy patriotism of some of the other characters he meets, is throughout the novel plagued by his own inadequacy, by his knowledge that his wife is having an affair with her manager, the brash and confident Blazes Boylan, and by his lasting grief for the death of his son 11 years previously. Ultimately, however, it is an optimistic and positive book: Bloom's befriending of Dedalus, his constant if undemonstrative feeling for his wife Molly, and his general kindness help him to an understated and restrained sort of triumph. Blazes Boylan is sent away, Molly commits herself to Bloom again, and good heartedness triumphs over bluster and bullying.

The final episode of the novel, an interior monologue delivered by Molly, ends with an affirmation of human warmth and affection. It encapsulates several of the particular qualities of Joyce's masterpiece: the unstructured flow of consciousness, the author's finely tuned ear that finds beauty in everyday speech, and tenderness and pathos in the very human situation of a young woman giving herself to her lover:

> … and then I asked him with my eyes to ask again yes and then he asked me
> would I yes to say yes my mountain flower and first I put my arms around him
> yes and drew him down to me so he could feel my breasts all perfume yes and
> his heart was going like mad and yes I said yes I will Yes.

These are just the last few words of Molly's monologue, which runs for some 25,000 words, divided into just eight sentences, the first of them around 2500 words long. This gives some hint of the great challenge that *Ulysses* presents to the reader. For a start, the novel is 250,000 words long – nearly a thousand pages. There is no page-turning storyline, rather an amassing of the infinite details of the world as we experience it from moment to moment, as images and thoughts elide with each other. The writing is often dense with allusion – literary, mythological, philosophical – and replete with parody, wordplay and Joycean neologisms ('He kissed the plump mellow yellow smellow melons of her rump, on each plump melonous hemisphere …'). Joyce himself observed: 'I've put in so many enigmas and puzzles that it will keep the professors busy for centuries arguing over what I mean.' And yet the book – full as it is with humour and high spirits – is as concerned with the mundane advertising jingle as with the esoteric theological reference, as focused on the progress of Leopold Bloom's bowel movements as with challenging the reader to spot a particular Homeric parallel.

Those who manage to finish *Ulysses* find it an enormously rewarding experience, and the book is accepted as one of the most original, ambitious and finely written novels ever published. Its development of the stream-of-consciousness technique paved the way for writers as diverse as Virginia Woolf (1882–1941), William Faulkner (1897–1962), Samuel Beckett (1906–1989) and Jack Kerouac (1922–1969). But like any great novel, its impact is not just literary: more than any other writer of the 20th century, Joyce articulated the quiet courage and determination of the common man. After Leopold Bloom, everyone could be a hero.

A MODERNIST POEM

In the same year that *Ulysses* was published, T.S. Eliot's 434-line poem *The Waste Land* appeared in the literary magazine *The Criterion*. Just as *Ulysses* became a beacon of modernism in the novel, so Eliot's equally challenging work overthrew the conventions of traditional English verse. Eliot was very deliberately following the diktat of Ezra Pound, his fellow modernist, to 'Make it new.' (The final version of *The Waste Land* was the result of heavy editing by Pound, and was dedicated to him.) The result was one of the most influential poems of the 20th century, whose echoes can still be heard in the voices of poets today.

Like the episodes of *Ulysses*, the sections of *The Waste Land* are written from various points of view, with different styles and moods. There is an overall sense of desolation, of fracturing and dislocation, in terms not only of narrative coherence and, sometimes, syntax, but also in the deployment of images (the phrase in the first section, 'A heap of broken images', might be taken as a reference to the poem as a whole), reflecting a world shattered by the First World War.

The Waste Land is also – again like *Ulysses* – heavily and provocatively allusive, with a vast range of echoes and references from classical, English and European literature, and from popular culture. It is the literary equivalent of a Cubist collage by Picasso, which, a few years earlier, had heralded the modernist movement in painting. But despite the similarities with *Ulysses*, Eliot's poem is at heart profoundly different. While Joyce cheerfully and optimistically embraces all aspects of what it means to be human, Eliot, a cultural pessimist, is disgusted by the modern age with its bar girls, its sex, its gramophones – amounting to no more, in Eliot's view, than 'a handful of dust'.

Lady Chatterley's Lover

1928

D.H. Lawrence

Without the intervention of the lawyers, D.H. Lawrence's *Lady Chatterley's Lover* might never have been anything more than one of the lesser-known works of a great novelist. It was finished in 1926, only four years before Lawrence died, and he spent the next two years trying to arrange publication. In the end it was privately printed, first in Florence, and then in Paris, but remained banned in both Britain and the United States for more than 30 years. Its explicit sexual content and four-letter words meant that potential publishers were scared off by the threat of prosecution under obscenity laws. Court cases, first in the United States and then in Britain, eventually allowed it to be published in 1959 and 1960 respectively, overturning not just the ban on *Lady Chatterley's Lover*, but the whole principle of book censorship.

The novel tells the story of Constance Chatterley, the wife of a landowner, Sir Clifford Chatterley, who is confined to a wheelchair, paralyzed and sexually impotent, as a result of injuries sustained during the First World War. When a young writer named Michaelis visits them at their home at Wragby Hall in the English Midlands, she takes him as her lover for a brief and unsatisfactory period, but then embarks on a passionate and highly sexually charged affair with her husband's gamekeeper, Oliver Mellors.

Mellors is the son of a miner, and speaks with a broad Derbyshire accent, but a spell as an officer in the Indian Army has left him able to adopt the manners, language and accent of a gentleman when he chooses.

Connie becomes pregnant by him, and then, when his estranged wife Bertha is threatening to cause a scandal, she confesses everything to Sir Clifford. Members of both her family and his, who had been prepared to countenance a discreet affair with a member of her own social class, are shocked and outraged that she should have given herself to a working man. The novel ends with Connie and Mellors temporarily apart as they hope for their divorces and the promise of a new life together.

The life of D.H. Lawrence

1885 Born in Nottinghamshire, England, the son of a miner and a former schoolteacher.

1906 Having left school at 15, gains a scholarship to study to become a teacher at Nottingham University College.

1912 Elopes abroad with Frieda von Richthofen, a married mother of three, six years his senior.

1913 Publishes the semi-autobiographical novel *Sons and Lovers*.

1915 Publishes *The Rainbow*; it is seized by police and declared obscene.

1919 Leaves with Frieda for Italy; he visits England only twice thereafter, for short visits.

1920 *Women in Love* is privately printed in New York, then in Britain in 1921.

1922 Starts his travels beyond Europe – to Sri Lanka, Australia, the United States and Mexico.

1925 Is diagnosed with terminal tuberculosis, and returns to Europe, settling in Italy.

1928 *Lady Chatterley's Lover* is printed privately in Florence; *Collected Poems* published.

1930 Dies in Vence, France.

1932 His *Last Poems* are published.

Lady Chatterley's Lover is as much about class as it is about sex, although it was the detailed and intimate descriptions of sexual activity – together with Lawrence's liberal use of four-letter words, which at that time were almost never seen in print – that led to the book being banned around the world. Reviewers who had seen it savaged it – one wrote that it 'reeked with obscenity and lewdness' – and those who had not read it were even more extreme in their condemnation.

Lawrence continued to defend his work, which he insisted was 'an honest, healthy book, necessary for us today', and even rewrote it twice in an unsuccessful effort to persuade publishers to take it. When that failed, he had it printed privately in Florence in 1928, and circulated 1000 copies through his close personal friends. A second edition, which he had printed in Paris the following year with an essay explaining the thinking behind the book, sold out within three months; pirated copies and expurgated versions also sold briskly.

But it was not until 1959 that the US courts overturned the American ban on the book. Emboldened by this decision, Penguin Books challenged the British courts in 1960 by publishing it. The landmark trial that followed was one of the last gasps of longstanding literary censorship in Britain. The old-fashioned and patronizing sexism and class prejudice implicit in the famous

'At your Ladyship's service'

In this extract, Connie and Mellors have begun their affair; but between them, apart from Connie's marriage to Mellors's employer, Sir Clifford, is the issue of class. The gamekeeper often stresses the gulf between himself and his lover by speaking with a broad Derbyshire accent and syntax – 'Shall us go i' th' 'ut?' – but here, bitter because he suspects he has been used, he slips into standard English.

'He looked at her, then again with the peculiar subtle grin out of the window. There was a tense silence.

At last he turned his head and said satirically:

"That was why you wanted me, then, to get a child?"

She hung her head.

"No. Not really," she said.

"What then, REALLY?" he asked rather bitingly.

She looked up at him reproachfully, saying: "I don't know."

He broke into a laugh.

"Then I'm damned if I do," he said.

There was a long pause of silence, a cold silence.

"Well," he said at last. "It's as your Ladyship likes. If you get the baby, Sir Clifford's welcome to it. I shan't have lost anything. On the contrary, I've had a very nice experience, very nice indeed!" – and he stretched in a half-suppressed sort of yawn. "If you've made use of me," he said, "it's not the first time I've been made use of; and I don't suppose it's ever been as pleasant as this time; though of course one can't feel tremendously dignified about it." – He stretched again, curiously, his muscles quivering, and his jaw oddly set.

"But I didn't make use of you," she said, pleading.

"At your Ladyship's service," he replied.

"No," she said. "I liked your body."

"Did you?" he replied, and he laughed. "Well, then, we're quits, because I liked yours."

He looked at her with queer darkened eyes.

"Would you like to go upstairs now?" he asked her, in a strangled sort of voice.'

Lady Chatterley's Lover, Chapter 12, 1928

OBSCENITY TRIALS

The history of literature is littered with acknowledged classics that have faced prosecution in the courts for alleged obscenity. James Joyce's *Ulysses* was banned both in Britain and the United States; Flaubert's *Madame Bovary* was prosecuted for obscenity; in 1857, the French symbolist poet Charles Baudelaire was fined 300 francs after his poetry collection *Les Fleurs du mal* (*The Flowers of Evil*) was declared to be 'an affront to public decency'. Six of the poems in the book remained banned until 1949.

The certain prospect of prosecution prevented publishers from taking on *Lady Chatterley's Lover* in both Britain and the United States for more than 30 years. In America, the eventual lifting of the ban on the book was followed by similar cases involving two other novels: *Tropic of Cancer* by Henry Miller (1891–1980), published in Paris in 1934, was eventually released in the United States in 1964; while *Fanny Hill* by John Cleland (1709–89), banned since 1821, was cleared for publication in 1966.

In Britain, the 1959 Obscene Publications Act allowed a new defence of literary merit in obscenity cases, which brought the novelist E.M. Forster (1879–1970) and the literary critics Raymond Williams (1921–88) and Dame Helen Gardner (1908–86), among others, into the witness box to defend *Lady Chatterley's Lover*. A similar defence was unsuccessfully mounted six years later, when the American novel *Last Exit to Brooklyn* by Hubert Selby Jr (1928–2004) was found to be obscene. This verdict was later overturned on appeal. Britain's last major obscenity prosecution was in 1976, when *Inside Linda Lovelace*, the controversial autobiography of a porn star, was ruled not to contravene the Obscene Publications Act. After the case, senior police officers were quoted as saying that if that book did not contravene the act then no book would.

In the United States, the courts have ruled that the First Amendment to the Constitution, which guarantees free speech, protects 'indecent' matter from prosecution, but not 'obscene' material. The distinction is presumably left to individual courts to decide in specific cases.

Subsequently, a government commission recommended that there should be no censorship of literature or purely textual material, but no action was taken on its report.

question posed by the prosecuting counsel to the jury – 'Is this a book which you would wish your wife or servants to read?' – were ridiculed even then, and the prosecution failed.

The successful defences mounted by supporters of *Lady Chatterley's Lover* in both the United States and Britain did not mark the end of obscenity prosecutions of books in either country – but they were the start of a new and more liberal age, and marked as such by the British poet Philip Larkin (1922–85) in his poem 'Annus Mirabilis', in which he asserts that sexual intercourse began 'Between the end of the *Chatterley* ban / And the Beatles' first LP'.

Some countries embraced the new attitudes; others rejected them for either religious or ethical reasons – India's Supreme Court upheld a conviction of *Lady Chatterley's Lover* for obscenity in 1966. However, there was a burgeoning mood of freedom of expression and permissiveness in lifestyle in many parts of the West, and in part that was the legacy of Lawrence, Connie Chatterley and Oliver Mellors.

The cultural importance of *Lady Chatterley's Lover* derives, ultimately, from its status as a *cause célèbre*. Few people claim that it is one of D.H. Lawrence's best books. He published a dozen other novels, including the more greatly admired *Sons and Lovers*, *The Rainbow* and *Women in Love*, along with ten collections of short stories, several books of poetry, and a number of plays, non-fiction works, translations and travel books based on his wanderings in Australia, Italy, Sri Lanka, North America, Mexico and France. But none of these books defined a cultural moment in the way that *Lady Chatterley's Lover* did.

The General Theory
of Employment,
Interest and Money

1936

John Maynard Keynes

John Maynard Keynes's *The General Theory of Employment, Interest and Money* was probably the most influential work on economics published in the 20th century. It mounted the first serious challenge to the classical theories of economics that had been developed over the preceding century and a half. The traditional view was that governments should not try to intervene in the working of the financial markets, but the crisis of the First World War and the misery of poverty, unemployment and worldwide economic slump that followed led Keynes to consider ways in which taxation and adjustments to the supply of money in circulation might mitigate the effects of economic recession.

The General Theory of Employment, Interest and Money, was primarily a theoretical study rather than a practical policy document. Keynes (1883–1946), known as a brilliant economic theorist at Cambridge University and a one-time adviser to the British Treasury, said that he hoped his book would be intelligible to non-specialists; but he was clear that it was aimed primarily at other economists.

Within that world of economics, however, his intention was from the start to bring about a revolution. A year before the publication of his book he wrote to the playwright George Bernard Shaw: 'I believe myself to be writing a book on economic theory which will largely revolutionize – not, I suppose, at once, but in the course of the next ten years – the way the world thinks about economic problems.'

The Victorian age and the decades thereafter had been dominated by free-market economics, built on the ideas of thinkers such as Adam Smith (1723–90), David Ricardo (1772–1823) and John Stuart Mill (1806–73), who opposed government intervention in the working of the economy. The title of Keynes's book, when it appeared, was a clear echo of *The General Theory of Relativity* that Albert Einstein (1879–1955) had announced in 1915. In the same way that Einstein had updated Newton's classical theories of physics, so Keynes was aiming to update classical ideas about the management of

The life of J.M. Keynes

1883 Born in Cambridge, England.

1902 Starts his studies at Cambridge University, where he becomes involved with the Bloomsbury Group of writers and artists.

1915 Becomes an adviser to the British Treasury.

1919 Attends the Paris Peace Conference after the First World War. Having resigned from the Treasury, warns against the terms of the Versailles Treaty in *Economic Consequences of the Peace.*

1923 Publishes his *Tract on Monetary Reform*; his warnings about the Versailles Treaty are borne out by German hyperinflation.

1925 Marries the Russian ballerina Lydia Lopokova; his earlier relationships have been with men.

1929 Following the Wall Street Crash, loses the fortune he had gained by successful investment, although soon recoups it.

1933 To counter the effects of the Great Depression, President F.D. Roosevelt introduces the New Deal in the USA, influenced by Keynesian thinking.

1936 Publishes *The General Theory of Employment, Interest and Money.*

1942 Created Baron Keynes.

1946 Dies at Tilton, East Sussex.

THE GREAT DEPRESSION

In the years after the First World War, while Great Britain suffered from a prolonged economic depression with record levels of unemployment, the American economy was powering ahead and creating unprecedented prosperity. In 1929, at the end of the so-called 'Roaring Twenties', unemployment in the United States was running at just over 3 per cent.

And then, on 24 October 1929 – Black Thursday – came the start of the Wall Street Crash. The US stock market, which one leading academic had declared only days before could only go up, began a collapse that would continue for nearly three years and see the value of shares fall by 89 per cent. By 1932 the Dow Jones Industrial Average was at its lowest level for more than 30 years. In 1933 one worker in four was out of a job, and America's standard of living had fallen by 52 per cent.

In the United States the crash marked the start of the Great Depression, which lasted through the 1930s. Much of the rest of the world also felt the effects of economic collapse. Wages, tax revenues and prices all tumbled in a vicious spiral as international trade slumped, businesses went bankrupt and workers were laid off.

Economists still argue about the causes of the Great Depression, but its effects were far-reaching and disastrous. Traditional free-market economics were largely discredited in many countries, and, in an effort to ease the pain, governments established interventionist programmes such as the 'New Deal' of President Franklin D. Roosevelt. Even so, there was political upheaval, which led in several countries – notably Germany – to the rise of fascist governments dedicated to massive programmes of state spending on arms. Many historians see the rise of Adolf Hitler and the Second World War as events made possible by the repercussions of the Great Depression.

the economy and the reduction of unemployment. Economic theories that had worked in the 19th century, he believed, were no longer satisfactory in the 20th.

Where free-market economists believed that the level of employment in society was essentially fixed by the price of labour, so that lower wages would automatically promote full employment, Keynes said that it was the level of economic demand within society that was the determining factor. In 24 densely argued chapters, *The General Theory* set out his case that, without positive action by government, under-employment and under-investment might be the result of unfettered economic competition. He was not putting forward a socialist case for full-scale central direction of the economy, but arguing for a measure of government intervention to work alongside market forces and protect the vulnerable. Increased government spending might be necessary, even if this resulted in governments running a budget deficit.

The General Theory was partly a product of the economic misery of the slump that had followed the First World War. Keynes had been developing much of the thinking behind *The General Theory* – how government action, together with market forces, could alleviate distress and promote the general welfare of society at large – for some 20 years before the book was published in 1936.

As representative of the British Treasury at the Paris Peace Conference of 1919, Keynes had argued passionately against the damaging reparation demands that were imposed on Germany. When his arguments were rejected, he resigned his Treasury position, and within two months wrote a book, *Economic Consequences of the Peace*, in which he warned prophetically that destroying the German economy would have serious implications for the rest of Europe.

Four years later, Keynes contemptuously dismissed the free-marketeers' assumption that the market would correct itself and solve problems of unemployment 'in the long run'. In his book

A Tract on Monetary Reform (1923), he famously pointed out 'The long run is a misleading guide to current affairs. In the long run, we are all dead.' In many ways, *The General Theory*, written 13 years later, is an expansion of this idea.

The General Theory was well received both by academic economists and by governments, and for a quarter of a century after the end of the Second World War it was widely accepted that economies could be successfully managed if a Keynesian policy of government spending was adopted, coupled with cheap money, a redistributive taxation policy and the maintenance of an agreed policy on incomes.

Keynes's adherents point to this period as a time of unprecedented real economic growth in the capitalist world, but by the mid-1970s, with incomes policies under strain, governments increasingly concerned about economic growth, and economists developing new ideas about inflation and employment, the Keynesian model fell out of favour. However, the fact that few modern economists would argue for completely unfettered competition is a mark of Keynes's influence. Markets, left to their own devices, do not always work. Some economists believe that the ideas in *The General Theory* have still not been properly applied, and the general consensus today is that although a properly functioning market will bring about equilibrium over a long period, Keynesian intervention can bring significant benefits in the short and medium term – and in times of real economic stress. *The General Theory* brought a lasting change to the terms of debate about how governments should manage a modern market-oriented entrepreneurial economy.

Channelling 'dangerous human proclivities'

The General Theory of Employment, Interest and Money was written as Britain was in the midst of the Great Depression, with grinding poverty and millions out of work. One of its central planks, as Keynes explains in this extract from the final chapter of the book, is the need to move towards full employment, and end what he believed was the 'arbitrary and inequitable' distribution of wealth and incomes.

'I believe that there is social and psychological justification for significant inequalities of incomes and wealth, but not for such large disparities as exist today. There are valuable human activities which require the motive of money-making and the environment of private wealth-ownership for their full fruition. Moreover, dangerous human proclivities can be canalized into comparatively harmless channels by the existence of opportunities for money-making and private wealth, which, if they cannot be satisfied in this way, may find their outlet in cruelty, the reckless pursuit of personal power and authority, and other forms of self-aggrandizement. It is better that a man should tyrannize over his bank balance than over his fellow-citizens; and whilst the former is sometimes denounced as being but a means to the latter, sometimes at least it is an alternative. But it is not necessary for the stimulation of these activities and the satisfaction of these proclivities that the game should be played for such high stakes as at present. Much lower stakes will serve the purpose equally well, as soon as the players are accustomed to them.'

The General Theory of Employment, Interest and Money, Chapter 24, 1936

If This is a Man

1947

Primo Levi

Primo Levi's account of his concentration camp experiences, *If This is a Man*, is a book whose resonances extend far more widely than its principal subject. The book, published in the United States as *Survival in Auschwitz*, concerns not just the Nazi camps, but also the effects of the most unimaginable misery on the human soul and man's ability to survive. It has changed our understanding of suffering and increased our awareness of mankind's almost limitless potential for good or ill.

Primo Levi (1919–87) was an Italian of Jewish descent, who participated in the Italian Resistance in 1943 until his capture at the age of 24. *If This is a Man* tells the story of his time in the notorious Auschwitz concentration camp system, from his arrest to his eventual liberation by the Red Army exactly one year and 45 days later. It was first published in Italian, as *Se questo è un uomo*, in 1947, when the wounds of the Second World War were still raw across Europe; fewer than 1500 copies were sold.

By that time, the realities of life in the concentration camps were well known, and many people simply did not want to be reminded. But in any case, *If This is a Man* is more than a simple piece of historical testimony: Levi admitted in his Preface to the book that it had nothing new to say about the atrocities which had taken place. 'It has not been written in order to formulate new accusations; it should be able, rather, to furnish documentation for a quiet study of certain aspects of the human

Arrival at Auschwitz

Words like 'comic' and 'tragic' have little meaning in *If This is a Man*. In this extract from the first chapter, Levi describes a glimpse of the future that awaits him in Auschwitz. He has been among 650 Jewish men, women and children transported from Italy on a four-day journey in a closed goods-train. When they arrive there, the women, children and old men have been separated from the men judged fit to work and taken away.

'In an instant, our women, our parents, our children disappeared. We saw them for a short while as an obscure mass at the other end of the platform; then we saw nothing more.

Instead, two groups of strange individuals emerged into the light of the lamps. They walked in squads, in rows of three, with an odd, embarrassed step, heads dangling in front, arms rigid. On their heads they wore comic berets and were all dressed in long striped overcoats, which even by night and from a distance looked filthy and in rags. They walked in a large circle around us, never drawing near, and in silence began to busy themselves with our luggage and to climb in and out of the empty wagons.

We looked at each other without a word, It was all incomprehensible and mad, but one thing we had understood. This was the metamorphosis that awaited us. Tomorrow we would be like them.'

If This is a Man (Survival in Auschwitz), Chapter 1, 'The Journey', translated by Stuart Woolf, 1960/1

mind,' he said. It is a book written by a man who has suffered, and meditated on suffering. Levi was a chemical engineer by training, but *If This is a Man* is above all the book of a philosopher.

From his earliest days in Auschwitz, in 1944, Levi was convinced that he might die at any moment, and yet was determined to survive in order to tell the rest of the world what had happened there. *If This Is a Man* documents the day-to-day suffering, the random hostility and friendliness, selfishness and generosity, of the other inmates, and the constant, overarching shadow of imminent death in plain and unemotional language.

It introduces several other inmates as individuals, characters in their own right, despite all the efforts of the concentration camp system to reduce them to creatures without minds or souls. There is Steinlauf, a Jewish ex-sergeant of the Austro-Hungarian army who won the Iron Cross in the First World War, and insists on washing himself and polishing his shoes to maintain a semblance of dignity; Walter Bonn, a Dutchman who tries to sell Levi a spoon for half a ration of bread and, when he refuses, lends it to him anyway; and the Hungarian chemist Somogyi, whose death from typhus and scarlet fever, hours before the Soviets liberate the camp, marks the end of the book.

One of the earliest impressions Levi records of the administration at Auschwitz is its apparent determination to destroy this individuality. Inmates are given numbers rather than names – Levi is *Häftling* ('Prisoner') 174517 – made to work until they are exhausted, and humiliated by being stripped naked and forced to stand in long lines for hours at a time. They are constantly at the mercy of the random brutality of the camp guards and other prisoners, but Levi also sees how the guards, as well as the prisoners, are caught and destroyed by the grotesque machine that has been created. Everyone, he says, is motivated by fear or hatred; the masters are slaves themselves.

Levi survived Auschwitz – one of only 20 from his original shipment of 650 Italian Jews to do so – largely because he was set to work in a synthetic rubber factory at the plant. Then, when the approach of the Red Army led the SS guards to march their prisoners out of the camp in an attempt to make their own escape, he was sick with scarlet fever. Those prisoners who left the camp with the SS were never seen again; the last chapter of the book, 'The Story of Ten Days', describes how Levi and the other sick inmates struggle to survive, abandoned in the ruins of the camp and under bombardment by the approaching forces, until the Soviet soldiers arrive.

In 1958, eleven years after its first publication, *If This is a Man* was reissued in Italian and soon translated into English and German. This time it was a major success, and Levi began writing a sequel, *La tregua* (*The Truce*), which traces his journey back from Auschwitz to Italy. The two books, which are often published together, have been compared to Dante's literary descent into Hell and back.

Other works that followed included *The Periodic Table* (1975), a collection of autobiographical sketches and short stories, and *If Not Now, When?* – a Zionist novel based partly on the experiences Levi had already recounted in *The Truce* about Jewish partisans fighting the Nazis.

Throughout the rest of his life, Levi dedicated himself to ensuring that the crimes of the concentration camps were remembered and understood, in spite of suffering from repeated bouts of depression, probably caused by the long-term effects of his sufferings in Auschwitz. When he died in 1987, after falling from an interior landing at his Turin apartment block, the coroner ruled that he had committed suicide.

The minority of people who still refuse, against all the evidence, to believe that the Holocaust took place at all will probably never be convinced. *If This is a Man*, Levi says, is intended as a warning against the belief, common in many nations, that every stranger is an enemy. It is also an intimate, chilling, but ultimately positive study of the psychology of suffering and survival. Few people who read it are unchanged by it.

ALEXANDER SOLZHENITSYN AND *THE GULAG ARCHIPELAGO*

The Nazi camps acquired a unique grimness in their genocidal aims. But the invention of the concentration camp for mass internment is credited to the British, during the Anglo-Boer War of 1899–1902, and the concept achieved its most elaborate structure in the Soviet Union. The nature of the Soviet labour camps was revealed by the dissident Alexander Solzhenitsyn (1918–2008), who was arrested in 1945 for writing a letter criticizing Stalin. He served eight years in the Soviet camps, followed by three years' forced exile.

Solzhenitsyn wrote about his life in the camps in the 1962 novel *One Day in the Life of Ivan Denisovich*, but was subsequently subjected to fierce official criticism and harassment, and his books were banned. Nevertheless, they circulated privately, via the thriving underground presses, and were published abroad. In 1970, he was awarded the Nobel Prize for Literature.

Three years later, despite efforts by the KGB to seize the manuscript, the first parts of *The Gulag Archipelago* were published in Paris (and the following year, Solzhenitsyn was expelled from the Soviet Union). *Gulag* was the acronym for the branch of the state security that administered the camps, and Solzhenitsyn's book brought the term worldwide notoriety. The book draws on Solzhenitsyn's own experience and the personal testimony of other prisoners to describe the arrest, interrogation, conviction, transportation and imprisonment of the camp inmates. It tells the history of the camps and the system of forced labour established in 1918, shortly after the Bolshevik Revolution, and hugely expanded under Stalin. But, as with Primo Levi's *If This is a Man*, it also focuses on the methods used to break down the resistance of the prisoners and destroy their personalities.

Like Levi, too, Solzhenitsyn spoke not just for the inhabitants of the prisons, but for the silent millions of victims of imprisonment, systematic ill-treatment and mass murder, under political tyrannies of all hues, across the globe.

BIG BROTHER

IS WATCHING YOU

Nineteen Eighty-four

1949

George Orwell

George Orwell's *Nineteen Eighty-four* – the archetypal dystopian novel – describes a nightmarish vision of the future, born out of the horrors of the mid-20th century. Portraying a world in which every aspect of life is controlled by the Party, the book is ruthless in its condemnation of totalitarianism, and many of the phrases coined by Orwell in the novel – 'Big Brother', 'Newspeak', 'Room 101', 'Doublethink' and more – have entered the language, providing a vocabulary of tyranny.

George Orwell (1903–50) is considered one of the most elegant stylists in English literature, but his books are mainly concerned with politics and social justice. He wrote, he said, 'against totalitarianism and for democratic socialism'. His first book, *Down and Out in Paris and London* (1933), an account of living in poverty, was followed a year later by *Burmese Days*, an anti-imperialist novel based on Orwell's time in the British police force in Burma. His other books include *The Road to Wigan Pier* (1937), a documentary account of poverty in northern England, *Homage to Catalonia* (1938), recording his experiences during the Spanish Civil War, and the satirical anti-Stalinist fable *Animal Farm* (1945). *Nineteen Eighty-four* was his last book before his death from tuberculosis.

Published just four years after the end of the Second World War, *Nineteen Eighty-four* took the fears and experiences of the 1930s and 1940s – the Nazi war machine, the Soviet purges, secret police, political torture and state propaganda – and projected them into a terrifying vision of

How many fingers?

In this extract, Winston is being interrogated under torture by O'Brien, who is demonstrating to him that not even the most private, secret opposition to the Party is possible. Eventually, he will be made to love Big Brother. It is not enough to obey – he must believe everything he is told. O'Brien holds up the four fingers of his hand, and asks how many fingers Winston will see if the Party tells him there are five.

'"How many fingers, Winston?"

"Four."

The needle went up to sixty.

"How many fingers, Winston?"

"Four! Four! What else can I say? Four!"

The needle must have risen again, but he did not look at it. The heavy, stern face and the four fingers filled his vision. The fingers stood up before his eyes like pillars, enormous, blurry and seeming to vibrate, but unmistakeably four.

"How many fingers, Winston?"

"Four! Stop it, stop it! How can you go on? Four! Four!"

"How many fingers, Winston?"

"Five, five, five!"

"No, Winston, that is no use. You are lying. You still think there are four. How many fingers, please?"

"Four! Five! Four! Anything you like. Only stop it, stop the pain!" ...

... "Just now I held up the fingers of my hand to you. You saw five fingers. Do you remember that?"

"Yes."

O'Brien held up the fingers of his left hand, with the thumb concealed.

"There are five fingers there. Do you see five fingers?"

"Yes."

And he did see them, for a fleeting instant, before the scenery of his mind changed. He saw five fingers, and there was no deformity.'

Nineteen Eighty-four, Part 3, ii, 1949

GEORGE ORWELL MEETS BIG BROTHER

While Orwell was writing about Big Brother in *Nineteen Eighty-four*, and for many years before that, he was himself under surveillance by the British security services.

Formerly secret files on 'Eric A. Blair, alias George Orwell', now available in the UK's National Archives, show that, as early as 1929, reports on his activities were being sent back to Scotland Yard. At that stage, the report noted that he was working for socialist newspapers in Paris, but added: 'He has not so far been seen to mix with Communists in Paris, and until he does –– [the name of the agent is deleted] considers that the French will not interfere with him.'

In England, however, the security services were clearly still keeping a close eye on him and the people he mixed with. There is a note from 1936 that Orwell was addressing a Communist Party meeting in Wigan, and a separate report saying that he was friends with a man who was 'known to hold socialist views, and considers himself an "intellectual"'.

There was some official confusion about Orwell's political allegiances. In 1942 a Special Branch officer described him as 'an unorthodox Communist, apparently holding many of their views but by no means subscribing fully to the Party's policy'. Another report about the same time referred to him as 'a bit of an anarchist in his day and in touch with extremist elements', and said he held 'undoubtedly strong Left Wing views, but he is a long way from orthodox Communism'.

No one who had read *Animal Farm* or *Nineteen Eighty-four* could have been in any doubt about Orwell's hatred of Soviet communism. At the end of his life he showed the police who had been following him for 20 years which side he was on. In 1949, already bedridden with the tuberculosis that would kill him a year later, he provided a friend who was working for the security services with a list of journalists, writers and public figures who, he said, were 'crypto-Communists, fellow travellers … inclined that way, and should not be trusted as propagandists'.

the world half a century on. Orwell had originally planned to call the book *The Last Man in Europe*, while the name of his leading character, Winston Smith, echoes that of Winston Churchill, who had warned that his Labour Party opponents might set up 'some kind of Gestapo'.

Nineteen Eighty-four is set in the future state of Oceania under the rule of the Party, which is committed to *IngSoc*, or English Socialism, and headed by Big Brother. It is an exaggerated version of postwar Britain, with bombsites, shortages and hopelessly incompetent public services. Winston Smith, a junior Party member, works in the ironically named Ministry of Truth, rewriting past documents so that they conform to the current Party dogma, but he comes to hate the total domination of the Party.

The first part of the book describes how, fascinated by vague memories of the past, he starts to write a diary, so that future generations may know something about his own life. Both knowledge of the past and diary writing are strictly forbidden by the Party's Thought Police.

In the second part, Winston begins an illicit affair with another Party member, Julia. They secretly rent a room in a poor part of town, since the working classes, known as 'proles', are not under the same constant surveillance as Party members. Winston also contacts a mysterious figure named O'Brien, whom he believes to be connected to an underground resistance movement, The Brotherhood.

But even in their secret room, it transpires that the lovers are being watched, and the second part of the book ends with their arrest. The third part describes Winston's gradual breakdown under physical, psychological and emotional torture, partly at the hands of O'Brien, who turns out to be a Party loyalist. Winston betrays Julia and eventually comes to love Big Brother – the invincible Party and the Thought Police have triumphed.

The life of George Orwell

1903 Born Eric Blair in Motihari, Bengal, India, to British parents.

1904 Travels to England with his mother.

1909–16 Attends an Anglican school; then St Cyprian's prep school.

1917 Attends Eton College, on a scholarship.

1922–7 Studies for Indian civil service exams and serves with the Indian Imperial Police, Burma.

1927–9 Lives in London and Paris, sometimes taking menial jobs.

1933 Publishes *Down and Out in Paris and London*, under the pseudonym of George Orwell.

1934 Publishes his first novel, *Burmese Days*.

1936–7 Fights in the Spanish Civil War, but falls out with his Marxist-aligned militia. Returns home after being shot through the neck.

1937 Publishes *The Road to Wigan Pier*, an account of working-class poverty in northern England.

1938 Publishes *A Homage to Catalonia*, about the Spanish Civil War.

1941 Works for the BBC as a propagandist for the Eastern Service.

1942 Begins as a regular writer for the *Observer* (until 1949).

1943–5 Becomes literary editor of *Tribune*, a left-wing weekly.

1945 Publishes *Animal Farm*, an anti-Stalinist satire.

1949 Publishes the dystopian novel *Nineteen Eighty-four*.

1950 Dies in London.

Big Brother and the rulers of Oceania want eventually to entrench their power by enforcing the use of Newspeak, a simplified version of English that is largely composed of abbreviations and compounds. *IngSoc* represents English Socialism, and *MiniTrue* is the Ministry of Truth. Some words, Orwell explains in an appendix to the novel, are deliberately misleading, so that *joycamp* is a forced labour camp (echoing the slogan the Nazis placed above the gates of Dachau and Auschwitz: *Arbeit Macht Frei* – 'work sets you free'). Others represent new concepts, so that *doublethink* is the ability both to believe and disbelieve the same idea at the same time. However, the main purpose of Newspeak is to diminish the range of possible thoughts by limiting the number of words and drastically restricting their possible meanings.

Nineteen Eighty-four is a bleak and depressing book, written at the end of Orwell's life and reflecting his disillusionment with political movements of both the Left and the Right. The only faint and vaguely expressed hope is the suggestion that eventually the proles, degenerate and corrupted as they are, might hold the key to the overthrow of Big Brother.

Where Orwell's predictions have turned out to be most accurate is less in the development of global, authoritarian regimes, but in the deepening loss of privacy and personal independence. Advances in technology and fears of crime and terrorism have contributed to a huge extension of the surveillance society: Big Brother really can be watching you on CCTV – and recording your phone calls, spending patterns and email traffic – in the 21st century.

Whether this is a good thing or not – whether the slogan 'Big Brother is Watching You' is ultimately threatening or reassuring – is open to argument. But the fact that many of us distrust excessive government power, the fact that we are aware of the malign possibilities of surveillance, and the fact that we understand how public opinion, private opinions and language itself can all be manipulated by governments and corporations, are all partly thanks to *Nineteen Eighty-four*.

The Second Sex

1949

Simone de Beauvoir

Simone de Beauvoir's *The Second Sex* stunned postwar France. A densely argued and highly intellectual two-volume philosophical treatise, it sold 20,000 copies in its first week of publication, and then swept through the English-speaking world. Women's right to vote having largely been won, *The Second Sex* heralded the second wave of the feminist movement, and de Beauvoir's book – a work of existentialist philosophy as well as a manifesto of women's rights – fundamentally changed the relationship between the sexes in the Western world. Is it because of the work of a French philosopher in the mid-20th century that a woman street-sweeper today is paid as much as her male counterpart? Not entirely, but de Beauvoir's book has been instrumental in changing beliefs and assumptions about equality, fairness and justice.

The central argument of *Le Deuxième Sexe* (*The Second Sex*) is that woman has been relegated over the centuries to be what de Beauvoir calls man's 'Other'. Man has established himself as the dominant sex, leaving woman, as de Beauvoir explains in her Introduction, as 'the incidental, the inessential, as opposed to the essential. He is the Subject, he is the Absolute, she is the Other.'

In the first of the two volumes, de Beauvoir looks at the way women have been depicted and interpreted through biology, psychoanalysis, materialism, history, literature and anthropology. All these disciplines, the books says, take women's inferior destiny for granted. None of them is sufficient on its own to explain the oppression of women, but together they have contributed to the development of a myth of womanhood – 'woman such as men have fancied her in their dreams'.

By constructing impossible ideals such as motherhood, virginity or the Motherland, society has trapped woman in what de Beauvoir calls the 'Eternal Feminine', while denying the ambitions and personalities of individual women. In particular, this section of the book looks at

The life of Simone de Beauvoir

1908 Born in Paris.

1923 At the age of 15, decides to be a famous writer.

1929 Achieves second place in the final philosophy exam at the Sorbonne; the first place goes to Jean-Paul Sartre, with whom she starts a lifelong relationship.

1931 Begins a career as a teacher.

1943 Publishes a novel, *L'Invitée* (*She Came to Stay*); gives up teaching to become a full-time writer.

1945 With Sartre, founds and edits *Le Temps moderne*, a monthly review.

1949 Publishes *Le Deuxième Sexe* (*The Second Sex*) in two volumes.

1954 Her novel *Les Mandarins* (*The Mandarins*) wins the Prix Goncourt.

1958 Publishes first volume of her autobiography.

1970 Publishes *La Vieillesse* (*The Coming of Age*).

1980 Jean-Paul Sartre dies.

1981 *La Cérémonie des adieux* (*Adieux: A Farewell to Sartre*) published.

1986 Dies in Paris.

the treatment of woman in literature, where she is treated as flesh, as nature, as the inspiration of poetry or as the one who shows the way to the supernatural, the heavenly and the eternal. If she declines or fails in these roles, says de Beauvoir, she becomes 'a praying mantis, an ogress' – but in any case, she remains essentially the channel through which man fulfils his own destiny.

In the second volume, de Beauvoir studies woman's life in the modern world, through childhood, youth, maturity and old age, and looks at particular situations such as motherhood, prostitution, love and social life. Without economic independence, de Beauvoir says, simply having the vote (which French women acquired only in 1944) does not mean women are free or independent. Whether prostitute, courtesan or wife, a woman remains dependent on men. 'She is not permitted to do anything, so she persists in the vain pursuit of her true being through narcissism, love or religion.'

In conclusion, de Beauvoir says that neither men nor women are satisfied with the current situation: both are victims of themselves and of each other. There will always be differences between the sexes, she says, and the final victory will be won when both sides unreservedly affirm their equality.

Such conclusions may seem unremarkable, even trite, today – but in 1949 they were profoundly shocking to the establishment. *The Second Sex* was placed on the Vatican's list of prohibited books and was the subject of angry controversy in France as soon as it was published. But de Beauvoir's thinking had hit a nerve, and it continues to resonate: an English translation in 1953, in which the

'One is not born, but rather becomes, a woman'

In the first book of *The Second Sex* de Beauvoir examines the different ways in which women's secondary status to men has been established. At the start of the second volume, she sets out her case that it is social indoctrination that maintains male dominance in society. From their earliest childhood, she says, girls are prepared for a submissive, second-class life.

'One is not born, but rather becomes, a woman. No biological, psychological or economic fate determines the figure that the human female presents in society; it is civilization as a whole that produces this creature, intermediate between male and eunuch, which is described as feminine. Only the intervention of someone else can establish an individual as an Other. In so far as he exists in and for himself, the child would hardly be able to think of himself as sexually differentiated …

The child is persuaded that more is demanded of boys because they are superior; to give him courage for the difficult path he must follow, pride in his manhood is instilled into him; this abstract notion takes on for him a concrete aspect; it is incarnated in his penis …

The adolescent girl at puberty … knows already that her sex condemns her to a mutilated and fixed existence, which she faces at this time under the form of an impure sickness and a vague sense of guilt. Her inferiority was sensed at first merely as a deprivation; but the lack of a penis has now become defilement and transgression. So she goes onward towards the future, wounded, shameful, culpable.'

The Second Sex, Book 2, Part 1, Chapter 1, 'Childhood', translated by H.M. Parshley, 1949

MARY WOLLSTONECRAFT

More than 150 years before the publication of *The Second Sex*, the 18th-century English philosopher Mary Wollstonecraft wrote her own contribution to the literature on women. In *A Vindication of the Rights of Women*, published in 1792, she argued passionately that girls should be given a full and rational education, so that as adults they should be able to be both companions to men and teachers to their children.

In the 18th century it was widely believed that woman were too emotional to be capable of rational thought. The French philosopher Jean-Jacques Rousseau had argued that the only reason to educate women at all was to give pleasure to men, and several leading moralists suggested that women should hide whatever learning they had, in case it made them less attractive to potential husbands.

Wollstonecraft is the most famous of several woman writers, both in Britain and France, who challenged these attitudes. Among the others were the English republican historian and writer Catherine Macaulay (1731–91) and the French playwright Olympe de Gouges, who published her *Declaration of the Rights of Women and the Female Citizen* in 1791, at the height of the French Revolution. She was guillotined in 1793.

Modern philosophers disagree over whether these writers can be called feminists – Wollstonecraft, for instance, conceded that men seemed 'designed by Providence to attain a greater degree of virtue'. But their works, and their lives, provided a clear inspiration to feminist writers and philosophers of the mid-20th century.

two volumes were published as one, has sold well over a million copies, despite repeated complaints that it fails to capture either the style or the thinking of the original.

For de Beauvoir, *The Second Sex* was a product partly of the existential philosophy that she shared with her lifelong partner Jean-Paul Sartre (1905–80). They believed that individuals, and not God, fate or society, are responsible for the definition of their own lives. The thinking of *The Second Sex* is partly an existentialist challenge to men and women in the modern world.

De Beauvoir is now considered one of France's leading philosophers and writers. Before the appearance of *The Second Sex* in 1949, she had already published several novels and philosophical works, starting with *L'Invitée* (*She Came to Stay*) in 1943. In 1970 she turned her attention to the position of old people in society, with the publication of *La Vieillesse* (*The Coming of Age*), and a year after the death of Sartre in 1980 *La Cérémonie des adieux* (*Adieux: A Farewell to Sartre*) appeared.

The relevance of the specific ideas of *The Second Sex* 60 years later is questionable, but there can be no doubt of the book's impact on feminist thinking since its publication. Simone de Beauvoir challenged both women and men to face the implications of society's treatment of the sexes, and the result of her challenge permeates the modern world. In the USA, the UK and France in particular, scores of books have been written analyzing and criticizing the position of women in modern society. *The Feminine Mystique* (1963) by Betty Friedan (1921–2006), *The Female Eunuch* (1970) by Germaine Greer (b.1939) and the essay 'Le Rire de la Méduse' ('The Laugh of the Medusa'; 1975) by Hélène Cixous all owe a debt to Simone de Beauvoir, as do the hundreds of university departments offering courses in Women's Studies. Whether or not women have achieved social, economic and emotional equality, there is more awareness today of the relationship between the sexes than there has ever been, and this is at least partly due to Simone de Beauvoir and *The Second Sex*.

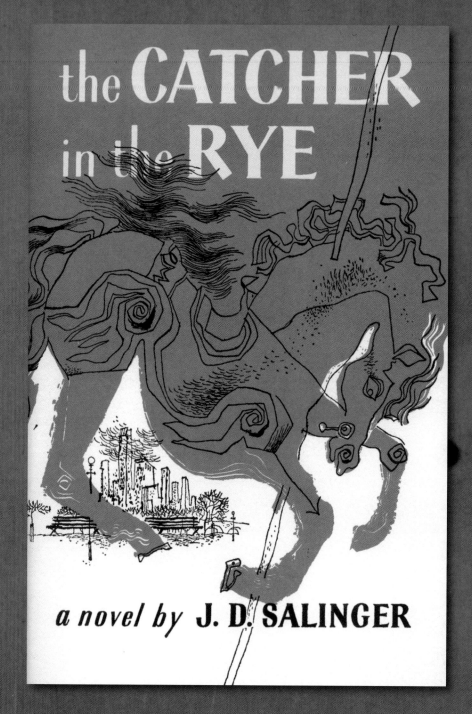

The Catcher in the Rye

1951

J.D. Salinger

J.D. Salinger's *The Catcher in the Rye* (1951) is the archetypal teenage novel. Originally intended for adults, it rapidly won acclamation as the first in-depth portrayal of adolescent uncertainty, ambition and disillusionment. What distinguishes it from other novels about young people is the uncompromising way in which it is written from its hero's point of view. The few scenes of teenage sexuality and the occasionally vulgar language – now rather outdated – have led to scores of attempts to have the book banned, or at least removed from school reading lists; but that has not dented its sales or popularity.

The US writer J.D. Salinger (b.1919) is a reclusive figure, with a slim *oeuvre*, who has fought several legal battles to protect his privacy, and who has produced only short stories and novellas after the massive success of *The Catcher in the Rye*. Most of them have focused on adolescent characters, particularly the various members of the Glass family, who had already featured in such stories as 'A Perfect Day for Bananafish' (1948), and who have reappeared over the years in *Franny and Zooey* (1961) and 'Raise High the Roof Beam, Carpenters' and 'Seymour: An Introduction' (1963). Most of Salinger's stories appeared in magazines, notably the *New Yorker*, before being published in book form. His most recent story, 'Hapworth 16, 1924', was published as long ago as 1965.

The Catcher in the Rye covers two nights and two days in the life of Holden Caulfield, a 16-year-old New Yorker who runs away from his school, Pencey Prep (Salinger himself frequently moved schools). It is told by Holden, a year or so later, while he is staying in a rest home to which he has been sent for therapy.

With a history of failure at school, he tells how he was to be expelled from Pencey after failing his exams, but walked out on his own late one night,

The life of J.D. Salinger

1919 Born Jerome David Salinger in New York City.

1932–6 Attends McBurney School, New York.

1934–6 Attends Valley Forge Military Academy, Pennsylvania.

1936 Takes classes at New York University, but drops out in spring 1937.

1939 Attends an evening class at Columbia University, taught by Whit Burnett, editor of *Story* magazine, who becomes his mentor.

1940 Publishes his first short story, 'The Young Folks', in *Story*.

1942 Drafted into the US Army and serves with the 4th Infantry Division in the Second World War. Meets Ernest Hemingway and starts a correspondence.

1948 Publishes 'A Perfect Day for Bananafish', 'Uncle Wiggily in Connecticut' and 'Just Before the War with the Eskimos' in the *New Yorker*.

1951 Publishes *The Catcher in the Rye*.

1953 Publishes *Nine Stories*.

1961 Publishes *Franny and Zooey* in book form, stories that originally appeared in the *New Yorker* in 1955 and 1957.

1963 'Raise High the Roof Beam, Carpenters' (1955) and 'Seymour: An Introduction' (1959) published as a book.

1965 'Hapworth 16, 1924', his last-published short story, appears in the *New Yorker*.

planning to spend a few days in secret in New York and give his parents time to hear the news of this latest expulsion. Over the next two days, he books into a hotel, visits nightclubs, has a brief and unsatisfactory encounter with a prostitute (with whom he simply wants to talk), and then gets beaten up by the hotel porter in an argument about the price. Much of the time, he is thinking about telephone calls he could make to people he knows, fantasizing about the tough, story-book character he might be, criticizing the adult world for being 'phoney' and talking about his affection for his brothers – one of whom is dead – and his younger sister, Phoebe.

Late at night, he goes back home secretly, hoping to see Phoebe without waking his parents. They are out, and Phoebe and Holden talk. In one of the most moving and evocative scenes of the book, he tells her his dream of protecting young children who might be in danger – of being 'the catcher in the rye', who prevents them from falling off a dangerous cliff as they play in the rye fields.

Leaving his parents' apartment, Holden visits his old teacher, Mr Antolini, who offers him a bed for the night; but he interprets Antolini's stroking of his head as a homosexual advance, and instead spends the night in a railway waiting room.

The next day, he makes a plan to hitchhike out west, and arranges to meet Phoebe to say goodbye. When she announces that she wants to go with him, he changes his mind, however, and agrees to go home. The novel ends on an optimistic note, as he watches her on a fairground carousel. 'I felt so damn happy, if you want to know the truth,' he says. He goes home, is sent to

'That's all I'd do all day'

The second night after he runs away from school, Holden Caulfield goes home secretly to talk to his younger sister, Phoebe. He is feeling ill after a night drinking in a club, and he wakes her up to find, to his relief, that both his parents are out. They sit and talk, and Phoebe challenges him to tell her what he would like to do with his life. His answer sums up the poetry, good intentions and ultimate dreamy unreality of his character, as he remembers a song he heard a child singing in the street. However, he has misremembered the quotation: nobody 'catches' anyone in the rye. The best he can hope for is to 'meet' them.

' "You know that song, 'If a body catch a body comin' through the rye'? I'd like …"

"It's 'If a body meet a body coming through the rye'!" old Phoebe said. "It's a poem. By Robert Burns."

"I know it's a poem by Robert Burns."

She was right, though. It is "If a body meet a body coming through the rye". I didn't know it then, though.

"I thought it was 'If a body catch a body'," I said. "Anyway, I keep picturing all these little kids playing some game in this big field of rye and all. Thousands of little kids, and nobody's around – nobody big, I mean – except me. And I'm standing on the edge of some crazy cliff. What I have to do, I have to catch everybody if they start to go over the cliff – I mean if they're running and they don't look where they're going I have to come out from somewhere and catch them. That's all I'd do all day. I'd just be the catcher in the rye and all. I know it's crazy, but that's the only thing I'd really like to be. I know it's crazy." '

The Catcher in the Rye, Chapter 22, 1951

THE DUCKS IN CENTRAL PARK

One of Holden Caulfield's questions in *The Catcher in the Rye* is: 'Where do the ducks in Central Park go to in the winter?' Twenty-nine years after its publication, the book and that particular question acquired a new, unwelcome notoriety on the night of 8 December 1980.

That evening, the former Beatle John Lennon was shot four times and killed as he returned to his apartment in New York's Dakota building. Afterwards, his murderer, the 25-year-old Mark Chapman, stood reading a copy of *The Catcher in the Rye,* until the police arrived. In it, he had written, 'This is my statement', and signed it 'The Catcher in the Rye'. According to Chapman's conversation with the police, Lennon 'knew where the ducks went in winter, and I needed to know this'.

Several trial witnesses said later that Chapman had become obsessed with Salinger's book after reading it repeatedly over the previous two years, and that he had fantasized about being Holden Caulfield. He told police that he had been hearing voices, and he added: 'The large part of me is Holden Caulfield, who is the main person in the book. The small part of me must be the Devil.'

There are many different theories about Chapman's fixation on *The Catcher in the Rye* and John Lennon. Possibly Lennon, whose immense wealth was at odds with his self-image as a 'working-class hero', seemed to be one of the 'phoneys' to whom Holden Caulfield takes such exception throughout the book; perhaps Chapman was simply attracted by the teenage angst and a sense that he was misunderstood. The only person who really knows the answer remains behind bars in Attica State Prison, New York.

the rest home from which he has written the novel and is to go to another school in a few months' time. Is he now prepared to make an effort to succeed there? 'I *think* I am, but how do I know? I swear it's a stupid question.'

At the heart of *The Catcher in the Rye* is what Holden Caulfield is, rather than what he does. Salinger presents a character who is filled with good intentions, but tortured by suspicion and distrust of the people he meets. He is frightened of growing up and dreams of protecting other children from the corruption of adulthood – a hopeless dream, which accounts for the regretful yearning with which the book is suffused. Yet, whether or not Holden applies himself to the challenge of his new school in the future, his uncompromising affection for Phoebe reveals an outgoing, loving character. There is a sense that the confusion he feels will be resolved.

Earlier writers had presented adolescent characters – Mark Twain's Huckleberry Finn is an obvious example – but no-one has described the angst, moral confusion and undirected emotion of the 20th-century teenager as evocatively as J.D. Salinger.

Things
Fall Apart

1958

Chinua Achebe

For centuries, Africa was regarded in the West as a source of gold, minerals and slaves. It was a powerful symbol, the Dark Continent, or in the title of Joseph Conrad's 1902 short story, the 'Heart of Darkness'. But few writers presented an African view of how White colonialism had affected Africans, and those who tried were not listened to. In *Things Fall Apart*, Chinua Achebe was the first Black African writer to reach significant numbers of readers with that story. It was with this novel that Africa began to examine itself, and speak for itself to the outside world.

Things Fall Apart was first published in London in 1958, at the start of a period when Britain's African colonies were achieving independence. It is set, however, more than 60 years earlier, at the height of the late 19th-century European 'Scramble for Africa'. A sombre novel, it deals with the tragic life and death of a proud member of the Ibo (Igbo) people of southeastern Nigeria, who is crushed by the power of the British Empire, by differences among his own people, and by his inability to comprehend the changing times. Through the story of this one man, Achebe – then working for the Nigerian Broadcasting Corporation – manages, in miniature, to convey the larger history of the crisis of African cultures under the pressure of European colonization.

The story centres on Okonkwo, a leading citizen among the people of the village of Umuofia, on the lower Niger River, in the 1890s. He has risen from nothing, and now has three wives and a productive yam plantation. He works hard, has a reputation as a fearsome wrestler, and expects instant obedience from his wives and his children.

A clash of cultures

After the imprisonment, beating, and humiliation of the elders of Umuofia by the British colonial powers, the villagers call a meeting to decide whether it is going to be possible to live in peace with the White men. Okonkwo wants to go to war, and when he sees messengers from the British approaching, he stops them. It is the confrontation that heralds the tragic conclusion of the novel.

'He sprang to his feet as soon as he saw who it was. He confronted the head messenger, trembling with hate, unable to utter a word. The man was fearless and stood his ground, his four men lined up behind him.

In that brief moment the world seemed to stand still, waiting. There was utter silence. The men of Umuofia were merged into the mute backcloth of trees and giant creepers, waiting.

The spell was broken by the head messenger. "Let me pass!" he ordered.

"What do you want here?"

"The white man whose power you know too well has ordered this meeting to stop."

In a flash Okonkwo drew his matchet [machete]. The messenger crouched to avoid the blow. It was useless. Okonkwo's matchet descended twice and the man's head lay beside his uniformed body.

The waiting backcloth jumped into tumultuous life and the meeting was stopped. Okonkwo stood looking at the dead man. He knew that Umuofia would not go to war. He knew because they had let the other messengers escape … They had broken into tumult instead of action. He discerned fright in that tumult. He heard voices asking, "Why did he do it?"

He wiped his matchet on the sand and went away.'

Things Fall Apart, **Chapter 24, 1958**

<hr>

THE DARK CONTINENT

Throughout history, Africa has been seen as a land to be exploited, a source of entertainment, slaves and riches. Lions, ostriches, zebras and other animals were brought to be slaughtered in the games at the Colosseum in Rome; African slaves were bought and sold for centuries, first in Rome, then in the Arab empires of the Umayyad and Abbasid dynasties. The trans-Atlantic slave trade, between the 16th and 19th centuries, resulted in an estimated 12 million people being seized in West Africa and transported to the Americas.

In the 19th century, Christian missionaries such as David Livingstone (1813–73) sought to eradicate traditional religious beliefs, alongside traders who exploited the tribes of the interior, enforcing their monopoly rights with their military power. The American journalist H.M. Stanley (1841–1904), who won fame by finding Livingstone in present-day Tanzania, coined the phrase 'The Dark Continent', which summed up the threatening mystery that Africa represented.

Gold, minerals and diamonds were mined and exported by foreign companies such as the Royal Niger Company and the British East Africa Company, and then in the last 20 years of the 19th century, European governments became involved in the 'Scramble for Africa', carving up the continent and sharing it out between them in their colonial enterprises.

The roughly 80 years of colonialism created the continent's present-day states and had other profound and still much-debated consequences. Some attribute the failure to prosper of many African states to the misrule of post-independence leaders; others condemn the legacies of colonialism as the underlying cause. It is part of Chinua Achebe's power as a writer that he can castigate colonialism while in no way remaining blind to the self-inflicted ills of his own society.

<hr>

The people of Umuofia wield considerable power in the region, and when a neighbouring village offers a young boy as part of a peace settlement, he lives with Okonkwo as a member of his family for three years; but when the priestess demands the boy's sacrifice, Okonkwo takes part in his ritual killing.

Shortly afterwards, he accidentally kills someone at a village funeral, and he is sent into exile with his family for seven years. When he returns, he knows he will have to work to reclaim his position, but while he has been away White Christian missionaries have visited Umuofia, gathering converts, building a church and establishing a thriving congregation. Some of the more fanatical converts start to show disrespect for the village's traditional religion, and when one of them rips the mask off one of the *egwugwu*, or spirits, at a village ceremony, outraged traditionalists set fire to his home and tear the church down. In response, British colonial officials seize the village elders, including Okonkwo, and handcuff, humiliate and beat them.

The villagers pay a ransom for their release, and gather for what Okonkwo hopes will be a great uprising. When messengers arrive from the White authorities to tell them to abandon the meeting, Okonkwo kills one of them. Realizing, to his despair, that the villagers are not going to follow his lead and attack the White men, he hangs himself. When the district commissioner arrives with soldiers to arrest Okonkwo, the villagers ask them to take down his body: to the villagers, suicide is shameful.

The novel ends with Okonkwo's treasured reputation among his people shattered, and the village of Umuofia clearly cowed and dominated by the White men. The bitter irony is clear as the district commissioner ponders whether the incident will merit a complete chapter or simply 'a reasonable paragraph' in the book he is planning on 'The Pacification of the Primitive Tribes of the Lower Niger'.

The title of Achebe's novel comes from the poem 'The Second Coming' by the Anglo-Irish poet and playwright W.B. Yeats (1865–1939), which contains the line 'Things fall apart; the centre cannot hold'; but his view of the effects of White colonialism can be seen most clearly in a different line of the poem: 'Mere anarchy is loosed upon the world'. What the colonists and imperialists see as a 'civilizing' mission wreaks destruction. But Okonkwo's personal fate exemplifies other tensions too: if colonialism and Christianity are the most overt challenges to his conservative sense of order and tradition, then the shifting allegiances and new tendencies among his people also undermine his sense of who he is and what he stands for. In death, he is defeated by the Europeans *and* rejected by his own. For the rigid-thinking Okonkwo, things do 'fall apart', and this sense of dislocation, of failure to comprehend a changing world, is powerful. Achebe's skill is to chastise colonialism but also to provide a subtle and penetrating analysis of the fragility of African tradition in a time of transformation. An Ibo himself, and the son of Christian parents, he was in a good position to appreciate such tensions.

Although attempts to promote the novel in West Africa were met with some initial bemusement and a lack of interest, critics around the world welcomed Achebe as an important new novelist. The first print run of 2000 books sold out rapidly, and in the years since publication the book has sold more than 8 million copies in over 50 languages.

Since *Things Fall Apart* Achebe has written a string of other books. In the earlier novels, such as *No Longer at Ease*, which is the story of Okonkwo's grandson, colonialism and its consequences figure largely. Later novels turn to the recent politics of Nigeria's imperfect democracy and its periods of military dictatorship. Along with his writing, Achebe's industrious career has taken in broadcasting, university professorships, publishing, forays into politics, and numerous honorary positions and awards. In a famous dismissal of Joseph Conrad's 'Heart of Darkness', Achebe complained that Africa is depicted as 'a metaphysical battlefield devoid of all recognizable humanity, into which the wandering European enters at his peril'. Achebe led the way in reclaiming from European outsiders the representation of African societies, and in *Things Fall Apart* he produced the first enduring master-piece of African literature in English.

The life of Chinua Achebe

1930 Born Albert Chinualumogu in Ogidi, Nigeria.

1948–53 Attends University College, Ibadan.

1954 Begins working for the Nigerian Broadcasting Corporation, rising to become director of the *Voice of Nigeria* (1961–6).

1958 Publishes *Things Fall Apart*, his first novel, to widespread acclaim.

1960 Publishes *No Longer at Ease*, a follow-up.

1964 Publishes the tragic novel *Arrow of God*, concerning African responses to British 'indirect rule'.

1966 Publishes *A Man of the People*, concerning postcolonial corruption.

1967 Begins his affiliation as research fellow, later professor of English, at the University of Nsukka, Nigeria. Espouses the cause of the secessionist Biafra and its Ibo people during the Nigerian Civil War (1967–70).

1971 Co-founds the literary magazine *Okike*.

1972 Takes up his first visiting professorship at an American university.

1975 Publishes the lecture 'An Image of Racism in Conrad's "Heart of Darkness"'.

1987 Publishes *Anthills of the Savannah*, a novel about postcolonial dictatorship.

2004 Issues his *Collected Poems*.

Silent Spring

1962

Rachel Carson

Rachel Carson's *Silent Spring* (1962) was the first book to provoke widespread concern about the impact that chemical pesticides can have on Nature and human health. By combining solid science with an emotional warning of the potential ill effects of humanity's interference with natural ecosystems, Carson was instrumental in bringing the science of ecology and the serious issue of environmental damage to the top of the international agenda. In so doing she helped to kick-start the modern environmental movement.

Carson opens *Silent Spring* with the image of a country town in harmony with Nature, until it is suddenly brought to ruin when its citizens thoughtlessly use dangerous pesticides on their farms, homes and gardens. The book's title was chosen to evoke the image of a spring where no birds sing, because they have all been poisoned by pesticides; it thus echoes the lines from Keats's poem 'La Belle Dame sans Merci': 'The sedge is wither'd from the lake, /And no birds sing.' Carson herself writes: 'Over increasingly large areas of the United States spring now comes unheralded by the return of the birds, and the early mornings are strangely silent where once they were filled with the beauty of bird song.'

In *Silent Spring* Carson traces the huge and rapid increase in chemical pesticides, such as DDT, since the Second World War. Many people at the time thought such pesticides delivered nothing but good: they increased agricultural production, made food cheaper, helped to reduce poverty, and also killed disease carriers such as lice (which spread diseases such as typhus) and mosquitoes (which spread many diseases, notably malaria). But Carson points out that DDT concentrates

A stricken world

Silent Spring is famous for its rigorous scientific attitude towards data and evidence, but it begins with an evocative image that Carson intends to use as a warning about what America and the world may be doing to themselves. This is the description of the 'silent spring' of her title ...

'There was once a town in the heart of America where all life seemed to live in harmony with its surroundings. The town lay in the midst of a checkerboard of prosperous farms with fields of grain and hillsides of orchards where, in spring, white clouds of bloom drifted above the green fields ... The countryside was famous for the abundance and variety of its bird life, and when the flood of migrants was pouring through in spring and fall people traveled from great distances to observe them ...

Then a strange blight crept over the area and everything began to change ... There was a strange stillness. The birds, for example – where had they gone? Many people spoke of them, puzzled and disturbed ... The few birds seen anywhere were moribund; they trembled violently and could not fly. It was a spring without voices. On the mornings that had once throbbed with the dawn chorus of robins, catbirds, doves, jays, wrens and scores of other bird voices there was now no sound ...

No witchcraft, no enemy action had silenced the rebirth of new life in this stricken world. The people had done it themselves.'

Silent Spring, Chapter 1, 'A Fable for Tomorrow', 1962

higher up in the food chain, interfering with the ability of insect-eating birds to breed; birds of prey that feed on these birds are even more vulnerable.

In a chapter entitled 'Elixirs of Death' Carson introduces the organic chemistry of chlorinated hydrocarbons such as DDT and other synthetic pesticides, and shows how such chemicals are absorbed by plants and animals, accumulate in adrenal glands, testes, the liver and kidneys, and enter the human food chain. Citing eminent scientists and public-health leaders, she outlines ways in which these compounds may be causes of cancer.

The book questions whether studies of the effects of these powerful poisons on rats have given regulators enough reliable information to set safety thresholds for their use, given their potential long-term effects and the way that several chemicals may have a combined impact on the human body. Carson predicts a rise in cancers and diseases of the nervous system if the widespread use of such pesticides continues.

Silent Spring chronicles a saddening array of cases where these poisons have already had devastating effects on wildlife. Campaigns to eradicate gypsy moths and fire ants, for example, decimated bird and animal life, although infestations of the pests remained as bad the year after the aerial spraying as before. Throughout, Carson suggests natural alternatives to synthetic chemicals, using ecology to defeat unwanted pests. She also puts academic entomologists under the microscope, pointing out that their research is compromised by the funding they receive from the chemical industry to undertake insecticide testing; they are thus biased against biological or ecological methods of pest control.

The book's concluding chapter, 'The Other Road', sketches the many alternatives to saturating the earth with poisons. Nature, Carson says, exists for more than man's convenience.

Silent Spring was serialized in the *New Yorker* magazine before appearing in book form in 1962, at the end of an era of postwar complacency and conformism. Multinational chemical giants were building plants and creating jobs, agricultural crop yields were booming, and there was little thought about the costs of this material progress. In 1962 the public was not used to questioning the authority or integrity of corporate executives, government officials, scientists or farmers. Carson was taking on an entrenched power structure.

The life of Rachel Carson

1907 Born in Springdale, Pennsylvania.

1932 Awarded MA in Zoology from Johns Hopkins University.

1936 Starts work as a government scientist with the United States Bureau of Fisheries (which later becomes the Fish and Wildlife Service).

1941 Publishes *Under the Sea-Wind*, about life on the ocean floor.

1949 Becomes editor-in-chief at the Fish and Wildlife Service.

1951 Publishes *The Sea Around Us*, which wins the US National Book Award.

1952 Becomes a full-time writer.

1955 Publishes *The Edge of the Sea*, the third of her popular studies of marine ecosystems.

1957 The US Department of Agriculture's programme to eradicate fire ants prompts Carson's interest in the environmental impact of pesticides.

1962 Publishes *Silent Spring*, bringing to public attention the dangers of pesticides, notably DDT.

1963 Testifies before President Kennedy's Science Advisory Committee, which largely backs her environmental and health claims.

1964 Dies in Silver Spring, Maryland.

1980 Posthumously awarded the Presidential Medal of Freedom.

THE ENVIRONMENTAL MOVEMENT

Largely thanks to *Silent Spring*, through the 1960s and 1970s the US government introduced a number of measures to tighten control over environmental risks. Shortly after its publication, President Kennedy announced that his administration was looking into the use of pesticides. Testifying to a congressional committee, Carson called for a new arm of government to protect the environment, and a few years later, in 1970, the Environmental Protection Agency was created along with legislation to regulate air and water pollution. Similar action aimed at protecting the environment was being taken in several other countries. DDT was finally banned in the USA in 1972.

In 1973 the UK's Ecology Party (later the Green Party) became Europe's first political party to concentrate specifically on environmental issues, and ten years later the German Greens won 27 seats in the Bundestag, the German parliament. Through the 1980s there was growing awareness of a new environmental threat: global warming. In 1992 the Earth Summit in Rio de Janeiro reached a framework agreement for stabilizing the amount of greenhouse gas emissions across the world. The Kyoto Protocol of 1997 was agreed by most industrialized nations, although the USA explicitly rejected it because it failed to control emissions by developing nations such as India and China.

There continues to be opposition to environmental regulation from various quarters. A bitter campaign has been waged, blaming Rachel Carson for the rise in malaria in Africa following a reduction in DDT spraying. One headline even claimed that she was responsible for more deaths than Adolf Hitler. However, most scientists today agree that mosquitoes have evolved to resist DDT and other poisons. *Silent Spring* suggests that spraying only makes the mosquito stronger by enabling it to develop resistance to poisons.

This challenge won her widespread acclaim within the nascent environmentalist movement, just as well-publicized environmental hazards were beginning to open the public mind. *Silent Spring* quickly became a bestseller in both the United States and Britain. Carson knew which buttons to press to get the public on her side. One year, she points out, an application of pesticides had made the nation's cranberry crop too dangerous to serve, an almost unthinkable absence from the American Thanksgiving feast. However, Carson knew that to have any chance of winning the scientific argument, she would need not only to trade on her credibility as a popular science writer, but also to ground her claims about pesticides in the academic and technical literature. She spent over four years researching *Silent Spring*, and listed fifty pages of sources at the end.

In any case, Carson's background was that of a serious scientist: she had a master's degree in zoology from Johns Hopkins University and had also spent time at the Woods Hole Marine Biology Institute in Massachusetts. From 1936 until 1952 she worked as a government scientist with the United States Fish and Wildlife Service, latterly serving as the agency's editor-in-chief. She published *Under the Sea-Wind* in 1941, and her second book, *The Sea Around Us* (1951), another study of the ocean, won the US National Book Award and became an international bestseller. After this success, her reputation enabled her to leave her job and take up writing full time.

Within two years of publishing *Silent Spring* Rachel Carson died of cancer, aged 56. After her premature death, a number of public-interest pressure groups came into being to promote reform in the USA, including the Environmental Defense Fund and the Natural Resources Defense Council. Others, such as the National Audubon Society (America's leading wildlife conservation organization), began to campaign against pollution.

Silent Spring pioneered a new genre of popular-science books that weave together scientific evidence and emotive appeals in order to arouse public concern and raise awareness of the environmental risks of industrial technology. Campaigning environmentalism as we know it received its start in life from Carson's book.

Quotations from Chairman Mao

1964

Mao Zedong

Marching past Mao Zedong in Tiananmen Square at the start of the Cultural Revolution in 1966, massed ranks of Red Guards saluted their 'Great Helmsman' by holding up copies of the *Quotations from Chairman Mao.* As the turmoil of the ageing Mao's last-gasp effort at permanent revolution continued, every Chinese citizen had to carry this compact compendium of Mao's thoughts. The political exhortations contained in what became known as the 'Little Red Book' were little more than vague exhortations to toe the party line and defeat the enemies of communism; but the personality cult and 'thought reform' that the book symbolized dominated China throughout Mao's three decades as supreme leader.

Mao was born in the decaying years of imperial China, with the country suffering more and more humiliations as the Western powers sought to dominate this once great empire, now crippled by traditional habits of mind and blind obedience to authority. He witnessed the 1911 Revolution that saw the overthrow of the last Chinese emperor after over two millennia of imperial rule, and encountered communism while a part-time student at Beijing University. In 1921 Mao was selected to attend the First Communist Party Congress, which was convened by the Soviet Union's Comintern, and began his career as a party organizer. At first the party was allied with Chiang Kai-shek's Guomindang (Kuomintang) nationalists against the warlords who had taken over many parts of China, but in 1927 Chiang turned on the communists, and civil war broke out.

Mao took part in the Long March, a devastating 8000-mile retreat by a 100,000-strong communist army from Jiangxi province, then under Guomindang attack. After several times falling out of favour with the party hierarchy, Mao seized the leadership when the surviving remnant of only 30,000 men straggled into remote Yan'an in Shaanxi province. China remained riven by Japanese occupation and civil war until Mao's victory in 1949 pushed Chiang and the nationalists out of mainland China to Taiwan. Mao led China from then until his death in 1976 at the age of 83.

'A revolution is not a dinner party'

The following extracts from the *Quotations from Chairman Mao* are from the 1964 Foreign Languages Press translation. They stress Mao's belief in violence as the means to achieve and maintain power, as in his famous dictum: 'Political power grows out of the barrel of a gun.'

'It is up to us to organize the people. As for the reactionaries in China, it is up to us to organize the people to overthrow them. Everything reactionary is the same; if you don't hit it, it won't fall. This is also like sweeping the floor; as a rule, where the broom does not reach, the dust will not vanish of itself ...'

'... A revolution is not a dinner party, or writing an essay, or painting a picture, or doing embroidery; it cannot be so refined, so leisurely and gentle, so temperate, kind, courteous, restrained and magnanimous. A revolution is an insurrection, an act of violence by which one class overthrows another.'

Quotations from Chairman Mao, Chapter 2, 'Classes and Class Struggle'

The life of Mao Zedong

1893 Born in Hunan province, China.

1918 Begins studies at Beijing University.

1921 Helps to found Chinese Communist Party.

1927 After communists break with nationalists, flees to establish guerrilla base in the mountains of Jiangxi.

1934–5 Participates in the communist army's Long March (retreat) from Jiangxi, and becomes party leader.

1937–45 Suspends fight against nationalists in favour of guerrilla war against Japanese invaders.

1945 Civil war between communists and Chiang Kai-shek's nationalist government.

1949 Foundation of People's Republic of China, with Mao as chairman.

1958–60 Inspires agricultural 'reforms' of the Great Leap Forward: tens of millions starve to death.

1964 The first edition of *Quotations from Chairman Mao* appears.

1966 Initiates Cultural Revolution, to reignite personal support and purge the Communist Party: the *Quotations* become an essential tool of Mao's personality cult.

1976 Dies in Beijing.

When the Communist Party established the People's Republic of China in 1949, its early campaigns for land reform and against 'counter-revolutionaries' involved the execution of between 1 million and 5 million people. There were several rounds of collectivization of agriculture during the 1950s, culminating in the disastrously impractical Great Leap Forward, which resulted in failed harvests, massive economic damage and huge loss of life. Those who opposed Mao's policies and attempted to restore orderly functioning to the economy were purged.

By the early 1960s, opposition to Mao had grown within the higher ranks of the party. Mao and his 'leftist' allies, notably his wife Jiang Qing and defence minister Lin Biao, decided to make a pre-emptive attack by launching the Cultural Revolution in 1966. The Cultural Revolution was the most far-reaching purge of the party yet and the most radical campaign so far attempted to control the minds of the Chinese people. It started out with children of party members forming Red Guard units to denounce their schoolteachers and professors; the Red Guards then went on to attack the party hierarchy, chanting slogans from the Little Red Book and accusing victims of being bourgeois reactionaries opposed to Mao. In public 'struggle sessions', people were forced into stress positions, beaten and bullied into self-criticism and confessions. Innumerable academics, technocrats, party officials and university students were sent off to the countryside for 're-education' as manual workers in agricultural communes. Any expression of individuality was crushed, and men and women were all obliged to wear identical 'Mao suits'. Attempts were made to obliterate all traces of the past, with the destruction of antiquities and historical sites. As many as half a million Chinese may have been killed or driven to suicide between 1966 and 1969, the peak years of the Cultural Revolution.

The *Quotations from Chairman Mao* played a key role in all this. The book had been compiled in 1964 from the leader's speeches and writings by the General Political Department of the Chinese People's Liberation Army on the instructions of Lin Biao. Lin used it initially to indoctrinate the army and ingratiate himself with Mao, who boasted that it put his thought on a level with that of Confucius, Buddha and the Bible.

The book's 426 paragraphs are arranged by topic, from the party and class struggle, through war and the army, to methods of thinking, ideological self-cultivation, criticism and self-criticism, and on to youth and women. Recurrent themes include the need for continual revolution, the dangers of Western (especially US) imperialism, the supremacy of the masses, and the over-arching dominance of Marxism-Leninism. The book is a collection of exhortations that demand instant obedience.

However, the maxims are vague and unspecific, with no analysis or context: nobody could know if he or she was following the guidance correctly without checking. The sayings are more notable for their forceful imagery than their political sophistication. Once the Chinese people are organized and united, the book says, an invader, 'like a mad bull crashing into a ring of flames, will be surrounded by hundreds of millions of our people standing upright, the mere sound of their voices will strike terror into him, and he will be burned to death'.

Lin – who was later vilified as a traitor and died in a plane crash after apparently attempting to mount a coup – had the book handed out at the start of the Cultural Revolution in 1966 to the Red Guards. It was subsequently distributed throughout Chinese society: over 5 billion copies were printed, and throughout the period of the Cultural Revolution people stopped in street checks were expected to produce their copies,

THE CULT OF PERSONALITY

Some societies, such as the South American Incas, have believed that their rulers were actually divine beings in their own right; others, such as the Romans, have deified their emperors after death as a political gesture; many, like medieval European kings, have insisted on immediate and unquestioning obedience. But the establishment of a ubiquitous, all-embracing cult of personality was essentially a 20th-century phenomenon.

Leaders such as Mao Zedong in China, Adolf Hitler in Nazi Germany, Joseph Stalin in Russia, Kim Il Sung in Korea and Saddam Hussein in Iraq did not rely on any supposed divinity, but on the exercise of unbridled power, mechanisms of control and notably the manipulation of the mass media. To ensure that their people were constantly dominated by the image, the voice and the thinking of the leader, they employed all the modern communication technologies that were available to them.

Hitler had himself described as the *Führer* ('leader'), Mao as the Great Helmsman, and Kim Il Sung as the Great Leader. But, despite the efforts used to maintain such personality cults, they can prove surprisingly – and reassuringly – fragile. It is rare for a cult of personality to survive the death of the object of worship; illusions, even mass ones, are quickly dispelled.

or face punishment. The essence of Maoism, expressed in the *Quotations*, was permanent revolution, violent struggle and a focus on peasants rather than urban workers. A leading Western historian of China has likened Mao to a medieval Lord of Misrule, sowing disorder and mayhem as a matter of principle, in part as a reaction to the excessive obedience to tradition embodied in the Confucian culture of the old empire.

After Mao's death in 1976, the Chinese communists rejected Maoism and adopted a pragmatic, capitalist style of management, navigating China into the global economy and sparking decades of tremendous economic growth. While Mao's image remains an icon in communist China, his thought is largely ignored. Outside China, Maoism and the thoughts expressed in the *Quotations* have influenced a number of violent revolutionary movements, including Pol Pot's genocidal Khmer Rouge regime in Cambodia, Peru's Sendero Luminoso (Shining Path) and Nepal's Maoist guerrillas. China's foreign propaganda service distributed the Little Red Book to many other countries in the late 1960s, and it briefly became fashionable among European leftists: Jean-Paul Sartre called Maoist violence 'profoundly moral'. From the perspective of the early 21st century, however, the Little Red Book is best seen as a cruel relic of the most ambitious attempt ever made to enslave the minds of an entire nation – a nation that comprises a quarter of the world's population.

Harry Potter and the Philosopher's Stone

1997

J.K. Rowling

When J.K. Rowling's *Harry Potter and the Philosopher's Stone* appeared in Britain in 1997, after a succession of rejections from various publishers, it was greeted as an amusing novel for children by an unknown writer. Several critics noted how closely it was modelled on an apparently outdated tradition of middle-class British boarding-school stories, and even though it won a succession of prizes for children's fiction, no-one saw it as the first of a series of seven worldwide record-breaking bestsellers, and the start of the greatest publishing sensation of the modern age. Within ten years, the Harry Potter books had sold more than 400 million copies in 67 languages, revolutionized the book trade and changed the reading habits of a generation.

In many ways, *Harry Potter and the Philosopher's Stone* is one of the least original and ambitious of the Harry Potter books. But within a few months of the publication of the first print run of 1000 copies, it had already won the prestigious Nestlé Smarties Book Prize in Britain and been bought by the US publisher Scholastic for $105,000, an unprecedented advance for a first-time children's author. Five years later, it had sold over 4 million copies and started the worldwide phenomenon of Pottermania, now valued at comfortably over £7 billion (almost $14 billion).

The Harry Potter books are set in a world where witches and wizards with magical powers live – mostly secretly – among the non-magical or 'Muggle' population. A 'Ministry of Magic', the British government's most discreet department, supervises magical life. Harry is introduced at the start of *Harry Potter and the Philosopher's Stone* living with his bullying Muggle aunt, uncle and cousin because of the death of his parents. He does not know that he is a wizard who has won fame in the magic world because, as a baby, he survived the attack from the evil Lord Voldemort which killed his parents.

On his 11th birthday, he is contacted by Hagrid, a daunting but amiable giant who is groundsman at Hogwarts School, a boarding school for young wizards and witches in Scotland. Against the wishes of his rigidly suburban aunt and uncle – who prefer to delude themselves that the magical world does not exist and have tried to keep the secret of Harry's magical powers from him – he is taken off to the school on the Hogwarts Express steam train, via the mysterious Platform 9¾ at London's Kings Cross station.

Once there, he is inducted into the strange but infinitely appealing world of spells, where, for the first time in his life, he is esteemed and acquires friends. He also discovers that it is a world quietly fretting about whether Voldemort, who was disembodied and almost destroyed in his attack on Harry and his parents, may be about to return and seize power.

The book culminates in Harry's first encounter with Voldemort as he attempts to capture the Philosopher's Stone, hidden at Hogwarts, which will enable him to regain human form and achieve eternal life.

Much of the appeal of *Harry Potter and the Philosopher's Stone* comes from the imaginative combination of traditional English public-school traditions with the 'magical' formula. Thus the talking Sorting Hat, for instance, assigns new Hogwarts pupils to particular houses (similar to US fraternities), and the game of Quidditch, which has its own complex rules and resembles a cross between rugby, polo and basketball, is played in mid-air on broomsticks.

Harry Potter and the Philosopher's Stone was followed a year later by *Harry Potter and the Chamber of Secrets,* and then in quick succession by five further titles. Each book occupies a year of the Hogwarts calendar, so that the series traces the life and career of Harry and his friends (and enemies), from age 11 to 17. It is part of Rowling's skill – and a key component of the series' fascination for its loyal young fans – that, as the characters (and readers) age, so the language develops, the characterization acquires nuances, the plots thicken, and the elemental clash between good and evil at the books' core becomes bigger, darker and starker. The books also grew much longer than is usual for children's fiction: where *Harry Potter and the Philosopher's Stone* is around 75,000 words long, *Harry Potter and the Order of the Phoenix* has over 250,000 words.

In the publishing trade, the Harry Potter books have been credited with revitalizing the world of children's fiction. They started children reading again, tempting them away from television, computers and video games, and, more specifically, managed to attract young boys, who had always been considered to be particularly difficult to persuade to read. As the phenomenon took hold, the publishers also found that adults were buying and reading the books for themselves, so that special editions with less child-oriented cover illustrations were produced to encourage this new market.

Each book was accompanied by huge publisher's hype and strict pre-publication secrecy, lest the plots be leaked. Long queues formed outside bookshops before the day of publication, as children – many costumed appropriately – tried to be the first to buy the newly published books.

Inevitably, a hugely profitable Hollywood film franchise followed – one film for each book – and at the time of writing is yet to conclude. Rowling achieved almost unprecedented influence for an author over the film adaptations of her books, using it to ensure that the British context was retained, the plots were faithfully followed

The Harry Potter novels and films

1997 Joanne (writing as 'J.K.') Rowling, an unemployed single mother, publishes her first book, *Harry Potter and the Philosopher's Stone*: it brings her wealth, fame, an ardent following and launches a publishing phenomenon.

1998 The US edition, as *Harry Potter and the Sorceror's Stone,* is published. The second novel, *Harry Potter and the Chamber of Secrets,* appears: from now on, US and British editions have the same titles.

1999 The third novel, *Harry Potter and the Prisoner of Azkaban,* is published.

2000 The fourth novel, *Harry Potter and the Goblet of Fire* is published.

2001 Film version of *Harry Potter and the Philosopher's Stone* is released.

2002 Film version of *Harry Potter and the Chamber of Secrets* is released.

2003 The fifth novel, *Harry Potter and the Order of the Phoenix,* is published.

2004 Film version of *Harry Potter and the Prisoner of Azkaban* is released.

2005 The sixth novel, *Harry Potter and the Half-Blood Prince,* is published. Film version of *Harry Potter and the Goblet of Fire* is released.

2007 The concluding novel, *Harry Potter and the Deathly Hallows,* is published. Film version of *Harry Potter and the Order of the Phoenix* is released. Rowling produces, in a limited edition of seven copies, *The Tales of Beedle the Bard,* fairy tales derived from the Harry Potter stories: one later sells for £1.95 million (over $3.5 million).

2009 Film version of *Harry Potter and the Half-Blood Prince* is released.

SCHOOL FICTION

Bestriding all the Harry Potter novels is 'Hogwarts School of Witchcraft and Wizardry', an institution that taps into a long tradition in British fiction for children. British 'public schools', which, counter-intuitively, are fee-paying and the equivalent of US private schools, have been a favourite setting ever since *Tom Brown's Schooldays* by Thomas Hughes (1822–96) in 1857. Because they were traditionally boarding schools, where their pupils lived, ate and slept for months at a time, they gave authors the opportunity to create a world largely occupied by children.

Teachers, as representatives of authority and the adult world, could be either menacing, like Mr Quelch in the extensive series of Billy Bunter stories by Charles Hamilton (pen name Frank Richards) (1876–1961), or sympathetic, like Mr Carter in the Jennings and Darbyshire stories of Anthony Buckeridge (1912–2004). In either case, they remained outside the private world of the children, which often involved misunderstandings, quarrels, plots, and rebellion, all frequently under the threat of strict physical punishment.

Generally, the children are depicted as having a firm code of ethics of their own. Individuals may break the code, by lying, drinking or even stealing, but the plots of the books almost always see right triumphant and misunderstandings satisfactorily resolved.

Other notable British examples of school fiction include *Stalky and Co.* (1899) by Rudyard Kipling (1865–1936) and the Nigel Molesworth books of Geoffrey Willans (1911–58). Most school fiction focused on boys' schools, but Enid Blyton (1897–1968) and Elinor Brent-Dyer (1894–1969), in their series set in Malory Towers and Chalet School respectively, were among authors concentrating on girls.

The genre has generally been less popular in the United States, although *The Catcher in the Rye* (1951) by J.D. Salinger (b.1919) starts by describing Holden Caulfield's predicament at Pencey Prep, and *A Separate Peace* (1959), by John Knowles (1926–2001), focuses on two boys growing up in school against the background of the Second World War.

(though the length of the later books precluded all their scenes being dramatized), and a British cast was employed.

Undeniably, then, *Harry Potter and the Philosopher's Stone* launched a phenomenon. Future generations, though, may remember the stories more for what they say about children and teenagers at the start of the 21st century. If J.D. Salinger's *The Catcher in the Rye* (1951) introduced the idea of the modern teenager in fiction, perhaps *Harry Potter and the Philosopher's Stone*, nearly half a century later, marks the extinction of the species. In the real world, young people increasingly progress from childhood direct to quasi-adulthood, with rights and responsibilities of their own, targeted as consumers of adult products, with their own disposable incomes; it seems as if the intermediate phase of teenagerdom has withered. Harry, aged 11, begins a series of elemental life-and-death struggles, his childhood rudely interrupted and beset with grave burdens. It is, literally – and ironically for a world of magic – a form of disillusionment, and in this sense *Harry Potter and the Philosopher's Stone* is a disguised and elegiac farewell to childhood.

Index

Page numbers in **bold** denote a chapter devoted to the subject.

Foreign-language book titles are cited, whenever possible, by their published English translations.

FOR PENNY

dulce ridentem Lalagen amabo, dulce loquentem

Picture credits

6 Frieze of a Roman sarcophagus showing death of Achilles; © akg-images/Erich Lessing. **10** Image of a 'Blemmyae' (headless man) from Schedel's *Nuremberg Chronicle*, 1493; © Beloit College. **14** Illustration of Confucius, 19th century Korean manuscript; © British Library/HIP/TopFoto. **18** Plato and his pupils in the garden of the Academy, after painting by Antal Strohmayer, 1834; © akg-images. **22** Title page of the King James Bible (Authorised Version), designed by Cornelius Boel, 1611; © Rischgitz/Getty Images. **26** Etching of Horace, 1754; © Getty Images. **30** Map based on Ptolemy's work, as reproduced in 1482; © TopFoto. **34** 'The private pleasure of Raja Dalpat Singh', illustration of the 17th-century Rathore ruler of Bikaner in western Rajasthan; © Fitzwilliam Museum, University of Cambridge/Bridgeman Art Library. **38** Decorated page from a 14th-century Egyptian Qur'an; Or. 1009, ff.302v-303 © 2008 The British Library. **42** Miniature from Avicenna's *Canon of Medicine* entitled 'The Doctor's Visit'; © Scala, Florence. **46** Chaucer dressed as a pilgrim, Ellesmere Manuscript (Facsimile Edition, 1911); © Private Collection/Bridgeman Art Library. **50** Portrait of Machiavelli by Santi di Tito (1536–1603); © Palazzo Vecchio, Florence/Bridgeman Art Library. **54** Title page to Gerard Mercator's *Atlas*, 16th century; © Royal Geographical Society, London/Bridgeman Art Library. **58** Title page to *Don Quixote* by Cervantes, Part I, 1605; © Mary Evans/AISA Media. **62** Title page to Shakespeare's First Folio, 1623; © TopFoto. **66** Engraving of a circulation experiment by Harvey; © Bettmann/Corbis. **70** Frontispiece of Galileo's *Dialogo*, 1632, showing from left to right, Aristotle, Ptolemy and Copernicus; © World History Archive/TopFoto. **74** Title page of Newton's *Principia mathematica*, 1687; © World History Archive/TopFoto. **78** Opening pages of Johnson's *Dictionary*, 1755; © Time & Life Pictures/Getty Images. **82** Portrait of the young Goethe; © Ullstein Bild/TopFoto. **86** French engraving of Adam Smith, 18th century; © Bibliothèque Nationale, Paris/Archives Charmet/Bridgeman Art Library. **90** Title page of Paine's *Common Sense*, 1776; © Bettmann/Corbis. **94** Engraving of Tintern Abbey's ruins, from *Romantic and Picturesque Scenery of England and Wales*, 1805; © Private Collection, The Stapleton Collection/Bridgeman Art Library. **98** Copy of the portrait in watercolour of Austen by her sister Cassandra, *c*.1810; © TopFoto. **102** 'Ignorance and Want' presented by a ghost to Scrooge, illustration by John Leech for *A Christmas Carol* by Dickens, 1843; © World History Archive/TopFoto. **106** Photograph of Karl Marx, *c*.1880; © akg-images. **110** An illustration by Rockwell Grant for the 1930 Lakeside Press edition of Melville's *Moby-Dick*; © 1930 by R.R. Donnelley & Sons, Inc. and The Plattsburgh College Foundation, Inc. All rights reserved. **114** Poster advertising *Uncle Tom's Cabin*; © TopFoto. **118** Caricature of Flaubert extracting Madame Bovary's heart, 1869; © akg-images. **122** Caricature of Darwin, 1859; © akg-images. **126** Portrait of John Stuart Mill; © Bettmann/Corbis. **130** Photograph of the young Tolstoy, shown as a Crimean Army officer; © Bettmann/Corbis. **134** Cover of the *New Haven District Telephone Directory*, 1878; © Christie's Images Ltd. **137** Photograph of Sir Richard Burton, 1864; © Getty Images. **140** Arthur Conan Doyle's *A Study in Scarlet*, as it appeared in *Beeton's Christmas Annual*, 1887; © TopFoto. **144** Photograph of Freud, *c*.1906; © Austrian Archive/Scala, Florence. **148** Title page of the English translation of the *Protocols*, *c*.1935; © Mary Evans Picture Library. **152** Owen's manuscript of 'Dulce et Decorum Est', 1918; © Scala, Florence/HIP. **156** Photograph of Einstein, *c*.1905; © Bettmann/Corbis. **160** Joyce and the publisher of *Ulysses*, Sylvia Beach; © Bettmann/Corbis. **164** A commuter on the London Underground reads *Lady Chatterley's Lover*, 1960; © Hulton-Deutsch Collection/Corbis. **168** Photograph of J.M. Keynes, 1940, reproduced in *Picture Post*; © Getty Images. **172** Prisoners at Auschwitz, after their liberation by Soviet troops on 25 January 1945; © akg-images. **176** Film still from *1984* (1956), based on Orwell's *Nineteen Eighty-four*; © TopFoto. **180** Photograph of de Beauvoir, 1945; © Roger Viollet/Getty Images. **184** Cover of the first edition of J.D. Salinger's *The Catcher in the Rye*, 1951; published by Little, Brown and Company, New York. **188** Photograph of Achebe, 1960; © Time & Life Pictures/Getty Images. **192** Photograph of Carson, 1961; © Alfred Eisenstaedt/Time & Life Pictures/Getty Images. **196** Red Guards' propaganda poster from 1967 during the Chinese Cultural Revolution; Private Collection, © The Chambers Gallery, London/Bridgeman Art Library. **200** A Harry Potter fan, 16 July 2005, the day *Harry Potter and the Half-Blood Price* was published; © Johannes Eisele/AFP/Getty Images.

Author's acknowledgements

I have had help and advice from many sources in the past few months. In the United States, my old friend Julian Bene, in Atlanta, was a mine of information and interpretation about Rachel Carson and Mao Zedong; Mark Riley, Professor of Latin at California State University, Sacramento, helped me with his thoughts on the poetry of Horace; and Stan Swihart, of East Bay, California, astounded me with the breadth and depth of his knowledge about the early days of the telephone system.

In the UK, Lynden Flint guided me through Newton's thinking, and Dr Nicholas White, of Emmanuel College, Cambridge, threw fresh light on Flaubert's *Madame Bovary*. And in China, Tamsin Roberts was kind enough not to laugh at my mis-spellings of Chinese names, and unfailingly helpful in interpreting the thoughts of Confucius. To all of them, my thanks – any errors that remain, of course, are mine alone.

I also owe a great deal, as always, to my agent Mandy Little, to Richard Milbank at Quercus, and to my editor, Mark Hawkins-Dady, a master of the creative destruction that every book requires.

My wife, Penny, read each chapter as it was written, argued over many of them, and put up with my sulking when she was proved right. And finally, as always, I should thank Dr Tim Littlewood and his NHS team in the haematology department at Oxford's John Radcliffe Hospital in England. All the others helped me with the book: they kept me alive.

Andrew Taylor

Quercus Publishing Plc
21 Bloomsbury Square
London
WC1A 2NS

First published in 2008

Copyright © Andrew Taylor 2008

A catalogue record of this book is available from the British Library

Cloth case edition:
ISBN 13: 978 1 84724 602 8

Printed case edition:
ISBN 13: 978 1 84724 254 9

Printed and bound in China

10 9 8 7 6 5 4 3 2 1

Publishing director: *Richard Milbank*
Art director: *Nick Clark*
Managing editors: *Mark Hawkins-Dady, Rosie Anderson*
Designer: *Terry Jeavons*
Copy editors: *Ian Crofton, Gillian Lindsey, Sarah Chatwin*
Picture researcher: *Caroline Hotblack*
Proofreader: *Gordon Lee*
Indexer: *Patricia Hymans*